CHILE, PERU,
AND THE
CALIFORNIA GOLD RUSH
OF
1849

Books Written by Jay Monaghan

Lincoln Bibliography, 1839–1939 (2 volumes)

*Diplomat in Carpet Slippers: Abraham Lincoln
Deals with Foreign Affairs*

Last of the Bad Men: The Legend of Tom Horn

The Overland Trail

This is Illinois: A Pictorial History

*The Great Rascal:
The Life and Adventures of Ned Buntline*

Civil War on the Western Border, 1854–1865

The Man Who Elected Lincoln

*Swamp Fox of the Confederacy:
The Life and Military Services of M. Jeff Thompson*

Custer: The Life of General George Armstrong Custer

*Australians and the Gold Rush:
California and Down Under, 1849–1854*

Books Edited by Jay Monaghan

John Hope Franklin, *Civil War Diary of James T. Ayres*
Robert L. Kincaid, *The Wilderness Road*
Philip D. Jordan, *The National Road*
John Drury, *Old Illinois Houses*
Theodore Calvin Pease, *Story of Illinois*
Francis Philbrick, *Laws of Illinois Territory, 1809–1818*
Mary Waters, *Illinois in the Second World War*
The Book of the American West
R. B. Townshend, *A Tenderfoot in Colorado*
The Private Journal of Louis McLane, U.S.N., 1844–1848

Jay Monaghan

CHILE, PERU,

AND THE

CALIFORNIA GOLD RUSH

OF

1849

UNIVERSITY OF CALIFORNIA PRESS
Berkeley   Los Angeles   London
1973

UNIVERSITY OF CALIFORNIA PRESS
BERKELEY AND LOS ANGELES, CALIFORNIA
UNIVERSITY OF CALIFORNIA PRESS, LTD.
LONDON, ENGLAND
COPYRIGHT © 1973 BY THE REGENTS OF THE UNIVERSITY OF CALIFORNIA
ISBN: 0-520-02265-3
Library of Congress Catalog Card Number: 72-78946
PRINTED IN THE UNITED STATES OF AMERICA

For Mildred, encore une fois

Contents

CONTENTS

Illustrations

PART I
The Rush Starts from Chile

1

Who Started the Gold Rush?

"Gold! Gold! Gold from the American River," Sam Brannan, the big-voiced Mormon auctioneer, storekeeper, real estate agent, and newspaper publisher, is reported to have shouted on the streets of San Francisco the second week of May, 1848,* while waving his hat and displaying a bottle of golden granules. According to H. H. Bancroft's history,[1] as well as the accounts of many historians who followed him, this episode started the California gold rush.

An entirely different story is told by Charles de Varigny, the French consul in San Francisco, who wrote in his native language a book published in Paris the same year as Bancroft's history. De Varigny claimed that the gold rush started when a Chilean supercargo in San Francisco offered to pay 60 francs ($12) an ounce in cash for all gold brought to him.[2] The local merchants were paying only $8 to $10 in cash for gold, or $14 to $16 in exchange for goods.[3] The Chilean's offer sounded very attractive, therefore, and many men started for the diggings.

Bancroft and de Varigny agree on the approximate time the first rush began, and both authors' accounts are probably true in part. The gold discovered on the American River during the last week in January, 1848, had been accepted with increasing frequency at Sutter's Fort and even in San Francisco, where the newspaper *Californian* made casual mention of it as early as March 15.

Of course this was not the first discovery of gold in California. A local rush had started in 1842 when a Mexican ranchman, seek-

* Hubert Howe Bancroft (*History of California* [San Francisco, 1884–1890], VI, 56) says the date was probably May 12, 1848.

ing lost cattle in southern California's San Fernando Canyon, found gold clinging to the roots of a wild onion he dug up with his knife—the beginning, perhaps, of the oft-repeated saying during the great rush that in California gold was so plentiful it could be mined with a knife.[4] This first little rush was short-lived. The neighboring Indians were dangerous[5] and California at that date belonged to Mexico.

The Chilean supercargo's offer of $12 in cash assured him a fine profit, since gold was quoted at $18 in Europe and $17 in Valparaiso. He knew gold and its value because his country had dealt in the precious metal for almost 300 years. The earliest explorer of Chile, Pedro de Valdivia, found little gold but he was determined to duplicate Pizarro's achievement in Peru. The king of Spain claimed a "royal fifth" of all gold found, and Valdivia is said to have magnified his discoveries by sending gold from the ornaments on his horsemen's spurs which they had brought from Peru. This extravagant publicity gave Chile's mountains and deep forests a reputation for riches which attracted scores of conquistadores. Indians killed Valdivia in 1553, and legends say his greed for gold prompted the red men to pour the molten metal down his throat.[6] But the tradition of golden treasures in Chile did not die with him. In 1782 Juan Ignacio Molina, who lived much of his life in France, was still intoxicated by tales of mineral wealth when he wrote in his *Historia de Chile* that the Bank of Santiago had for many years received a million and a half pesos in gold annually. This gold, he said, had purchased lavish ornaments for Chilean churches, luxurious furniture for Chilean homes, and exquisite jewelry for Chilean ladies.

By 1848, the year of the great discovery in California, Chile's meager gold mines were exhausted, but poor people, still hypnotized by dreams of Pizarro's wealth, panned the stream beds diligently when unemployed.* Gold—even the thought of it, as the supercargo knew—had never been washed out of the bloodstream of a true Chilean. In his country prices were still quoted

---

* Frederick Gerstaecker, who visited Chile during these years, says that even in Valparaiso peons panned the stream beds for gold after floods (*Narrative of a Journey round the World* [New York, 1853], p. 116).

in *onzas*, or ounces, a monetary unit equal in value to an ounce of gold.

Many words common in Chile would be adopted by California Argonauts. The word "placer," derived from *plaza*, had been used in Chile for gold-bearing sand since 1757.[7] "Jerky," the dried-meat ration later to be a mainstay of California miners, was the Spanish *charqui*, the meat cured in the high, dry air of the Andes. Latin-American use of the word *ley* may also have been accepted by the Californians. In South America, "ley" was slang for the amount of ore in a prospector's load of pay dirt.[8] In North America a prospector wishing to say, "I started with this and this is what I got," might say, "This was my ley," or perhaps "lay"? The word was never written and may have referred to a gambler's layout.

Chilean prospectors had learned that the best sacks for carrying gold dust, sacks without seams through which the heavy dust might leak, were made from the scrota of butchered rams (*escrotos de los carneros*). In North American mining camps, puckish geniuses perverted this practice by using the scrotum of a dead man as a purse for small change—conduct usually ignored in Victorian accounts of mining camps but remembered by survivors of those days.[9]

All Chileans had been reared on detailed descriptions of the process of mining gold, but whether the new discovery would start a gold rush to California remained to be seen. Wealthy Chileans were busy managing their estates or vacationing in Europe. Their *inquilinos*—sharecroppers, serfs, peons, call them what you will—seemed much too poor and closely attached to the land to leave their ancestral allotments. The one class that might emigrate, and make trouble if they did, consisted of *rotos*, or landless vagabonds who worked occasionally and robbed often, proving themselves dangerous highwaymen or excellent guerrillas. They had formed the core of the army that drove Spain out of Chile and then seemed eager to fight in any revolution headed by ambitious politicians. Reckless, vindictive fighters, these ragged gangsters cared little for their own lives and not at all for the lives of others. Always gay, happy, and laughing as they stabbed in terrifying fights, they had repeatedly defeated the armies of their Latin-American enemies. Chileans boasted that rotos never lost a battle.[10] With so belligerent a tradition, one thing seemed certain. If a stampede started from Chile to California, many of the men who emigrated would be aggressive fellows who knew much more about panning gold than most Americans did.

The Chilean supercargo who bought the first gold in San Francisco came on the brig *J.R.S.* to trade for hides and tallow. His vessel anchored in the bay on May 3, 1848,[11] bringing a cargo of assorted merchandise valued at $4,000 which sold readily,[12] but the amount of gold purchased by the supercargo is unknown. The brig was owned by José Ramón Sánchez, a wealthy resident of Valparaiso whose credit was certainly good should the supercargo draw on it. The *J.R.S.*, commanded by Alfredo Andrews, was one of Ramón Sánchez' smaller vessels, a craft of only 193 tons. The ship remained in San Francisco six weeks, and during that time the gold excitement steadily increased. The village had a population of only 800 to 900 people* and boasted less than 200 buildings, many of them shanties, but ten new residences were already under construction[13] and American occupation promised a fast growth.

The first news of the gold discovery interested only the adventurous and the unemployed in San Francisco. Perhaps many people distrusted noisy Sam Brannan because he owned real estate and a store in the area where gold had been discovered and would profit by a boom. But a week later a launch arrived from Sutter's Fort with a large quantity of gold, one man carrying three pounds he had "gathered of Sundays"[14] while working at Sutter's mill. This event really excited San Franciscans, and Captain Andrews must have seen people leaving on horseback or by boat, and a few on foot. Soon half the village houses stood empty.[15]

The disturbance spread south to the seat of government at Monterey, where the United States naval agent, Thomas Oliver

---

* Ralph P. Bieber, "California Gold Mania," *Mississippi Valley Historical Review*, XXXV (June, 1948), 7. Andrew F. Rolle (*California: A History* [New York, 1963], p. 211) says the population was 812 in March, 1848.

Larkin, heard the rumors and saw soldiers at the nearby post deserting their commands to search for riches at the distant diggings. On May 26 Larkin wrote the military governor, Colonel R. B. Mason, that the agitation was becoming uncontrollable. Larkin was a man of probity, careful, exacting, economical, dull but durable. He had come to California in 1832 with one ambition: to make a fortune. By diligence and an advantageous marriage he had succeeded. Under Spanish rule the Franciscan missions had monopolized the hide and tallow trade, but after Mexican independence this business was opened to all; Larkin, with his knowledge of eastern markets, became a wealthy trader.* Now his thorough knowledge of California and its people made his statements important.

Captain Andrews may not have known about Larkin's letter, but his supercargo had been buying gold for at least a fortnight when loud-mouthed Brannan came back to San Francisco the first week in June. This time he brought three bottles containing 20 pounds of gold worth almost $5,000. His appearance started a general exodus. Schoolteachers, doctors, mechanics, cooks, gamblers, and even the sheriff left town. All the young men in the *J.R.S.*'s crew deserted. Obviously the little town would soon be abandoned, leaving only women, children, and infirm old men, probably less than a hundred altogether.[16]

On June 14 San Francisco's second and only surviving newspaper, the *California Star*, ceased publication, both editor and typesetter having gone to the diggings. On that same day[17] Captain Andrews, with the brawny oldsters who had stayed on the job to "cat and fish" his anchor, sailed the *J.R.S.* past Alcatraz (Spanish for "pelican") and out through the Golden Gate, so designated on the map published by Frémont that spring.[18] To the northwest, Andrews sighted those distant seagirt rocks towering above the horizon known as the Farallones, a name borne by a mountain in his native Chile. His destination, Valparaiso, was in the South Pacific, almost due south of Boston, Massachu-

---

* George P. Hammond, ed., *The Larkin Papers* (Berkeley, 1951–1964), I, vii–ix. Larkin also served as agent for Loring & Co., a firm of Valparaiso ship chandlers, with authority to advance money on drafts presented by whaleship masters (see advertisement in the *Californian*, July 3, 1847).

setts, so he steered south-southeast down the coast of California. For the next 1,500 miles he could count on the prevailing westerly winds which combed the crests of rolling breakers, sending white spray flying like the white manes of galloping horses. In this steady wind, studding sails could be set. No man need go aloft, and always, day after day, the high outline of mountains on the eastern horizon—a jagged silhouette in purple every sunrise, misty snowcaps against the blue sky at noon, a zigzag wall at sunset—assured a navigator of his position. "Si, Señor!"

The captain's name, "Andrews," did seem odd for a Chilean, but it was not odd in Valparaiso, where he planned to land. One-third of that city's population were foreigners, and one newspaper, the *Neighbour*, was printed in English. This weekly was edited by the Reverend David Trumbull of the Foreign Evangelical Society who had lived in Valparaiso since December, 1845.[19] The journal's alleged object was "not gain, but the diffusion of intelligence, correct opinions, and sound morality."[20] A copy sold for two reales (25¢). A year's subscription cost one "ounce" ($17).[21] The paper carried ship news, and articles from its pages were reprinted as far away as New Orleans.[22]

Families with non-Spanish names were numerous in Valparaiso. The *J.R.S.*'s cargo was consigned to G. L. Hobson y Cía.,[23] a firm reckoned to have a capital of $1 million and a net annual income of $200,000 to $225,000. The Hobsons were notable. William Hobson had resided in Valparaiso for more than a decade. He lived in style, returned once to "the States," and brought back a wife whom he could afford to indulge with lush "invalid treatment" in the sulphur springs at Talcahuano.[24] When the gold rush began he was the first person from Chile to establish a commission house in San Francisco. Joseph Hobson was also in business in Valparaiso, and G. G. Hobson had been United States consul there.[25] In those days a conflict of interest for government officials was accepted practice.

Another wealthy resident of Valparaiso was William, or Guillermo, Wheelwright. Born in Rhode Island in 1798,[26] he went to sea on a merchant ship at the age of twelve, and ten years later was commanding a trading brig. In 1825 he became a commission merchant in Guayaquil, Ecuador.[27] Moving to Valparaiso, he became known to easygoing Chileans of wealth as a pestiferous promoter obsessed with one idea he pushed constantly. Servants were instructed "never to admit that mad man."[28] He proposed building a railroad from Valparaiso to Santiago as early as 1842 and, after ten years' struggle, succeeded in interesting English capital.[29] In 1847 he induced some wealthy Scotsmen to help him finance the Pacific Steam Navigation Company, just in time to compete successfully with English sailing ships during the gold rush.[30] The Chilean government eventually awarded him a gold medal for the introduction of steam navigation.[31]

Other non-Spanish surnames were common among commission agents and shipowners. Among them were Cook, Wilson, Mickle,* Hemenway, and Alsop of the New York and Connecticut banker-merchant family. The German firm of Schutte y Cía. had begun business in Valparaiso as early as 1822, the year after independence from Spain; Germans liked to boast that a Teuton, Partolomaus Blumen, had helped Valdivia found Santiago in 1541. The name Blumen, they said, was changed to Flores, the name of a distinguished family in Chile.[32]

The favorable westerly wind that allowed the *J.R.S.* to scud down the coast stopped blowing south of Baja California. This area was close to the Tropic of Cancer, and from there on the brig had to depend on trade winds that, both north and south of the equator, blew contrary to its plotted course. To make headway against the winds the *J.R.S.* had to tack far out into the Pacific, and the last land her crew would see for weeks was Cabo Falsa, the Spanish name for Baja California's gullied tip with its nearby islets that stood like pyramids in the sea.

The next delay always came in the equatorial doldrums, where a vessel might lie becalmed "as idle as a painted ship upon a painted ocean," often so glassy that it reflected the clouds. At dawn the tropical sun peeped above the horizon's taut gray line.

* Many of these foreign businessmen married into prominent Chilean families. Mrs. Mickle was the daughter of General Ramón Herrera (*Report on Consulate at Valparaiso*, 31st Cong., 1st sess., Senate Exec. Doc. 16 [Washington, 1850], p. 5).

A few diamonds on the distant water indicated a breeze, but it might pass, leaving the brig without a flap of sail. Experienced Chilean sailors murmured complacently:

Viento y ventura	Wind and good luck
Poco dura.	Never last long.

Monotonous inactivity frayed the tempers of green hands but old seamen remained calm, especially old Valparaiso seamen who sincerely believed all Chileans superior to other South Americans.

In colonial times Chile was a department of Spain's vice-royalty of Peru but, far distant down the coast from the capital at Lima, she had been neglected for almost 300 years. During this time Chileans learned to be self-reliant. Even the sailors quartered before the mast prided themselves on their virility and independence, characteristics those young men who had deserted in San Francisco might display at the diggings.

Since gaining their independence, Chileans had voiced contempt for Spain and her imperialism. Chileans liked to say that they did not even speak Spanish: "No, Señor, ablamos castellano" ("We speak Castilian").[33] Many of them were of Basque descent as the "ch" and "rr" in their names disclose. These proud mountain people never forgot that their ancestors, with rotos perhaps, had defeated one of the armies of Charlemagne in A.D. 778 at the Pass of Roncesvalles—certainly a braver tradition than the North American Anglos' defeat in 1066 by that Frenchman, William the Conqueror!

Lacking records, we may only surmise the thoughts, plans, and conversations of Captain Andrews, his supercargo, and the crew on the long voyage south with their California gold. They knew that a great rush had started from San Francisco to the diggings and that the *J.R.S.* was one of the first vessels to carry the news to the outside world. Also deep in the subconscious minds of all Chileans lurked a lingering tradition of the conquistadores. Pizarro, the lowly swineherd, had achieved noble status and founded a great house.[34] Unlike estates in Anglo North America, haciendas in Chile, once acquired, seemed permanent. Independence from Spain and succeeding revolutions had not destroyed the landed gentry. The great *patrónes* had not been deprived of their inheritances, and it was still illegal to divide a large plantation.[35] Who could say that "the men of the sea" who had deserted in San Francisco might not be following the Spanish-American tradition!

The *J.R.S.*, sailing southeast, came abreast of the Chilean coast more than 1,000 miles north of Valparaiso, yet Chile was a relatively small country. At no place was it more than 250 miles across, and mostly its width was a scant 100 miles. From north to south, however, Chile stretched out for a distance equal to that from Labrador to Panama. The *J.R.S.*, depending on the trade winds, sailed far out of sight of the narrow coast. Her captain navigated by dead reckoning and, when weather permitted, by a daily reading of the sextant. The southern trade winds do not extend as far south as usual in August,[36] so the *J.R.S.* must have reached the variables that month. During the third week of August, when Captain Andrews transferred the figures from his noon reading of the sextant's scale to his nautical almanac, he learned that he was 33 degrees south of the equator—as far south of that line as San Diego, California, and Charleston, South Carolina, are north of it. Knowing that he must now be opposite Valparaiso, he ordered the helmsman to steer to the east.

The coast was continually hidden by a wall of fog[37] some 20 miles offshore, caused by the cold Humboldt Current flowing along the sun-warmed shoreline waters. The *J.R.S.* had to glide blindly into this wall and then coast for perhaps an hour in its brilliant whiteness. Mists moistened the men's faces; rivulets dripped from their oilskins. No sound could be heard except the faint creaking of the cordage and a satin-like rustling of water along the brig's sides. A pale, ghostly rainbow told them that the sun still shone above.

Suddenly the *J.R.S.* emerged on a bright blue ocean with a fresh breeze under a cloudless sky. Ahead of her the snowy Andes peeped above a long level coast which stretched north and south as far as the eye could see.[38] Flocks of angular-bodied cormorants flew across the bow and pelicans plummeted with bombshell precision onto unlucky fish beside the vessel—but Valparaiso was nowhere in sight.

The city, always difficult to locate from the west or the south, lay concealed behind a peninsula which extended 4 miles to the north.[39] It gave the anchorage good protection except from northers which sometimes whistled in during the winter months of June and July, tossing ships about, pulling up anchors, and on one occasion piling helpless vessels against the shore while waves roared up the cobbled streets.[40] The surrounding ridge also caused unpredictable squalls, and mariners were instructed to enter the harbor with double- or triple-reefed topsails.[41] Yet, poor as the anchorage proved to be, Valparaiso was the unloading place for Chile's capital at Santiago, and the city had grown faster than the much safer port of Talcahuano, 300 miles farther south. In August the *J.R.S.* could expect to find tranquil water.

Captain Andrews knew that a lighthouse stood on the point that hid Valparaiso, and he must have searched for it with his telescope. The circular tower's construction had been promoted by the notorious Guillermo Wheelwright. Painted white, it stood 197 feet high[42] but was difficult to see by day.[43] At night its light could be sighted by ships 20 miles at sea.

If the lighthouse proved difficult to locate, seafaring men used another peculiar landmark to guide them to Valparaiso. Sailing in from the west, a ship approaching the coastal ridge soon lost sight of the snowcapped Andes. There was, however, a gap in the ridge 8 miles north of the city through which the mountains could still be seen. One peak, although 100 miles from the ocean and invisible at its misty base, served all navigators well. Sharply outlined against the sky, rugged, bald-headed Mount Aconcagua loomed up 22,835 feet—higher than any peak in North America*—and a helmsman who steered his craft straight for Aconcagua, as he saw it through the gap, would skirt the lighthouse peninsula, safely passing the rocky point where huge ocean waves painted an ever-changing collar of

* California's Mount Whitney is only 14,495 feet high, and Alaska's Mount McKinley, the highest mountain in all North America, reaches only 20,300 feet. Six peaks in the Andes rise above 20,000 feet.

white foam. Beyond this hazard the captain of the *J.R.S.* could see through his telescope a distant white line of surf below an irregular string[44] of butter-colored houses, with here and there a tall building. This was Valparaiso, Valley of Paradise, a settlement destined to send more gold seekers to California than any other city in South America. Behind Valparaiso, on the 1,000-foot encircling slope, stood many white mansions.*

Founded in 1543, almost a century before Boston, Valparaiso had remained a small town until Chile gained independence from Spain. Freed by that revolution from domination by the viceroy of Peru, who had directed most shipping to Lima's port at Callao, vessels flocked into Valparaiso and the city mushroomed amazingly.[45] Captain Andrews may well have seen this seaport grow from a village of 15,000 to a town of more than 30,000.† The city had become one of the busiest ports in the world, certainly in the Pacific.[46] No wonder its citizens cursed Spain and gloried in independence.

Such growth breeds "go-ahead people," able and eager to cope with the exigencies of a gold rush, and Captain Andrews was bringing the first news from California. Or was he? Other vessels had left San Francisco ahead of him, but they were not bound for Valparaiso. Yet later ships might have beaten his sixty-four-day sailing time, which was fast but not exceptional. If so, the exciting information might already be common knowledge.

Captain Andrews, gliding into Valparaiso harbor under reefed topsails, could only wonder how widely the news had spread while he was at sea. As a matter of fact, the startling tidings reached Hawaii three days after the *J.R.S.* had sailed from San Francisco,[47] and fourteen or fifteen vessels carrying more than

---

* Chester S. Lyman (*Around the Horn* [New Haven, 1924], p. 21) judged this ridge to be 2,000 feet high. Charles Wilkes (*Narrative of Exploring Expedition* [Philadelphia, 1845], I, 166) estimated its height at from 800 to 1,500 feet. Modern topographical maps show the ridge to be from 800 to 1,000 feet high, with a knoll farther east which rises to 1,600 feet.

† James Melville Gilliss (*Chile: Its Geography, Climate* [Washington, 1855], p. 229) says the population of Valparaiso in 1847 was 22,000, and that by 1850 it had increased to 30,826. Lyman (*op. cit.*, p. 22) gives the population in 1846 as 50,000. Wilkes (*op. cit.*) says Valparaiso had a population of 15,000 in 1822 and 30,000 in 1839.

100 gold seekers were immediately laid on in Honolulu for California. The news was spreading around the world fast because ships from Europe, South America, and the Orient made regular stops at the Islands.

On June 28, 1848, two weeks after the *J.R.S.* had left California, moneymaking Larkin wrote another historic letter from Monterey, this time to Secretary of State James Buchanan, in Washington, saying: "Every Mexican who has seen the place says throughout their Republic there has never been any placer like this one."[48] Larkin's letter certainly had not yet reached Buchanan, nor had it caused any great stir in world affairs, but it is interesting for another reason. The Mexicans mentioned by Larkin may have been Chileans. A platoon of rotos under Juan de Dios Calderón had fought in the Mexican War. They were discharged in California, and knowing gold they would be among the first to pan for it. Certainly Larkin knew *Californios* too well to confuse them with Mexicans, but did he differentiate between a Sonoran and a Chilean,* both of whom would refer to "their Republic"? In this connection note that Larkin wrote his letter in June and that the first Sonoran caravan of record left Mexico in October,[49] though individual Sonorans did go to California earlier.

In any event, Larkin's letter caused little excitement during the days the *J.R.S.* was at sea. The letter that really started the rush from the eastern United States was written by the military governor of California, Colonel R. B. Mason, to the adjutant general in Washington. Dated August 17, two days before Captain Andrews landed, the letter said in part: "There is more gold in the country drained by the Sacramento and San Joaquin rivers than will pay the cost of the present war with Mexico a hundred times over."[50] This startling statement could not have

---

* A search has failed to reveal much information about the Chilean rotos described by Roberto Hernández Cornejo (*Los Chilenos en San Francisco* [Valparaiso, 1930], I, 43). A Chilean was killed in the battle of Natividad on November 14, 1846, according to Edwin Bryant (*What I Saw in California* [Minneapolis, 1967], p. 363). Larkin, serving as agent for a Valparaiso commission firm, should have been able to differentiate between a Mexican and a Chilean, but a Chilean from the Mexican army might be considered a Mexican. Juan de Dios Calderón was a wealthy shipowner in Peru, for whom a street in Lima was named.

been received in Washington until many months later. Oddly enough, an obscure writer described the California gold discovery in an article published by the *New York Times* on August 19,[51] the day Captain Andrews landed in Chile. Other letters carried by a naval courier who arrived in Washington on September 16, 1848,[52] confirmed the report, but many readers remained skeptical. The rush from the East did not begin until President Polk reiterated Colonel Mason's statement in his annual message to Congress on December 5, 1848: "The accounts of the abundance of gold in that territory are of such an extraordinary character as would scarcely command belief were they not corroborated by authentic reports."

Three to six months from the date of Polk's message would pass before Easterners could reach California, and the *J.R.S.* had arrived in Valparaiso three and a half months before the presidential message was delivered. Thus Chileans were sure to learn about the gold discoveries long before the North Americans; Captain Andrews—if no other ship preceded the *J.R.S.*—brought really important news.

The gold rush had developed in a minor way in San Francisco during the sixty-four days the *J.R.S.* was at sea. Ships arriving from Hawaii were reported to be selling potatoes at the diggings for $1 a pound, and blankets might fetch $50 to $100 each.[53] These large potential profits attracted the attention of money-making Thomas Larkin in Monterey. He saw an opportunity to double, triple, or quadruple his fortune by investing in a series of business ventures, ventures that eventually made him one of the richest men in California. His first project was to import boatloads of merchandise from Mexico. Chilean merchants, however, could ship at once and beat him to the anticipated market. Likewise, Chilean gold seekers could reach California almost a year ahead of the first forty-niners, and with their age-old skills they might skim the cream from California's mother lode.

Nothing Is More Timid Than a Million Dollars

Gold, gold! Gold, gold!
Bright and yellow, hard and cold,
Hoarded, bartered, squandered, doled,
Spurned by the young but hugged by the old.
—Thomas Hood

Captain Andrews, snug at last in Valparaiso harbor on August 19, 1848,[1] found ten other seagoing vessels at anchor there. Had news of the discovery come on any of them? The flags drooping over each ship's taffrail showed four to be British, two French, two from Hamburg, one from the United States, and one, the maverick *Ann McKim*, from God knows where. This famous forerunner of the clipper ships had been a pet of her former Baltimore owner. Her red copper bottom and her raking masts, set for speed like a slaver's, would be recognized anywhere. Though the *Ann McKim* was now sixteen years old, her deck was still resplendent with Spanish mahogany rails, brass capstan heads, and bells. On the death of her first owner, she was purchased by Howland & Aspinwall of New York and in 1847 had been sold in Valparaiso. She was registered as Ecuadorian.[2]

The captain saw no activity on the decks of the assembled craft or in the harbor. Nothing indicated that a gold rush to California had begun, and the number of vessels was not unusual. Since Valparaiso served all ports in the Pacific, many vessels stopped there. During the stormy month of July, just past, fourteen British, six American, and five French ships had called at this port—a total of twenty-five in one off-season month, all engaged in routine business.[3] In addition, Chile's own national merchant fleet of 100 barks, brigantines, and schooners[4] carried grain, flour, metal, lumber, and coal to Peru, Ecuador, and New Granada (Colombia and Panama), bringing back fruits, cocoa, coffee, and sugar.[5] These vessels, along with some 700 New England whaleships now sailing the Pacific, kept Valparaiso shipwrights busy and made the town very prosperous.[6] The masters of these many vessels were equipped to transport gold seekers, should a rush develop, but as yet there was no sign of one. *Olé!* The *J.R.S.* was the first to bring the news!

Captain Andrews could not dock his brig. Valparaiso's harbor, although 2.5 miles wide,[7] was too deep for the construction of many piers; one small mole served all vessels. Large amounts of cargo were unloaded into lighters, rowed to landing beaches, and carried ashore on the backs of men.[8] Standing on the deck, Captain Andrews could see, at the foot of the circling ridge, tall business houses at the western end of town. The flat ground there was too narrow for more than a row or two of buildings, and two walls of the spacious customhouse at the end of the mole were up against solid rock.[9] Near it he could see the Exchange, which welcomed all seafaring men to elegant reading rooms containing the principal European newspapers[10] as well as a large framed portrait of Guillermo Wheelwright.[11] A telescope enabled businessmen to identify incoming vessels and arrange commercial transactions before anchors were cast. Captain Andrews also knew that curiosity seekers used that scope to spy on deck occurrences which were sometimes amusing.[12] He may have wondered if, at this moment, some observer was watching him.

East of the tall buildings the level ground below the crescent ridge became wider. On this plain stood the cathedral beside the plaza,[13] the Episcopal church, partly supported by the British Parliament,[14] and a theater—Valparaiso's principal place of entertainment[15] since bullfighting had been abolished by the revolution's humanitarians. The opera, a good hotel, and a club made Valparaiso a happy stopping place for foreign naval officers.[16] From his anchored vessel Captain Andrews could also see long adobe walls, the common front of many houses, with doors and occasional barred windows opening on cobblestoned alleys. These flat-roofed dwellings were thatched with palm fronds which drooped over the brown walls. Here lived the city's laborers, stevedores, and always a few of those unpredictable rotos.

Cross streets led to fine houses on the ridge behind the town and the bay. The residences of English, French, American, and German merchants[17] were set like jewels in groves of orange, fig, and almond trees. At the 300-foot level a fine mansion housed the former consul, G. G. Hobson, and his family.[18] From some balconies homeowners could enjoy the sunset's play of lights on bald-headed Aconcagua's snowy summit, 100 miles away.[19]

The rich men's gardens, with the approach of spring in late August, were brilliant with roses, heliotropes, pinks, callas, and violets.[20] Geraniums grew to a truly gigantic size. Captain Andrews probably did not know Goldsmith's line, "Flowers grow best where broad ocean leans against the land," but he must have remembered the days when this Chilean coast was as bare and treeless as California's stark shore.

The ridge encircling the harbor was cut by steep gulches which formed three distinct knobs known as Fore, Main, and Mizzen Tops. On the last of the three stood Chile's naval academy, and Captain Andrews, looking through his telescope, could see promenading middies in odd uniforms, as British as could be, from the billycock hats on pig-tailed heads to the dirks strapped beneath their short, closely fitting jackets.[21] The naval academy, founded almost a generation before Annapolis, had been established by Thomas Cochrane, eldest son of the ninth Earl of Dundonald. He was a British naval officer expelled from Parliament for questionable financial practices.

The disgraced nobleman became an admiral in Chile's rebel fleet during the revolution and swept Spanish vessels from the Chilean coast, assuring the country's independence.[22] Like Wheelwright, he is credited with bringing the first steamship to the Pacific; at least he brought a sailboat with auxiliary engines in 1822.[23] Steeped in the Nelson tradition, Cochrane had his own "Lady Hamilton," a young, genial, bold horsewoman fond of picnics, parties, dancing, and music. The puritanical clerk on an American warship complained that she used too much rouge, thus setting a bad example for other Chilean ladies. "I should like them very much," he commented, "if they kept their Boosoms covered." [24]

Naval officers everywhere admitted that Cochrane's academy, modeled on British standards, equaled any in the world. Many foreigners served in the Chilean navy, both as officers and as men. One English-speaking seaman from this fleet would lead an anti-Chilean riot in San Francisco during the gold rush soon to begin [25] (an incident described later).

Vessels arriving in Valparaiso were always met by guttersnipes in small boats who offered fruit and sweets for sale, "fares" to shore, or advice concerning cheap lodgings with pretty women. These boatmen, meeting so many British and American vessels, spoke English, shouting, "Want a boat?" [26] To them, American whalemen were Yankees or gringos, a new word meaning "foreigners" but not necessarily North Americans. The word may have been derived from "Griego" or "Greek," as used in the sentence, "It's all foreign—or Greek—to me." [27] The *J.R.S.*, flying Chile's lone-star flag with its broad white and red stripes, was sure to be addressed in Spanish, and the captain, when he went ashore with his supercargo, undoubtedly climbed down a Jacob's ladder into a landing boat. They had to report to G. L. Hobson y Cía. and receive orders for disposal of their cargo, including the California gold.

Surely the hides and tallow would not be landed, because Chile was a cattle country raising more livestock than it consumed. Yet hides could be transported more cheaply by ship from California and Hawaii [28] to Valparaiso than by oxcart from Chilean haciendas only 100 or less miles away. In any event, some 30,000 hides were shipped annually from this port, [29] many in the emptied holds of New England and European vessels which came loaded with machinery, bolts of cloth, shoes, furniture, and books. [30]

Captain Andrews and his supercargo, when they jumped from the boat to shore, did not emulate Sam Brannan by shouting, "Gold! Gold! Gold from the American River!" Instead, they seem to have walked unnoticed up the street, and it is easy to picture the captain striding along the broad avenue around the bay,[31] followed closely by his supercargo and a few trusted "men of the sea" carrying the precious gold. The wide pavement was decorated by white stars and crosses said to have been made from the bones of Spaniards killed in the revolution. A chain gang of prisoners swept it daily.[32] The buildings on the land side of the street displayed the names of shipping agents, often printed on signs swinging above the entrances to their counting rooms. Wide-open warehouse doors disclosed coils of cables, spools of rope, bales of canvas, blocks, tackle, oilskin hats, and yellow slickers with red flannel collars turning idly in the breeze. The smell of tar, hemp, salt water, and lye soap filled the air.

Few carriages appeared on the streets. Fruits and vegetables were peddled from the backs of donkeys. An occasional shrill squeal announced the approach of an ox-drawn *carreta* with ungreased hubs. A law prohibited lubrication lest the vehicle slip quietly into town without paying customs.[33] Pedestrians walked out in the street as often as on the sidewalk. Merchants in frock coats and tall beaver hats sauntered along, swinging canes. Laborers darted about in white, wide-legged trousers and cotton shirts. Their woolen ponchos, colored red, green, or yellow, were gaily striped.[34] An occasional gringo female was clad in bonnet and hoops, her figure distorted with corsets.[35] The native women, full-bodied and bareheaded, walked proudly erect. They parted their hair in the middle and two black braids hung below their waists, making excellent handholds for the children tagging *mamá*.

This scene of leisurely opulence changed suddenly with the ringing of church bells. Doors opened everywhere and women flocked into the streets, all dressed in coarse black woolens. Black scarves of the same material covered their heads and faces, except for the eyes. Harsh as this apparel looked, some of the wearers were evidently well-to-do because the white hand that held the scarf displayed costly rings of precious gold.[36]

The sailors, trudging along with the captain and his gold, may have looked longingly toward Mizzen Top whose terraced slope was occupied by cheap boardinghouses, grogshops, gambling dens, and brothels of the worst sort.[37] Yet it might be a mistake to believe that all of the *J.R.S.* crewmen would spend their hard-earned pesos in such places. In those gaudy rooms English, American, and French sailors often seemed more numerous than natives.

What did the captain and his supercargo have on their minds when they entered the counting room of Hobson y Cía.? Unfortunately little is known about their reception. The handsome sum of $17.50 an ounce was paid for the gold,[38] and Hobson y Cía. may well have reaped an additional 50¢ for it in Europe. Certainly they entered into separate negotiations with Captain Andrews, who quit his service with Don José Ramón Sánchez for reasons that became clear a few days later. Perhaps the good news was kept a secret from Don José. Perhaps that wealthy shipping hidalgo, being far above "men of the sea," considered the news trivial. At any rate, neither of Valparaiso's Spanish newspapers mentioned the California gold discovery,[39] although the news may have been withheld from them to favor certain merchants, as was done in Australia. However that may be, the *J.R.S.* sailed under a new master, not to California but on a coastal cruise to Guayaquil, carrying an assorted cargo,[40] and life in the city proceeded in its customary manner. Before long Captain Andrews's new plans came to light.

In the meantime ships arrived and departed, often six or eight in one day. Sailors landed for a spree, and after dark the streets were policed by *vigilantes*, a word that would have sinister significance in California. These men blew official whistles as every pedestrian passed, thus marking the stroller's route; no prowler could move unnoticed.[41] Throughout the night the *vigilantes* called the hour, singing, "Viva Chi-li, viva Chili, las diez and-a y see-re-na." At dawn they added a prayer, shouting, "Ave María purissima las cinco y media."[42]

For two and a half months the press ignored the discovery, but the news must have spread rapidly among seafaring men who met on the avenue and gossiped at ship chandleries. Merchants, no doubt, discussed the hearsay stories while sipping *tintos* of black coffee at the little tables covered with their white cloths, set temptingly along the side streets.[43]

The rumor certainly swept like a good south wind through

the rows of adobe houses with their single doors opening onto the cobblestone streets. Sailors from the *J.R.S.* surely had families or friends living in these squalid quarters. The rooms inside had whitewashed walls, bare except for a possible wooden crucifix or a cherished religious picture. The bed was invariably a reed mat on an elevated platform in a corner of the room. A brazier for charcoal stood nearby.[44] Only the rich could afford the coal shipped by boat from Talcahuano, almost 300 miles to the south. A sailor visiting in one of these homes would be invited to share the owner's maté, sipped from a common bowl through a silver tube passed from mouth to mouth.[45]

Visiting sailors were sure to report the exciting discovery in California and to tell about the younger men on the *J.R.S.* who had deserted to seek fortunes, "como el Pizarro, si?" They told many persons about the 450 residents of San Francisco who left their homes as "candidates to be millionaires"[46]—a neat Spanish expression—leaving only the lazy to unload vessels and catch fish as they had always done.[47]

Such stories braced these poor people like strong drink. Many of them panned gold in nearby gullies after every rain, seldom collecting more than a half-peso's worth in a day.[48] Think of becoming "more rich" in the new El Dorado! A short trip to California and a quick return as men of wealth! Then they might sip maté all day, or even sit in a chair at one of those neat little tables, drink tintos, and talk with important friends. When a rich man spoke, people listened and smiled agreement with his wise observations, thus making him feel "more good." If he told a joke everybody laughed and repeated it to friends as an example of his ready wit. Finally, after many happy years, the rich man would be laid to rest in the well-kept Catholic cemetery under a splendid monument like the one erected by the wealthy Señor Waddington, another prominent Chilean with an English name. Such an end to life was a glorious prospect for a roto who, if he died a poor man in Valparaiso, would be laid in a common grave 10 feet deep, packed like a sardine with his worthless fellows.[49] Poor people talked many hours about these things, about life and death, visions they had seen, and miracles that had happened to friends. Now one of those miracles might come true in California!

Six days after Captain Andrews's arrival with the gold, while stories concerning it were still unconfirmed rumors passing from man to man, an odd notice appeared in the newspaper, *El Comercio de Valparaiso*. Printed in both English and Spanish, the item announced the sale at auction of the 215-ton bark *Undine* to the highest bidder on August 31 by the captain, Thomas S. Baker of New Brunswick, New Jersey, U.S.A. This unfortunate fellow on his way to California had sailed into Valparaiso with a cargo insufficient to pay for the necessary repairs on his bark.

Available records reveal little about Thomas Baker. The *Undine* was built in New Brunswick in 1845, although Baker is not listed among the captains sailing from that port.[50] The announcement of his sale, however, marks a prelude to the rush from Valparaiso. The negotiations for the purchase of the *Undine* were complicated, but the Hobsons were involved and they employed Captain Andrews to be her master. This explains why he quit the service of wealthy José Ramón Sánchez.

Before the *Undine* could be readied for California another vessel, the 289-ton *Virjinia*, was laid on. The ship was chartered by José Waddington[51] and Hobson y Cía.[52] supplied her cargo. José was the son of Don Josué Waddington, born in York, England, in 1792. He moved to Valparaiso in 1817, founded the commercial house of Waddington, Templeman y Cía., and by 1830 was considered the wealthiest man in Valparaiso,[53] with interests in mines, hospitals, and charities. Like so many successful Anglos he married into a Chilean family, established his sons in prosperous businesses, and built the ornate Waddington mausoleum a quarter of a century before his death. Don Josué's greatest accomplishment was the building of a canal from the Aconcagua River to irrigate his vast estate 20 miles from Valparaiso, near Quillota.[54] This village was the birthplace of California's outlaw, Joaquín Murieta, according to latter-day Chileans, as will be explained in due time.

The *Virjinia* booked forty-five gold-seeking passengers,* in-

* Enrique Bunster (*Chilenos en California* [Santiago de Chile, 1965], p. 75),

cluding many family men with wives and sons. Almost half of
the passengers bore English names, such as Don Tomás O. Neill,
with his wife and three sons; Don Juan Ellis, with his wife, three
sons, and a servant; Don José Ware and Don Samuel S. Crocker
each with a servant. Ware and Crocker were carpenters[55] and
their "servants" may have been carpenters' helpers. Their skilled
trade, appreciated in South American coastal towns, promised to
be more valuable in booming San Francisco. Undoubtedly the
name Crocker would mean something in California. The Chilean
daredevil Carlos Armstrong purchased tickets for his wife and
eight husky rotos,[56] the first of many *cuadrillas* or peon troops
who washed California gold. All were supplied with picks,
shovels, pans, and bars, along with firearms and camp equipment. All the peons listed for the passage had Spanish names,
indicating that they lacked Anglo blood. But English names tell
little about backgrounds in an international port like Valparaiso.
These gold seekers may have been second-generation Chileans,
or they may have been Anglo adventurers who had recently
arrived.

A forlorn misfit also embarked on the *Virjinia*. Don Enrique
Poett was a doctor who continually expected to do better in
another location. Always he was sure he would prosper somewhere else.[57] Was he typical of many pioneers? Yes and no! With
him sailed his wife, six sons, and a sister.[58]

The excitement in the harbor interested Faxon D. Atherton,
a successful North American resident of Valparaiso who was
always on the lookout for profitable investments. He knew
Thomas Larkin and decided to send him a letter by the *Virjinia*
along with a packet of the newspaper, *Neighbour*,[59] which reported Valparaiso's shipping news in English. In his letter Atherton described the agitation which the newspapers were still
ignoring. As a conservative businessman, he questioned the story
that California was "all gold." Instead, he hoped that pioneers
there might discover a good mine of coal, a mineral that would

---

Roberto Hernández Cornejo (*Los Chilenos en San Francisco* [Valparaiso, 1930],
I, 20), and Ramón Pérez Yañez (*Forjadores de Chile* [Santiago de Chile, 1953],
p. 250) all say that the Virjinia booked forty-five passengers, but *El Comercio
de Valparaiso* puts the figure at thirty-seven.

be salable in Valparaiso, especially for steamships. "That there are both copper and silver mines in California which may prove very rich," he wrote, "I have not the least doubt." Evidently impressed by the gangs of mine-trained peons going with the gold seekers on the *Virjinia*, he added: ". . . and were I to go there, would take some of these country miners who know how to look for them."[60]

Atherton was a New Englander who, like Thomas Larkin, had come to the South Pacific to make money. A man now in his early thirties, he had left the States fifteen years earlier with a motley cargo of goods valued at $500. It included cigars, cologne, brushes, shoes, German harps, and so on.[61] He sold the cargo to Augustus Hemenway, of the Hemenway commission firm, and accepted employment from Elishu Loring, another Valparaiso shipping agent. After working for a year Atherton sailed to Hawaii, investigated business opportunities there, then returned to Valparaiso and engaged in the hide and tallow trade which was making Larkin wealthy. In 1839 Atherton sailed back to New England with 540 hides valued at about $1,000. A promoter always, he sold the hides in Boston and tried to raise $4,500 there to build a highway from Valparaiso to Santiago. Failing in this endeavor, he returned to Chile with a $250 rotary printing press and a supply of enamel "address cards." In 1843 he married a plump, laughing, witty young woman of the prominent Goñi family,[62] whose wildest dreams could never have matched her fabulous future in San Francisco.

During the Mexican War, Faxon Atherton's wealth increased remarkably; as early as December 13, 1846, he wrote Larkin that he had accepted drafts for $300,000 from whalers and that all had been honored.[63] Atherton really needed no gold but, like Valdivia 300 years earlier, he would take all the precious metal he could get, and what Faxon Atherton eventually got made him another of the richest men in California.[64] He also became the father-in-law of Gertrude Atherton, well-known California author. In 1860 the Athertons moved to San Francisco and established a residence in Valparaiso Park.* In September, 1848, how-

* Oscar Lewis, *Sea Routes to the Gold Fields* (New York, 1949), p. 228; Doyce B. Nunis, Jr., ed., *The California Diary of Faxon Dean Atherton, 1836–*

ever, Atherton watched with scornful eyes the eager gold seekers making arrangements for passage on the *Virjinia*. Did the small amount of gold Captain Andrews had brought justify the Chileans' wild excitement? "A little glitter has blinded them," he told Larkin in his letter.[65]

In California, Larkin, the money-maker, knew better. He had developed a plan to increase his fortune by trading with the thousands of incoming Argonauts, and, in order to amass sufficient goods, he had entered into partnership with Job F. Dye, a fellow merchant in Monterey.[66] These two men had chartered the schooner *Mary* which, at the moment Atherton was writing, was sailing down the Mexican coast to fetch supplies from Mazatlán.[67] That ancient colonial harbor, used by the Spaniards in their trade with the Philippines, was the nearest Mexican port to San Francisco. Since it was also the principal port of entry for foreign goods shipped to all northwestern Mexico,[68] merchandise of many kinds could be bought there.

In spite of the *Mary*'s head start, the *Virjinia* with her gold seekers and ample cargo from Valparaiso would surely beat her to the San Francisco market. Thus Chilean goods as well as gold seekers would be among the first in California. On September 12, 1848, the *Virjinia* was ready to make sail for her historic voyage. All passengers were aboard and all cargo was stowed. As she was the first ship to go, it is easy to envision the captain on her quarterdeck gazing with practiced eye at the pennant on her mainmast. That little flag told him what he needed to know about the wind before he decided on the best sails to set.

Then, at the last moment, a strange incident occurred. The 98-ton schooner *Adelaida* entered the harbor and attracted everyone's attention. Surely one extra vessel arriving or departing on that day should have been unimportant; in fact six sea-going ships had already cleared for different foreign ports. But

---

1838 (San Francisco, 1964), p. xvi. Gertrude Atherton (*My San Francisco* [Indianapolis, 1946], pp. 38–39) describes lavish parties at the Atherton mansion in the days when no woman of quality would "expose an ankle, but it was the fashion to exhibit the upper part of the body so far south as just to avoid the mammalian point." The Chilean Señora Atherton evidently did not watch her diet; her daughter-in-law described her as a 200-pound woman who, when she beheld Mrs. Mark Hopkins in a dress sparkling with diamonds, said in broken English, "She looka like the crystal chandelier."

this schooner came from California, and her errand may have been broadcast by the flag-signal code that Admiral Cochrane had introduced in Chile.[69] In any event, her business was soon known and it stirred the *Virjinia*'s passengers to new ebullience. The *Adelaida* had come from San Francisco without waiting for a cargo of hides, but she brought 2,490 pesos' worth of gold,[70] presumably for the purchase of supplies to be carried back at once to California—another shipload to beat Larkin and Dye's schooner *Mary*.

By now there should have been no question about the gold discoveries. The *Virjinia*'s passengers sailed away with fresh dreams of wealth,[71] but on shore Faxon Atherton and many well-to-do Spanish-speaking shipowners paid little attention. The newspapers still printed no word verifying the questionable El Dorado. Did the conservative men of means say to themselves, "Let the Hobsons, Waddington's ambitious son, José, and other money-hungry young sprouts speculate. We established businessmen are making substantial profits from our usual cruises! Why take a chance?" The old saying, "Nothing is more timid than a million dollars," seemed true, indeed.

The Hobsons, however, continued to speculate. With their newly purchased *Undine* repaired, they ventured a second cargo aboard her for California. With Captain Andrews in command, she sailed on September 23, carrying passengers in cabin class and also stowed tween decks.[72] Her supercargo, Alejandro Cross, would establish a San Francisco commission firm in partnership with William Hobson of Valparaiso. Also on board was a man named Tomás King, who carried dispatches from Washington. He, like Cross, had originally booked on the *Virjinia*, as had also another passenger, a Captain John Johnson of the United States Navy.[73] The *Undine*'s cargo was an odd assortment of dried fish, brogans and braces, cowhide whips, bolts of cotton cloth, shawls, Paris snuff, English cutlery, glassware, inkstands, desks, and writing paper. She also carried the forge that had been advertised for sale in James Harris's shop at a price said to be below its cost in England.[74]

In spite of the Hobsons' two shipments, conservative Spanish-speaking merchants remained skeptical. Owners of the Chilean schooner *Adelaida*, which had brought such glowing news from San Francisco, did not send her back to California. Instead they purchased trade goods with the gold she had brought and dispatched her on a cruise to the Marquesas Islands.[75]

On the other hand, José Ramón Sánchez, who had not returned the *J.R.S.* to California after she brought the first gold, now changed his mind concerning opportunities in San Francisco. On October 12 he advertised the 337-ton *Mercedes*, the biggest ship yet to go, as being available for transporting freight to the goldfields. He promised to sail in ten days but her holds filled so rapidly he sent her three days earlier than planned.[76] Her cargo consisted of the oddest imaginable assortment of goods for a gold rush, including children's toys, straw hats, Spanish playing cards (forty-card decks), books printed in Spanish, small-toothed combs, jewelry, Irish linen, cotton unbrellas, tent rugs, silk stockings, blankets, shoes, clothing, white calico, earthenware, cooking utensils, rice, sugar, dried sweetmeats, cinnamon, French preserves, cigars, chewing tobacco, jerked beef, champagne, brandy, shovels, hoes, and axes.[77]

The interest of Chilean merchants in California was obviously growing, despite the silence of the press. Many persons looked ahead to an era of new prosperity. Perhaps it was only a coincidence that on October 21, 1848, a large advertisement printed in both Spanish and English on the back page of *El Comercio de Valparaiso* informed readers that a seminary was opening for students of mathematics, writing, and bookkeeping. Teachers, according to the proclamation, had just arrived from London and a French instructor was on his way. Another advertisement stated that Don Carlos Blay had "the honor of announcing he will teach English."[78]

On October 23, 1848, the 124-ton Chilean schooner *Seis de Junio* arrived from California with only one passenger. He confirmed the stories of fabulous discoveries,[79] but newspapers continued to ignore them. Day after day, vessels arrived in Valparaiso from, or departed for, various parts of the world: England, France, Hong Kong, Singapore, and Batavia in Java. Finally, on October 25, *El Comercio* published an article entitled "ESTADOS UNIDOS EN EL PACIFICO." Readers were told that

North Americans' interests had recently shifted from whaling and the China trade to exploiting the new territory of California —but the discovery of gold was not mentioned.

Five days later, the American *Minerva*, a whaling bark, skimmed into the harbor[80] among the many foreign craft. *El Comercio* noted her arrival and said that Captain Perry, sixty-six days out of San Francisco, had brought 150 barrels of whale oil, but again there was no printed word about gold.[81] The press seemed to be boycotting all reference to the precious metal. Then, with thunderbolt suddenness, the newspapers headlined accounts about amazing discoveries in California! The vessel that started the unprecedented publicity was the 177-ton Chilean brigantine *Correo de Talcahuano*, Captain H. Mangot,[82] which arrived on November 3, 1848.

3

Chilean Newspapers and the Gold Rush

Why did Valparaiso's two daily newspapers refrain for more than two and a half months from printing any account of the California gold discovery? Why did *El Comercio de Valparaiso* complain, ten days after Captain Andrews had returned from San Francisco, that the current month had seen few events of interest? Also, why did this silence stop suddenly with the arrival of the Chilean brigantine *Correo de Talcahuano*?

Several explanations are possible, none of them thoroughly satisfactory. In the first place, gold discoveries were an old story in Chile and this was not the first one reported from California. People remembered the 1842 discovery. The fact that the new one was said to be making such a commotion in San Francisco was hearsay evidence based on questionable sources—stories told by plebeians. Chile had remained an essentially aristocratic country because the revolution that freed her from Spain had been democratic in name only. The great landowners had merely assumed the role of the throne. Commerce and industry were considered occupations for the lower classes, for foreigners, and for a few wealthy citizens like the Waddingtons. The activities of the captain of a small merchant ship and his supercargo were of minor interest. Such men did not rank with the elite. Newspapers described the great explorers, navigators, and merchant seamen as rotos who extended Chile's trade along the entire Pacific coast. These men were referred to with pride and extolled for their hardihood and bravery, but they were not classed with intellectuals.[1]

Socially important citizens were the landed gentry and professional men such as clergymen, lawyers, doctors, and scholars, especially if they were connected with landowning families.[2] A middle class was growing rapidly, however, and social distinctions were crumbling. On feast days public balls were open to all who could afford to attend. This practice, although democratic, was ironic, because the balls were aristocratically formal, often with an intermission for hairdressers to rearrange the ladies' coiffeurs. Females might attend these gaieties either masked or unmasked! What could be more democratic than that?

The leading Valparaiso newspapers printed announcements of the February 2, 1848, treaty with Mexico which ceded California to the United States, thus making a concession to the shipping interests, those unintellectual commercial people! The papers also published accounts of England's expanding transportation lines and of the latest improvements in steamships.[3] Of apparently deeper interest to the upper classes, however, was news concerning events in France. Of all the foreign residents the French were most acceptable socially, and they outnumbered other nationals in Valparaiso.[4] France, since Chile's independence, had become the nation's beau ideal.[5]

All cultured Chileans had studied in France, or at least had visited that country. The best shops in Valparaiso carried French furniture, French clothing, French bonnets. The opera *Lucia di Lammermoor*, at that time receiving great acclaim in Paris, was presented and praised in Valparaiso.[6] Pupils in school, even in the larger country towns, were taught French along with Latin,[7] and the Virgin in Chile's more up-to-date churches was dressed in French modiste fashion.[8] The newspapers considered accounts of French affairs in the Pacific singularly important,[9] and when the priest in Honolulu was appointed bishop of Hawaii he sailed down to Valparaiso for confirmation.[10] Napoleon's reactions to the revolutions in Europe during the summer of 1848 interested "important" Chilean readers more than the possibility of finding gold in distant California.[11] On September 27, *El Comercio de Valparaiso*, ignoring the adventurous departure of the *Virjinia* and the *Undine*, devoted its entire front page to the new phase of the revolution in France and the death of the archbishop of Paris, but not a word was said about California.

The threat of a revolution much closer than France may have crowded accounts of California discoveries from the Valparaiso papers. In neighboring Bolivia an insurrection was simmering and a Peruvian general had made secret purchases of arms in Chile to foment the uprising. The Chilean government ordered Captain Roberto Simpson to intercept the arms, and the situation quieted down, but the affair was of public interest while it lasted. Roberto Simpson was another of those Chileans with English names. Born in England in 1799, he came to Chile at the age of twenty-two to serve in the navy under Admiral Thomas Cochrane. When twenty-six years old, Simpson commanded his first frigate and ten years later he distinguished himself in a war against Bolivia.[12]

Revolutions and threats of revolutions at home and abroad filled only a part of the newspapers in the autumn of 1848. The editors also informed their readers about the *Communist Manifesto* of Marx and Engels, which in the hands of rotos and inquilinos might destroy the Chile that had become so successful since independence from Spain. Already, lawless fellows were making trouble; if they learned to read, the *Manifesto* might give them uncontrollable ideas. Some of these rotos had accumulated money by smuggling cattle across the Andes from Argentina. The traffic became so flagrant that the Chilean government appointed Juan Antonio Rodríguez, a cowboy in that region, to police the district. This rascal knew how to control wild, border horsemen. An expert with a knife, versed in the gaucho's deadly upper stroke with the cutting edge held inward,[13] he ruled his district so well that he declared himself the caudillo of an independent nation, thus becoming guilty of treason. His trial and execution in the spring of 1848 caused wide dissatisfaction among rotos generally, and a bloody insurrection in his name might still be festering underground.[14]

A threat of revolt was naturally more important news in Valparaiso than the discovery of gold in California, yet strangely enough it was connected with the rush. Vicente Pérez Rosales, the only Chilean who wrote a published account of his 1849 experiences in California, smuggled cattle out of Argentina, and he may have known more about Cowboy Rodríguez than he cared to admit. Pérez Rosales, born into a patrician family on April 5, 1807, later became an important Chilean administrator. His parents had participated, with San Martín, the Carreras, and the younger O'Higgins, in Chile's war for independence from Spain.[15] Shortly before the final victory Vicente was sent to school in France. Returning in 1828, he lived a sheltered life until financial reverses bankrupted his family. A period of nondescript adventures followed. Vicente prospected for gold, visited worked-over Chilean goldfields, and experimented with new methods of extracting "colors" from abandoned placers.[16] Dreaming of his country's fabled past and hoping to renew his family's fortunes, he explored the Andes probably as far south as the Chilean lakes where Valdivia had found gold and established a village which he named Villarrica.[17] Indians destroyed the "camp" and also a subsequent settlement there. Years later, when Pérez Rosales returned to that region, Indians and a few equally savage white outlaws were still in control.[18] Instead of finding wealth anywhere along the Andes, Pérez Rosales found only an opportunity for smuggling cattle from Argentina.

Little is known about this part of Vicente Pérez Rosales' life,[19] or about the locale of his smuggling. Many years later, after returning from his California adventures, he proved himself acquainted with the lake region some 250 miles south of Cowboy Rodríguez' bailiwick, a long distance for civilized, sedentary people but not for wilderness horsemen. The Andes, along the Argentine border which Pérez Rosales knew, stand like a jagged white-toothed wall thrust through a black carpet of pines. Passes across the mountains to Argentina are located at the head of deep gorges with narrow trails along steep slopes where cattle, if driven in herds, would crowd one another into deadly chasms. Yet smugglers who knew the habits of livestock could, by resorting to a clever artifice, get the animals across safely. Even when the grass is good, cattle will not stay long in the vast silence above timberline where condors nest and camel-necked guanacos thrive. If driven up, turned loose, and prevented from returning, cattle would therefore find the dangerous trails down the western slopes and proceed along them in slow-paced, single files, thus smuggling themselves into Chile's pine forests.

No grass grows under the dark Chilean conifers. In the sparse, sunny spaces along brawling streams cattle would find no feed— only stunted soapbark trees and tufts of unpalatable, bristling, blue-gray herbage. Seeking green pastures, cattle were sure to emerge in the lush, verdant country farther west, where grass grew knee deep and sapphire lakes with black sand beaches made safe watering places for livestock. Chilean cowboys, or *huasos*, who dared face the Indians might round up these cattle and drive them across rolling prairies to the coastal cities.

Pérez Rosales' part in such adventures is vague. His whereabouts for six or eight years are also vague, and it could have been more than a coincidence that he left the Andes at the time the first German immigrants to southern Chile made smuggling precarious by trekking back toward the lake country to establish homesteads.[20] In later years Pérez Rosales possessed more than common knowledge of the details of huaso Rodríquez' last days.[21] His California adventures indicate that he also remembered the exhilarating taste of dry, timberline air and the unforgettable sound of the peregrine falcon's piercing cry on the lofty slopes of the Andes.

When Pérez Rosales left the Andes for Valparaiso, he joined a group of ambitious writers in that growing city, and in 1842 he succeeded in having one of his philosophical "letters" published by *El Comercio*.[22] At thirty-five[23] he was older than many of the gifted scribes who had been attracted to the city's liberal press, a press that would have considerable influence on Chile's attitude toward the gold rush. Newspapers since colonial days had been the principal medium for urging political change. To support the revolution for independence a printing press and a typesetter were imported from the United States, and Chilean readers, like those in North America during their Revolutionary War, were steeped in the doctrines of Voltaire and Rousseau.[24] After Chile gained independence, the generation reared on vociferous liberalism sought a new cause, and in 1827 a new newspaper, *El Mercurio*, appeared in Valparaiso with the avowed

purpose of offering a forum for expressions of the new national-
ism, of newborn literature and art.

El Mercurio was first printed in a store owned by Alsop, Wet-
more y Cryder. Alsop belonged to the Connecticut banker-
merchant family whose commission firm would be strangely
connected with the gold rush from South America. The typesetters for this early-day newspaper were named Wells and
Silva, the former a fellow countryman of Alsop's.[25] The type for
the paper had been purchased from the heirs of Benjamin Franklin, and the top of the front page on early copies displayed the
American eagle and the seal of the United States.[26]

In 1842 a Spanish bookseller, Santos Tornero, purchased *El
Mercurio*. He and his brothers had come to Chile in 1834.[27] They
did not foresee the possibility of a gold rush to California, and
when it developed they fought it consistently in their newspaper. They had been attracted to Chile by the country's growing prosperity, the establishment of her international credit,[28]
and the growth of her navy[29] which enabled her to defy Argentina by occupying the Strait of Magellan, a serendipity destined
to be important to gold seekers sailing around the Horn.

Soon after the purchase the Tornero brothers began using
their presses to print pamphlets and books which they advertised
in their newspaper—a clever opportunity, yes! They planned
also to publish another newspaper, *the Valparaiso English Mercury*,[30] to compete with the *Neighbour*. Among the writers flocking to this new literary mecca was Andrés Bello from Caracas,
Venezuela. A scholarly man, he had served in Bolivar's government and admired that great revolutionist.[31] Priding himself on
being a liberal, Bello lectured at the University of Santiago and
wrote copiously for the newspapers on art, drama, and social
customs. Agreeing with *El Mercurio*'s opposition to the gold
rush, he became one of its editors and aspired to a seat in the
Chilean Senate where he could shape his adopted country's
policy toward gold seekers.

The liberalism of Andrés Bello's youthful days had become
conservativism by 1848; or were the younger generation of liberals too liberal to conform with other liberals? In any event,
the sixty-eight-year-old Bello found himself opposed by thirty-

seven-year-old Domingo Faustino Sarmiento, the member of a
new leftist group eager to display its intelligence by arguing
with him through letters in the press.[32] Sarmiento would make
a lasting, although backhanded, contribution to the literature of
California's gold rush. His vigorous, realistic style, very different
from Bello's flowery rhetoric, attracted the attention of ambitious
Pérez Rosales,[33] who would join the gold rush and write about it.

Perhaps Sarmiento's background added to Vicente's interest
in him. Sarmiento came from Argentina, knew huasos (called
gauchos on the pampas),* and had ridden several times with
questionable companions across the Andes[34] where Vicente had
been strong and young, so happy and so free. Although Sarmiento was four years younger than Pérez R., he had begun writing
earlier, cultivating an original style that differed radically from
the classical formalism that perfumed the compositions of Bello
and other Spanish authors.[35] He had taught in a country school[36]
where he found and read Franklin's autobiography. This book,
and the study of English which it engendered, may have helped
produce the simplicity of Sarmiento's sentences and his unpre-
tentious use of words, although he never mastered the English
language.[37] However that may be, Vicente admired Sarmiento's
narrative style and soon developed the same frank realism in his
own writing which would give life, color, and earthy humor to
his descriptions of life in California.

As noted above, the newspaper's silence concerning California
ended suddenly[38] with the arrival of the *Correo de Talcahuano*
on November 3, 1848. The *Correo* had made the trip from San
Francisco in fifty-nine days, bringing seven passengers, an assorted cargo, and a large quantity of gold.[39] The exact amount of
gold is controversial, but one man was reported to have returned
with $25,000 worth, which in those days made him well-to-do
in Valparaiso.[40]

The size of the shipment, however, compared with earlier im-
portations, was not large enough to stir up sudden interest by the

---

* "Gaucho," or "huaso," is spelled "guaso" by some travelers. Walt Whit-
man, in "Salud Monde," used the word "Wacho." Gaucho is said to be a corruption of "wáhcha," meaning "vagabond" in Quechua, a language spoken by
the Peruvian Inca. (See *The American Heritage Dictionary*, p. 546.)

press. Something else must have prompted *El Mercurio* to headline an article the next day: "LAS MINAS DE ORO DE CALIFORNIA." Under this banner Chilean readers could see in print, not just hear by word of mouth, the magnificent opportunities for acquiring a fortune in California. The source of the new information is plain. The *Correo de Talcahuano*, a mail-carrying vessel, had brought San Francisco newspapers, and the editor of *El Mercurio* broke the news by translating a story from the August 14 issue of the *Californian*. In this account Chileans were told that Alta California had changed from rural country, controlled by a few wealthy merchants, to a land of laborers who had suddenly become rich. Four thousand whites, the editor said, were reported to be working at the placers with many more than that number of Indians. Capital was unnecessary; all men worked together as equals while they panned gold. In some places, the editor told his readers, a miner needed only a common knife to get gold—again that knife story! A man with a pan could earn $30 to $40 a day until he acquired enough money to buy a round-bottomed machine made of boards. This contraption, 10 feet long and 2 feet wide at the upper end, enabled miners to make $75 to $150 a day. A laborer's daily wage was one ounce, figured at $16.[41]

With this exciting description *El Mercurio* scooped the conservative *El Comercio de Valparaiso* which catered to the established shipping and commercial interests. Eager to discredit his rival, *El Comercio*'s editor saw a small error in *El Mercurio*'s account and proceeded to make the most of it. That paper, he said, was wrong in telling its readers that the *Correo* had sailed from Valparaiso. She had left Talcahuano for the Sandwich Islands. Later she stopped at San Francisco. Not knowing that United States customs officers had arrived there her supercargo was surprised to learn that some of his goods could not be sold duty free.

The question of admitting Chilean goods was important, and the two papers debated the issue of international reciprocity for days, each accusing the other of being ignorant or illogical. The quarrel finally created a situation detrimental to the relations between the United States and Chile at the beginning of the gold rush. In those days journalism in Valparaiso, with its eager young intellectuals and exuberantly quarrelsome editors, was a philosophical avocation in which readers took part by writing letters to the press. In arguing the case of the *Correo de Talcahuano*, editors and correspondents of both papers displayed their profound knowledge of geophysics, navigation, philosophy, and international jurisprudence, and they all used it to cover up their meager knowledge of California and the facts in the case. *El Mercurio* made the final mistake of saying that misunderstandings between the two countries should be referred for clarification to the United States minister in Santiago, "a distinguished diplomat and excellent lawyer."[42]

Once again *El Comercio* took exception to its rival's statement, not to the reasoning but to the premise that the United States minister, who was really a chargé d'affaires, was a "distinguished diplomat and excellent lawyer." Seth Barton, *El Comercio* pointed out, was neither one; he was a "disgraceful character, disliked by everybody." Six months earlier, in May, 1848, the Chilean minister in Washington had requested Barton's replacement but was told that Barton could not be dismissed as he had committed no offense. Moreover, President Polk sustained Barton for his part in negotiating the recent treaty with Mexico, the treaty that gave California, with its newfound gold fields, to the United States.[43]

Part of Seth Barton's unpopularity may have stemmed from his report, early in 1848, that Chile had violated her treaty with the United States by giving Spain more favorable importation rights than she granted the Yankees.[44] Barton was one of those undiplomatic officials who are often sent by democracies to countries with a totally different culture. To Barton, all Chileans were "spigotties," and their capital, in spite of its population of more than 70,000, was an uncivilized collection of mud huts.

In truth many of Santiago's houses were built of adobe blocks, an excellent building material for earthquake country. Also, most of them stood only one or two stories high, but the city, founded in 1541,[45] could hardly have been called uncivilized. A fine cathedral graced one side of the broad, central plaza. A block-long government office building stood across from it. On the other two sides of the plaza Roman-arched arcades[46] sheltered shops selling jewelry, French clothing, furniture, and objets d'art. French architects were cutting "Parisian passages" through many old business blocks, making arcades with entrances between street corners.[47] This kind of city may have differed sharply from the upstart North American cities Barton knew, but Santiago's residents were certainly civilized.

The capital of Chile prided itself on being the nation's cultural center; its inhabitants were a bit skeptical of those literary radicals in Valparaiso. Santiago supported schools of painting, art, and music. The National Library shelved 21,000 books, the Law Library an additional 1,700, all open to the public. Two theaters offered performances but, also unlike Valparaiso residents, the people of Santiago were not theatergoers.[48] One of Valparaiso's municipal services was noteworthy. The city provided free daily garbage collections.[49] Did Seth Barton's much touted North American communities offer that civility? Surely no city in Barton's country had a finer thoroughfare than Santiago's O'Higgins Boulevard. Water from the Andes babbled along gutters at the roots of a long line of Lombardy poplars. Beneath the trees, benches tempted promenaders to rest. Urchins with little boxes of glowing punk offered *para una propina* to light strollers' cigarettes.[50]

Many of Santiago's city streets looked drab and dull to gold seekers on their way to California, but the rough adobe walls with an occasional barred window sometimes masked a fine residence. A guest stepping through the front door entered a patio often shaded by a magnolia or a Norfolk Island pine imported from New Zealand's South Pacific islands and hauled by oxen over the mountains from Valparaiso. In the reception parlor, or *sala*, glowing coals for the visitor's cigarette could be found in a silver *brasero*.[51] As in most old civilizations, some aristocrats who could not afford servants[52] clung to their big houses which carried on the venerated tradition of gracious living. But no matter what the financial circumstances of a true gentleman, he would invariably welcome a guest by presenting him with a rose or some other small token, and his universal greeting was, "The house, and all it contains, are wholly at your service."[53]

Perhaps Seth Barton took advantage of these hospitable words. He may have shown brash contempt for the venerated manners of Chileans, for certainly his behavior prejudiced them against North Americans at the dawn of the gold rush. In June, 1848, he further disgraced himself in the eyes of Santiagoans by driving recklessly through their streets, which often lacked sidewalks and were often too narrow for vehicles to pass. Pedestrians complained, rotos rioted, and the *vigilantes* were called out to maintain order.[54]

Then, shortly after the newspapers commenced printing fantastic stories about the gold in California, Barton created a scandal by marrying a divorced woman, mother of two sons and member of a good family in impoverished circumstances.[55] Unpleasant as such a union might be to conservative Chileans, Barton made it worse by arranging for the nuptials to take place when United States warships were anchored at Valparaiso. The commodore and his suite attended the ceremony, as did some members of the diplomatic corps, but the archbishop wrote the lady telling her that she was living in sin and if she felt rewarded in this life she would suffer during eternity.[56]

The archbishop also sent Barton a note expressing a wish that he leave the country within twenty-four hours. Barton appealed to the Chilean government, demanding that the archbishop be arrested, tried, and punished for insulting a citizen of the United States. The government denied responsibility for the archbishop's act, and Barton, in a huff, closed the United States legation, saying that Chile had violated the treaty of 1833[57] which specified that citizens of the two countries would be unmolested for their religious beliefs. In making this statement Barton was ignoring the implications of paragraph 11 of the treaty, which added that citizens would be unmolested "so long as they respect the laws and established uses of the country."[58] Instead, he vowed the United States would insist on indemnifications, with force if necessary. Here was an ugly threat of war at the time when thousands of North American gold seekers in unarmed vessels were due to stream north on the Pacific.

Almost half a century later, in 1890, when a United States minister showed sympathy for an antichurch liberal, a Chilean mob attacked a party of sailors on shore leave from the cruiser *Baltimore*. Two were killed and several wounded. In that case the United States insisted on reparations, threatening war until the Chilean government agreed to pay $75,000 in damages to the injured and to heirs of the dead. How would a Chilean mob react in the gold rush? Certainly they had already made life unsafe for Barton.[59]

The crisis in 1848 was not taken lightly by the Chilean government. The minister of foreign relations submitted to the Chilean Congress a defense of the republic's actions covering 103 octavo pages.[60] The debates that followed were a prelude to the constant threat of revolution which developed later when reports came back to Valparaiso concerning the abuse of Chileans who had emigrated to California.

4

California Has Made
Another "New World"

Twilight and evening bell,
And after that the dark—
And may there be no sadness of farewell,
When I embark.
—Tennyson

The gold rush came as a great relief to Chile's Rear Admiral
Carlos Whiting Wooster, for it allowed him a means of escape.
He was an outlawed and broken man. His fighting temper had
earned him high naval honors, but eventually it rang his "evening bell" and darkness obscured the record of his brilliance.
Born in New Haven, Connecticut, in 1780, he went to sea at the
age of eleven, was commanding a ship at twenty-one, and as a
privateer in the War of 1812 captured twenty-two prize ships,
thus becoming a wealthy man.[1]

Wooster's wife died in 1816, and with no war, no wife, and no
business in New England he became interested in a proposition
offered him by a foreign visitor. Don Miguel Carrera, seeking
aid in the war for Chile's independence, offered Wooster a captain's commission in the Chilean navy if he would buy and command a cruiser to help in the fight against Spain. Wooster accepted the proposal and with the new ship he sailed around the
Horn. On October 28, 1818, he became a national hero by board-
ing and capturing the Spanish warship *Reina María Isabel* in
Talcahuano.[2] When Thomas Cochrane arrived to assume command as admiral of the Chilean fleet, Wooster served under him
in the 1820 occupation of Callao which deprived Spain of a port
of entry to Lima, causing her eventual defeat. Wooster's fighting

temper, though excellent for a privateer, prevented him from serving under others. He rebelled at Cochrane's discipline and resigned.

In 1822 Cochrane left the Chilean service and Wooster accepted the top command. Fighting now for President Ramón Freire,[3] whose name would mean much to Chilean gold seekers in a California riot, Wooster won another naval victory on Chiloé Island in 1826, driving Spain from her last foothold on Chilean soil. In 1829 he was commissioned rear admiral, but again his fighting temper prevented him from cooperating with the successive victors who assumed power after political upsets. In self-defense, Wooster became implicated in a revolution that failed; he lost everything except his life and the precious jeweled medals awarded him by grateful Chilean governments for his naval victories. Aged sixty-eight, he fled to California as supercargo on a vessel loaded with wheat.[4] He was lucky to get away, and doubly lucky because he did not see the tragedy ahead of him. The date of the rear admiral's escape cannot be determined. Fleeing under disguise, he probably left before the arrival of the *Correo de Talcahuano* or shortly thereafter, for during the rush that soon developed he might have experienced serious difficulty in getting the job of supercargo. Many men, both rich and poor, were negotiating for transportation to California.

The frenzied quest for passage was new to shippers, and the first to cater to the demand was another of the Waddington sons, this time Jorge W., who on November 7, 1848, advertised his brigantine *Talca* as a passenger ship with ample accommodations. She would sail, he said, early in December.[5] Two days later José Cervero offered space on his *Correo del Pacífico*. Then auctioneers began announcing sales of vessels in the harbor, as well as of equipment and supplies. When owners of the British bark *Collooney* advertised her for sale, the notice was printed in Spanish only; the next day it appeared in both Spanish and English.[6] The two big newspapers, even as they published these advertisements, fulminated over the excitement. One urged people to go; the other advised them to be sensible and stay home.[7]

The demand for passage changed the routine schedules of

many ships, and again José Ramón Sánchez, the successful businessman, changed his mind. He had failed to send the *J.R.S.* on
a return trip to California after she brought the first gold in
August. In October, when the shipping rush began, he dispatched, posthaste, his big *Mercedes* with the odd cargo that
included umbrellas and children's toys for California miners.
Then, on November 3, the *Correo de Talcahuano* arrived with
printed accounts of the true situation, and within nine days Don
José loaded and sent the 225-ton *Dolores* to San Francisco carrying a more appropriate cargo in charge of Francisco Álvarez
y Hijo. Francisco's only son, Francisco Salvador Álvarez, was on
board; he hoped to become an auctioneer in San Francisco.[8]

The size of the *Dolores* and of her cargo indicated the importance of the new market. Furthermore, men seeking adventure
—men like Pérez Rosales—must have noticed that the *Dolores*
carried three patrónes engaged in an enterprise others could
readily copy. Don Alejandro Smith, Don Eduardo Desemberg,
and Don Télesforo Sarabia were taking a force of husky peons
armed with the usual mining tools, picks, bars, and shovels. Such
laborers were easy to employ in Valparaiso since a day's wage
was only one or one and a half reales (12.5 or 18.5 cents).[9]

Four days later, on November 16, *El Comercio* printed a long
editorial on the front page, "EMIGRACIÓN A CALIFORNIA," which
said, in substance, "A true fever of emigration is afflicting part of
our population, a fever specialized in by North Americans who
hope to use California for their commercial interests and to dominate trade from Cape Horn to Panama. Exploiting their mines
and monopolizing the shipping, they will profit by an increased
number of laborers and consumers. Their prosperity will not
make less sad or lamentable the experiences of our emigrants.

"We do not doubt for one moment all that is said about California, but in a rapidly increasing population the splendor of a
great fortune obscures the poverty of others. When America
was discovered, the search for gold caused thousands of people
to leave homes and families in search of a fortune. The same
thing will be repeated in California. History tells much about
gold discoveries, but it omits the bitterness of failure, especially
the bitterness of self-inflicted failure."[10]

The newspapers admitted that the emigration was true to Chile's roto tradition. These hardy people had always been tireless navigators, audacious explorers, a glory to the flag, heroes in wars to extend civilization. Chile, one editor wrote, was founded on the outskirts of the world, at the foot of gigantic mountains and at the edge of the immense ocean. Starting with miserable little villages of miners, fishermen, and farmers, Chile had achieved a splendid destiny. During colonial days rotos traded as far north as Panama and Mexico. They became acquainted with the coasts of California and Lower California, although trade with these regions was prohibited. In Chile's fight for independence her rotos made up the infantry and her cowboys the cavalry which together defeated Spain, thus liberating not only Chile but Peru as well.[11]

At the time of these lavish pronouncements in the press, a vessel entered Valparaiso harbor with information that really kindled the gold rush. She was the British warship, *Constance*, carrying letters describing the ever growing opportunities in California, opportunities not only for merchants who might make 400 percent profits,[12] but for laborers who could make a 1,000 pesos a month.[13] The shipping of passengers, not freight, became a new business in Valparaiso, and men walked fast from counting rooms to booking offices.

Next day another vessel sailed in, and men who walked fast along Valparaiso's streets began to run. The mail schooner, *Lambayeque*,[14] came from California with even more exciting news. She had carried an army lieutenant taking an official report of the discoveries to Washington along with a tea caddy filled with gold dust for the president of the United States to see. Leaving the schooner to cross the Isthmus of Panama, he must now be well on his way. Due to an odd coincidence, his trip had already started the gold rush from Peru, as will be described later.

A sudden demand for passage to California from Valparaiso caused the editor of *El Mercurio* to print a startling report. On November 20 he wrote that a vessel announcing at 11:00 in the morning that she was sailing to California could sell all her passenger space by 2:00 P.M. the same day. This report disturbed the editor, who suspected the city's financiers of engaging in undercover trickery. Fares to California were expensive, and the average person, even in the growing middle class, could not raise sufficient funds in so short a time. Always critical of the established classes, he surmised that one of two adverse circumstances loomed ahead: either many capitalists were taking their money out of the country, leaving it destitute, or the various commercial houses had joined together to purchase all tickets, corner the market, and resell them at a handsome profit.[15]

El Mercurio's competitor, *El Comercio de Valparaiso*, true to the old rivalry between the two sheets, immediately began attacking the liberal paper's statements. The renewed battle of rhetoric lasted a fortnight. In the joy of forensic discourse, editors on both sides soon lost sight of the gold rush. The liberal *Mercurio* became strongly conservative in its desire to stop the rush. The emigration, according to the editor, had been of little importance at first. Only a few people had gone, but now uncounted numbers were departing to seek questionable treasures in an unknown land. Every vessel sailing from Valparaiso, the editor said, snatched away a portion of Chile's invaluable population, all good industrious citizens, some of them men of substance. The poor and worthless could not raise the necessary 100 pesos for passage. In addition to the loss of population the editor noted that an increase in the world's gold supply would cheapen the value of gold and that the inflation would also affect silver currency. With dismay he pointed to the "world crisis," saying that "now as never before" something must be done "*before it is too late*"—the three clichés voiced so often in English by concerned moralists before his day and many times since. Becoming lyrical, the editor even called readers' attention to the fact that the ocean currents flowed northward, taking in that direction the nation's hopes, aspirations, and prosperity.

This last observation served the rival paper well, and instead of sending a reporter to get a firsthand story from a departing gold seeker at the harbor, the editor of *El Comercio* replied under the headline, "LAS CORRIENTES DEL PACIFICO." Accusing the opposition paper of inaccurate reporting, he granted that some ocean currents flowed north, but insisted that many others flowed south and that some remained stationary. (An odd way to "flow"!) As for the northbound currents, not all of them took Chile's hopes of prosperity to California. They took Chilean merchant ships to Peru, Ecuador, New Grenada (Colombia and Panama), and Mexico, as well as to California and Oregon. Trade with the ports of all these countries had made Valparaiso a great city. Trade influenced navigation more than ocean currents.

The discovery of gold in California, according to *El Comercio*, would not hurt Chile. Instead, it would bring more ships from all nations to the Pacific. Then, matching the poetic allusions of *El Mercurio* and at the same time demonstrating a mastery of English literature, the editor stated in Spanish that Chileans should remember "the picturesque language of Washington Irving," who commended the Genoese navigator, Columbus, for giving us a "new world." Now the discovery of gold in California had made another "new world" out of the Pacific. Readers were urged to remember that Venus of antiquity was born of the ocean's foam; perhaps "the Pacific's foam will give birth to another new and beautiful world."[16]

The editor of *El Comercio*, evidently fascinated by his references to mythology and literature, reminded his fellow citizens that they all resembled the child who watched the genie in *A Thousand and One Nights* produce a giant studded with diamonds and rubies. Then, with the assurance of a professional conversationalist who scores a neat point, the editor added: "No one should disapprove of the gold discoveries in California. Instead, everyone now has a great opportunity to display inventive and constructive imagination." Finally, resorting to parables, he concluded by saying: "If the net of the fisherman is broken in the sea, he uses another method to catch fish. Chileans must now do the same, and they will prosper by increased shipping from their ports and by the sale of Chilean products, thus making money, not for the few as in the past, but for all."[17]

At this stage of the debate between the two newspapers, mobs of prospective gold seekers, many of them rotos and inquilinos lacking money for subsistence as well as passage, crowded Valparaiso's cobbled streets. They presented a new problem to *vigilantes* who were accustomed to dealing only with the small crews of sailing vessels, but instead of reporting incidents in the crooked streets, the papers continued their bandying of words. On November 21 *El Mercurio*, in a two-column article, warned readers that all accounts of California riches were translated from English, and that translations were notoriously inaccurate. As for *El Comercio's* statement that the rush might be good for Valparaiso, *El Mercurio* told its readers: "The illusions about California have many facets. Will they be good or bad for the interests of Chileans? Nothing is absolute in the firmament. Certainly a new market is opening for our products, but will Chile be ruined by her geographical position and the peculiarity of her products? Will the prosperous development of California help or hinder Chile? If we find a new market for our supplies, yes; but if the North Americans build a railroad across the Isthmus of Panama, then the trade route to India and China will no longer be by Cape Horn, and Valparaiso will suffer."[18]

Next day, November 22, *El Comercio* continued the inconsequential debate, saying: "It is impossible for us not to talk about California when it is the topic of the day, the subject of conversation on all occasions, the direction of the thoughts of all who desire greater wealth and more commerce; it even usurps conversation about fashionable clothes and books. We have said that the discoveries will call the world's attention to the Pacific, bringing vessels of all nations, bringing civilization to the Pacific."

Perhaps these long newspaper discourses furnished diversion for the more literate gold seekers crowding Valparaiso, jostling one another for berths on the vessels anchored in the bay. Shopkeepers and restaurateurs had become desperate for supplies. Some of them climbed the steep roads leading out of town, racing with one another to be first to meet the squealing carretas loaded with farm produce. These men paid exorbitant prices on the road and then doubled the amount they charged their customers in town.

The gold-rush agitation soon extended inland, disturbing inquilinos on the big haciendas. It also reached across the mountains to Chile's capital, Santiago. That city of red tile roofs, plazas, and imposing churches[19] lacked Valparaiso's large foreign population; it was more conservative, but certainly not Spanish. Most ladies had discarded the high comb and mantilla for French bonnets, but always, even when exquisitely dressed, they wrapped themselves in shawls. The best homes in Santiago lacked central heating. Wood was scarce, and so were fireplaces.[20] On a social call ladies might be invited to remove their shawls and keep warm by dancing.

Religious customs were also more strict in Santiago. In Valparaiso, where Protestants were numerous, a man might be ignored if he failed to uncover his head, kneel, and cross himself when the Host, with lamp carriers and ringing bell, passed along the street. In Santiago such a blasphemer would feel his coattails twitched by some ragged fellow until he complied. As in other societies, the lower classes—the peons and the rotos—were apt to be the most exacting and the least tolerant.[21]

In Santiago many working people discussed the gold rush at two public places: at the fountain in the plaza[22] and at the foot of Santa Lucía, a sharp-pointed hill topped by a fortress protecting the city. At both these gossip centers donkey boys filled kegs in their panniers with water to be sold, along with the news, at distant doorways. From nearby residences servant girls brought pottery jars to fill with water. They carried the jars on their heads—a practice that required their erect and universally admired posture. For them, woman-empty California offered a tempting opportunity, and great plans were made to send there "200 young, white, poor and virtuous girls to be . . . honorably married to the thousands of North Americans and other strangers who have made their fortunes at the mines."[23]

Santiago's three newspapers voiced diverse opinions about the gold rush. El Araucano, an official publication, printed proceedings of the Chilean Congress and also national statistics. In this sheet the debates over the gold rush which led to a national crisis and eventually to revolution were printed. That meticulous scholar, Andrés Bello, the liberal turned conservative, served as one of the editors.[24] Bello's literary rivals, including Sarmiento,[25] wrote for El Progreso, a paper that criticized all government actions. Conservatives called the paper socialistic, and indeed it could be counted on to use the gold rush as an aid to social change in Chile and to laud North American "liberty" and "democracy." The third journal, La Tribuna, posed as the paper of the people, that is, of the conservative people, the silent majority. Subsidized by the government, it always approved or excused the administration's acts.[26]

Santiago was only 60 air miles from crowded, excited Valparaiso, but the distance was 80 miles by the shortest road,[27] which ran across two steep mountain ranges, La Cuesta Zapata and La Cuesta del Prado. A road paved with red stones had been started by the elder O'Higgins under the rule of Spain, but it had been neglected since the revolution[28] which, like most revolutions, benefited a new privileged class, creating a new vested interest. In 1821 an American operated a lumbering stagecoach line to carry passengers from Santiago to Valparaiso in two, sometimes three, days, with changes of horses at stations along the way, but it had failed.[29]

The means of transportation which became popular during the gold rush was the *birlocho*, a two-wheeled rig with a grating for a seat. Three men with twelve horses, valued at an "ounce" each,[30] operated a birlocho. Two or three galloping horses pulled the vehicle. One, the wheelhorse, was hitched between shafts. A second horse pulled beside him on the right. A postilion on a third horse also helped pull with a rawhide riata attached to a ring in his saddle girth. Another horseman galloped behind the vehicle, driving nine or ten loose horses to spell the harnessed teams as they tired.

Passage from Santiago to Valparaiso by birlocho cost three ounces—surely an expensive trip, but a traveler could make it in fourteen to eighteen hours.[31] Although this indicates that the birlocho traveled only 4.5 to 6 miles an hour, it really moved much faster because time was lost by changing horses. Short as the overall time seems, most travelers, even the eager gold seekers, called a halt for rest at one of the stage stations. The usual time for departure from Santiago was midday,[32] when shops were closed for the siesta and the streets were so quiet that a pedestrian could hear his own footsteps. A sudden shout, shrill as a huntsman's wild halloo, told the relaxed city that a birlocho had started.

Horses drew the vehicle at a gallop through the city's dilapidated gate and along the road that stretched straight as a plumb line to La Cuesta del Prado.[33] For the first mile or two, passengers saw loosely thatched adobe houses, each with a beehive oven at the rear. Ragged children and scrawny dogs stared at the travelers.[34] Beyond these squalid huts, the road passed through vineyards and olive orchards. Long lines of Lombardy poplars served as windbreaks. At the foot of La Cuesta del Prado, the rolling hillsides were dotted with *espinos* which, in the heat of December, had shed their yellow blossoms and looked for all the world like neglected peach trees, with last year's dry grass waving beneath the spindly trunks. In this counterfeit orchard the drivers stopped their birlochos and, throwing riatas with dexterous casts across the backs and manes of the loose horses, they snared fresh animals for the gallop up the ridge ahead. The road zigzagged across the steep, almost bare slope, and a birlocho usually reached the crest in midafternoon. From there the passengers cold look across a hilly valley below them and see the next mountain wall, Cuesta Zapata, which they hoped to reach before dark.

On the downgrade ahead a birlocho made good time, skidding breathlessly around hairpin turns which sent pebbles flying from the wheels and made passengers clutch the latticework seats. Arriving at the foot of the ridge they found the valley ahead sparsely settled, except for a few farms along one little stream. On the entire trip from Santiago to Valparaiso travelers saw only one or two fine country mansions. Few of the proud landowners lived permanently on their estates. This custom might soon change because bitter debates and recent enactments had qualified the law of entail. The ancient haciendas might soon be broken up, especially if roto gold seekers brought back new ideas of democracy.[35]

The days were long in December when birlochos were used for the rush to Valparaiso, and with good luck a traveler topped Zapata's summit by sunset. From that point the next valley looked as green and flat as a billiard table. A straight red line across it was the road to Valparaiso. Fifteen miles away, Casa Blanca, the last stage station on the trip, was visible in the clear, dry air, as sharply distinct as an image seen through the wrong end of a telescope.

From Zapata's summit travelers could also see a tiny village below them at the foot of the slope, where the green tableland began. Curacaví was a Chilean country town in which the houses were joined together as in a city. The main road, like a city street, ran for at least 100 yards between two walls with doors and occasional windows. Some birlocho travelers stopped here for the night.[36] Others rattled through the town after dark. Town lights were expensive luxuries, seldom used. Peons "rose and set" with the sun.

Beyond Curacaví a birlocho entered farm country where passengers, riding at night during the early months of the gold rush, could smell the first cutting of hay. The road was level and straight. Drivers, eager to reach the next stop, shouted "Andela, caballos! Andela!" to the galloping horses, but midnight invariably passed before they reined to a stop at Casa Blanca. This stage station, an adobe village 30 miles from Valparaiso, supported some 500 souls,[37] all dependent on the overland traffic. At Casa Blanca men broke horses, traded them, and repaired wagons. Women cooked for their men and catered to travelers' wants. Children, some of them toddlers hoping someday to be cowboys or *birlochoderos,* carried coils of twine instead of toys in their little hands and constantly practiced lassoing dogs and chickens. In the station proper, food and wine were served along with the latest newspapers from Valparaiso.[38] Most passengers rested at the station until morning.

At Casa Blanca several roads joined the highway and, after the gold rush started, the thoroughfare to Valparaiso became crowded. Birlocho drivers had to shout their way past drays, squealing carretas, groups of horsemen, and many peons, barefooted or in sandals. Each of these fellows wore a poncho around his neck—the only bedding he needed—a dagger at his waist, and a leather money belt or a sash with a few reales knotted in one end. All faces beamed with hope of riches in the new El Dorado. These devout and eager pilgrims reminded one writer of the Crusades from medieval Europe.[39] A birlocho traveler, delayed by such a mob, often felt the sinking sun in his eyes, despite his broad-brimmed sombrero, before he glimpsed the Pacific. Constantly he watched for the row of pipestemmed wine palms along the rim surrounding Valparaiso. When they were sighted, a traveler knew that after one or two more rough riding miles his birlocho would spin down a 1,350-foot slope[40] into the city's crowded streets.

Valparaiso was unprepared for such a mass of almost destitute humanity, but speculators, intent on reaping profits in California, saw their opportunity and enlisted peons by the score. One North American sea captain booked passengers without money, stipulating in writing that they pay their fares by panning gold for a master in California.[41] In other words, the captain planned to sell them as bond servants in San Francisco.

The exodus from Chile disturbed José Victorino Lastarria in Santiago. He was one of the liberal writers[42] of his time, a popular academician devoted to progressive education and to ideas of liberty, democracy, and social justice.[43] A vigorous champion of causes, he scorned the complacent people who lacked concern. His letters to El Mercurio[44] were read widely, discussed, and answered. He was a scholar versed in Latin, French, and English. A much younger man than Pérez Rosales, he was already widely known as a writer. He had studied under Andrés Bello at the university and by the time of the gold rush had probably outstripped his former master in literary importance.[45] Laying down his pen for politics, he served as minister of the interior in 1843 and in 1862, a "little more later," as Spanish speakers say, he became minister of state.[46] He was a great admirer of the English historian, H. T. Buckle, sharing his views on the relation of geography, climate, and soil to a nation's history. By the time Lastarria died in 1888 he was acclaimed as the father of Chilean literature.[47] Like so many of his fellow liberals, he opposed emigration to California, as he made clear in December, 1848:

The reports of riches in California which have caused such a stir in Valparaiso have also created much agitation in the habitually sedate Santiago. A spirit of adventure has induced people to forget the resources of their own country and go to an unknown land. They ignore the fact that copper may be developed profitably here in Chile, and so much undeveloped agricultural land remains unplowed that the government has dispatched, at the height of this rush, an emissary to Europe to offer the heads of families free passage and homesteads tax free for twelve years. Native Chileans fail to see these opportunities at home. They are unable to see the reverse side of the gold coin they seek in California. The spirit of adventure, like the tides on the beaches of Valparaiso, draws them away to the California of the Mexicans who, with their usual laziness, neglected the country that has become the center of world interest. All wish only to be first in the land of a portentous future. They go arming themselves with only a pick, or shovel, or even a knife to dig gold by handfuls.[48]

5

Pérez Rosales Joins the Rush

From their folded mates they wander far,
Their ways seems harsh and wild;
They follow the beck of a baleful star.
Their paths are dream-beguiled.
—Richard Burton, *Black Sheep*

Romantic-minded Chileans read Dumas's novels, and his characters were very real to many of them. They admired d'Artagnan, with his ready sword and his winning ways. The immensely popular *Three Musketeers* had been published in their beloved French, only four years before the gold rush from Chile began. The all-conquering Gascon may not have been one of the Chileans' own Basque forefathers, but he came very close to it. The rush to California became more than a search for gold. It presented the possibility of another great crusade, and instead of dressing in coats of mail many Chilean gold seekers wore the hats and cloaks of French *mousquetaires*.

Vicente Pérez Rosales, a cowboy d'Artagnan and an occasional correspondent for the Valparaiso press, soon felt the excitement that intoxicated so many daring young men. He was determined not only to join the rush but to keep a journal of his experiences, a journal that proved to be of some importance to California history. As the son of a prominent family[1] he had been admirably educated with books in Europe and not so admirably by smugglers in the Andes—two schools that certainly qualified him for a California adventure. As early as November 10, 1848, in the flurry of ship sales which followed the arrival of the *Correo de Talcahuano*, he must have noticed the announcement of an auction scheduled for November 20.[2] Captain Witzel was selling, to the highest bidder, his 321-ton *L'Orient* to pay for her recent refittings.

The captain described the vessel as a copper-bottomed craft constructed in Bordeaux of the best materials,[3] a vessel ready to sail at once for California. Vicente, having gone to school in France and knowing that the French residents of Valparaiso ranked among the wealthiest, must have watched the approach of this sale intently. Indeed, he may have negotiated with the French Fauché brothers to take part in the bidding. He had seen the California fever grow from a few venturesome speculations to heavy investments by conservative shippers. He had seen ship after ship arrive with sacks and casks of gold, and he knew that José Ramón Sánchez had sent the *Dolores* to California without waiting for the returns from the *Mercedes*. He had also heard that men of means tripled and quadrupled their investments in a single round trip, and he saw the mobs in the streets—patrónes and *peónes*—clamoring for passage. This new El Dorado, this new frontier, might have many similarities to the Andes he knew so well.

Four days before the auction[4] an incident occurred which proved important to the career of Pérez Rosales. A French ship, the 235-ton *Staoueli*[5] commanded by Captain Pigno Blanco, sailed in from Le Havre with twenty-four passengers, all refugees from the revolution, bound for California.[6]

As the date for the auction approached, the demand for vessels increased daily, and shipwrights for new construction were hard to find even at exorbitant prices. The excitement stimulated newspaper editors to new denunciation or new approval of the gold rush, and the editorial bombardment lasted for weeks. When *El Mercurio* made its usual complaint about the exodus, *El Comercio* replied, true to form: "Is there anything wrong with it? Nothing! All this will help the Pacific in general and Chile in particular. We are told that our population will leave for California. If so, better people will come to take their places. Notice the scientists, artists, skilled artisans, and merchants. Not many days have passed since a boatload of such people arrived from France."[7] If the editor of *El Comercio* was referring to the French refugees who had arrived on the *Staoueli*, he was certainly mistaken, because those energetic liberals were already infected with the gold fever and planned to continue their voyage.

During the newspapers' exchange of literary shots, ship auctions continued and the Fauché brothers bid in *L'Orient*.[8] Pérez Rosales' part in the purchase is obscure, but he did make some arrangement for passage on *L'Orient* to California for himself, three brothers, a brother-in-law, two servants, and three peons.[9] The cost would have been $1,000 to $1,200, but he may have paid only part of it. Certainly he and his companions moved their baggage and equipment on board: spades, axes, picks, a big iron kettle, gunpowder and lead for bullets. They also loaded tents and six sacks of beans, 400 pounds of rice, a barrel of sugar, two barrels of Concepción wine, and six sacks of toasted flour, a Chilean preparation that needed only the addition of water to make it edible.[10]

Storage space for so many supplies was very expensive in Valparaiso since the gold seekers had crowded the city, and Pérez Rosales may have felt lucky to find a place for his equipment. As noted above, there must have been some manipulation in the sale because the purchasers were so confident of buying the vessel that they advertised for passengers on the day of the sale. Surely their advertisement had been filed at the newspaper office the night before.

The paper that carried the advertisement ran another on the same day which may have disconcerted Pérez Rosales. Agents for the *Staouelí* advertised passenger space, and within half an hour applicants had lined up to purchase tickets. Vicente may have wondered why these people preferred this vessel to *L'Orient*. Had he invested in the wrong ship? The *Staouelí* was scheduled to sail in fifteen or twenty days and *L'Orient*'s agents assured passengers she would go "in a few days."[11] *L'Orient* might therefore leave first, and Pérez R. may have felt that he had engaged passage on the best vessel—but had he? The next few weeks would tell.

Other vessels, fully booked, set off from time to time. Six days after the auction, the schooner *Rosa* sailed for California with a cargo shipped by Jorge Wilson y Cía.,[12] and among her passengers she carried one who belied *El Comercio*'s prophecy that the gold rush would bring artists to Chile. Instead, the *Rosa* was taking away the French artist, Ernest Charton, a longtime resident of Valparaiso. He had studied under Paul Delaroche, a name familiar to everybody in that sophisticated town. Engravings of Delaroche pictures were in vogue on both sides of the Atlantic. Only five months before, Ernest Charton had announced that he was returning to France, and he began selling all his paintings, his personal art collection, paints, brushes, and palettes. But now, after news of the gold discoveries, he changed his mind and decided to join the rush.[13]

Among other passengers on the *Rosa* were four "gentlemen," or "dons," with Spanish names, and also many workmen. Most notable among the passengers was a woman, Doña Carmen López, her daughter, and a servant. She was a widow seeking a son who had embarked furtively on an earlier vessel for California.[14]

Next day the American *Minerva*, a 195-ton whaling bark hastily converted to a transport, sailed for California under Captain Perry. The assorted cargo, dispatched by Loring y Cía.,[15] consisted of beads, jewelry, prints, pillows, and soap. The ship also carried gold scales, quinine, and Seidlitz powders[16] which would make the voyage effervescent if they got wet. The *Minerva's* passenger list included many English names, a fact that may have had no significance. English names, of course, were common in South American coastal towns. Not all the passengers were Anglos, however. Four, obviously patrónes of Spanish descent, had enlisted groups of from two to twelve peons carrying mining tools. More unusual was Don Carlos Rosillón who booked steerage passage for four Indians. Two married couples, Eduardo Devon and Napoleón Dumonlin and their wives, occupied what were described as cabins barred like jails—but whether to lock the ladies in or to keep prowlers out, the records say not.[17]

Vicente Pérez Rosales, seeing these vessels depart, became more and more impatient to be off. *L'Orient*, on which his and his companions' baggage was stowed, seemed ridiculously slow in preparing for the voyage. On December 2 her owners discontinued advertising although her berths were still unfilled. Then, a week later, a new advertisement announced that *L'Orient* had been rechristened the *Julia*, under Chilean registry, and would sail "this month." The *Staoueli* promised to go on December 20, so it was still uncertain which ship would leave first. In addition to these two, three other vessels announced sailing dates, but none of them interested Pérez R.[18]

In the meantime, on December 3, Mickle y Cía. dispatched the famous *Ann McKim*. Of the sixty passengers, fifty-eight arrived in San Francisco—a moderate loss of life in the days of sail.[19] Her cargo seemed strange indeed for a gold rush. In the hold were bolts of cotton and wool cloth, bales of shawls, ponchos, blankets, pillows, towels, stockings, and gloves, boxes of thread, brass and bone buttons, silk umbrellas, rolls of oilcloth for tables, boots, shoes, lead pencils, spoons in two sizes, sugar tongs, sperm candles, looking glasses, razors, brushes for hair, teeth, and shaving, gold watches, shovels, nails, powder horns, spurs, tobacco, "American chairs," ale, champagne, port and white wine, tea, and chocolate. Indeed, what more could California gold seekers want to purchase![20]

On December 5 a lookout at the Exchange telescope reported the American bark *Tasso* coasting in under reefed topsails. She had come from San Francisco in sixty-six days and she brought Mickle y Cía. 3,968 ounces of gold worth almost $68,000.[21]

Seven vessels were now laid on for California, the largest number at one time so far.[22] Fortunately the 112-ton *Correo del Pacífico* was almost loaded, and two days later, on December 7, she set sail with twenty-one passengers, the usual assorted cargo, and a complete line of medicines.[23] By now the gold-rush excitement had reached a high pitch. Don José Ramón Sánchez, who had sent both the *Mercedes* and the *Dolores* to California, decided to risk a third vessel in the San Francisco trade. His *J.R.S.* returned from her routine cruise to Guayaquil on December 6, and five days later he advertised for passengers and freight, promising that the vessel would leave for San Francisco within the month.

The slowness of the *Julia* in preparing for the voyage perplexed Pérez Rosales, and he was obviously attracted to the *Staoueli*. Both barks promised emigrants exceptional meals and an ample supply of medicine; the *Staoueli* carried a doctor. Both charged the same fare: cabin passage, 10 ounces of gold; tween decks, 5 ounces; and cargo, 20 pesos per ton.[24] Of the two, the *Julia* was the larger vessel, and since her refurbishing she offered excellent staterooms for forty cabin-class passengers and an ample forecabin for those in steerage. The smaller *Staoueli* may have seemed more attractive. She was only nine years old,[25] and her remarkable china table service may have appealed to aristocratic Pérez Rosales.

Yet the equipment seems to have been unimportant, for many gold seekers were willing to sleep on deck during the entire voyage or be crowded into the hold. Their chief concern was to reach California,[26] *muy pronto,* and thus beat the *norteamericanos.* Governor Mason's letter describing the magnitude of the gold discoveries in California was now well known in Valparaiso,[27] and by this time his letter may have reached President Polk. A rush from the East might start any day, but the distance from New York to San Francisco was 19,300 miles and storms around the Horn sometimes delayed a vessel for thirty days.[28] Valparaiso was only 6,700 miles from California, with clear sailing all the way.[29]

Eagerness to reach California in the shortest possible time infected everybody. Pérez Rosales gave up waiting for the *Julia.* Her sailing date was never fixed more definitely than "in a few days" or "in December,"[30] whereas the *Staoueli* promised to go on December 20, for sure![31] This specific commitment may have convinced Vicente that the smaller vessel would get him and his party to California first, and he decided to buy passage on the *Staoueli* for himself and his ten companions, which required a nice outlay of capital. His baggage, already stowed on the *Julia,* would be expensive to transfer, and the freight charges to San Francisco seem to have been paid in advance. Otherwise he would probably have taken the baggage with him, because the cargo charges on both vessels were the same. But what advantage he might gain by arriving ahead of his gold-digging equipment remains a mystery.

The gold rush had reached a stage when emigrants became lyric. On December 13, *El Comercio* devoted two columns to a

poem entitled "Embarcación," subtitled in Spanish, "The Gold
and the Regrets." With apologies to the author the entire poem
may be translated and condensed to:

> Good-bye, fair ones, good-bye!
>   Good-bye, sweethearts.
> I go for adventure,
>   Hoping to return with gold.
> If I die of yellow fever,
>   I have satisfied my dreams,
> And if I return well sheared
>   It will hurt me little
> Because in that event
>   I shall have gained more sense.

Two days later *El Comercio*, always more sympathetic to the
gold rush than the politically liberal *Mercurio*,[32] published a
sonnet by another gold seeker who had recently departed for
California, perhaps on the 600-ton North American *Chile* which
had stopped on December 14 on its cruise from New York to
San Francisco with a cargo of government stores.[33]

During these exciting days of embarkation in the first fortnight of December some twenty-one adventurers enlisted peon
cuadrillas.[34] Among them were Tomás Anderson and José María
Edwards—another instance of men with English surnames who
would be condemned in California as "Chilean foreigners." There
was also bilingual Samuel Price, a fat, jolly chap who, claiming
to be a bona fide Chilean, served his people well in San Francisco. Pérez Rosales, having a few peons and servants in his
party, must have noticed that many of his fellow adventurers
feared that their servants would desert on arrival in California.
To prevent such desertion, many patrónes organized societies
or brotherhoods to hold any wages or property the men might
have until sufficient gold was discovered to pay for their transportation. Some hacienda owners drafted ten to twenty of the
inquilinos on their estates and, binding them with a promise of
a percentage—usually small—of the gold to be found, placed
them on vessels waiting in the bay.[35] Don Tomás Harwood embarked with no peons but took his wife and five sons.[36] Many
stowaways undoubtedly lurked in the crowds on these vessels.[37]
No one foresaw the next interruption to the rush.

The *Staouelí* was scheduled to sail on December 20, 1848, but for some reason she failed to do so. At 10:00 A.M. the booming of cannon at the entrance to Valparaiso Bay started men running,[38] ponchos flapping, along the city's cobblestone streets. Some vessels in the harbor listed dangerously as the peons, packed on board like sheep, crowded along the bulwarks to see the cause of the uproar. A sudden gust of wind might have swamped them. Cannon often announced a ship's arrival. It was a common custom, but the newcomer was no common craft. She was an odd-looking vessel whose tall foremast carried yards for main-, top-, and topgallant sails. Behind the mast a large smokestack stood in front of a fore-and-aft sail.[39] She was the North American sidewheeled steamship *California* which registered more than 1,000 tons, or better than twice the size of most goldrush vessels.

Steamboats from Britain were not new in Valparaiso, and the American firm of Howland & Aspinwall had already sent two steamships to the Pacific, but this vessel was the first of three Aspinwall steamers sent to connect Panama and San Francisco. The venture had been subsidized by a government grant for carrying the mail from New York to San Francisco and Oregon via Chagres and Panama. The *California's* sister ship *Oregon* had left New York on December 8 and was now paddling south in the Atlantic. The *Panama*, last of the trio, was due to leave New York in February.[40]

Valparaiso's three newspapers reported the *California's* arrival, the *Neighbour* printing good details in English. Within a few months, however, all the English-speaking compositors working for the newspaper would be seduced by the gold rush. Without them the Reverend David Trumbull carried on for another year, employing men who could set in type his words written in English, although they spoke only Spanish.[41]

People watching the incoming *California* noticed that she carried few if any passengers. Here was an opportunity for excellent accommodations to California! But when the big vessel dropped anchor they were disappointed. Although equipped to accommodate sixty persons in cabin class and a hundred and fifty in steerage, the *California* had left New York with only six passengers;[42] still, Captain Cleveland Forbes refused to accept any more at Valparaiso. When he left New York the Aspinwall company planned to send later California-bound travelers by other vessels to the Isthmus of Panama, and he was ordered to pick them up at Panama City as he steamed north in the Pacific. After he left New York the gold rush started and the number of passengers to be taken aboard at Panama increased tremendously. Obviously the *California* would be filled to capacity from that port to San Francisco.

Captain Forbes was an able seaman, hard and square, but he had suffered a lung hemorrhage and constantly feared another.[43] Regardless of the eager and threatening passage seekers in Valparaiso, the ill man remained obdurate. Orders were orders, and persons in New York who had purchased tickets to California would be waiting at Panama. They must be served. Valparaiso's disappointed gold seekers turned next to Alsop y Cía., the *California's* agent, but this firm could not change the captain's mind. In spite of his failing health, Captain Forbes remained master of his ship, although the company did place on board a new captain, John Marshall, in the event that Forbes became incapacitated.[44]

On December 21 barges loaded with coal came out to the *California*. A series of platform steps were placed down her side, and stevedores lifted bags of coal up this precarious stairway. As they labored, Pérez Rosales must have watched another vessel with dismay. The two-masted, 100-ton schooner *Progreso* glided away for California while the *Staouelí*, although due to leave the same day, remained at anchor. Had he chosen the wrong ship again? The *Progreso*, loaded with a large cargo sent by Mickle y Cía., carried ten cabin patrónes, most of them with Spanish names, and an unspecified number of peons.[45]

Next day, December 22, 1848, while excited gold seekers still clamored for berths, the *California* steamed away under full sail at 4:30 in the afternoon.[46] Captain Forbes had set all sails, even topgallants, for the fresh southwest wind. His next port of call was Callao, Peru, 1,300 miles to the north.[47]

On board, Christmas was celebrated by the ailing captain despite premonitions of another hemorrhage. With a seaman's appreciation for the white-capped grandeur of a turbulent sea, he noted in his journal that the steamer's canvas was bending merrily in the wind.[48] On December 26 the wind abated. The limp sails were furled but paddle wheels pushed the craft ahead. At this latitude finback whales often wallowed around vessels, amusing the crew.[49]

On December 28, 1848, the *California* steamed into Callao and reported again to Alsop y Cía. Here this firm played a baffling trick on the dour and determined captain, a device that was to have far-reaching effects in 1849 on all gold seekers in California.

6

The Cruise of the Staoueli

Vicente Pérez Rosales must have felt that he had been swindled when he watched the *California* steam out of Valparaiso almost empty on December 22 while the *Staoueli*, scheduled to sail two days earlier, remained at anchor. Next day he saw the decrepit Chilean *Eleodora* wallow off for California.[1] She was strictly a freighter, with no accommodations for so large a party as Vicente's. The *Staoueli*, though booked to capacity and fully loaded, for some reason failed to leave; she was still at anchor a week after scheduled departure. Another Chilean freighter, the bark *Confederación*, set sail on December 27, and the *Julia*, which carried Vicente's camp equipment, had decks cleared ready to go. On the 28th, to Pérez Rosales' delight, the *Staoueli's* captain, Pigno Blanco, ordered men aloft to bend glowing white square sails to the yards athwart her masts. The anchor was weighed and the *Staoueli* glided off, surrounded by the usual assortment of large and small seabirds which followed vessels from the harbor to that mysterious wall of fog along the Valparaiso coast.[2]

Pérez Rosales, in his account of the voyage, said he sailed on the *Stranguéli* on December 20 but contemporary records in Valparaiso give the date as December 28. Moreover, the bark's name was *Staoueli*, not *Stranguéli*. On board were four cows, eight pigs, three dogs, seventeen sailors, and ninety passengers,[3] almost half of them French radical refugees wearing beards to display their objection to the smooth-shaven Napoleonic establishment.

In Pérez Rosales' journal he adds three women to the passenger list. Certainly women were on board; one of them, dressed in gaudy silk clothes, and carrying a parasol, was the famous "Rosa . . . , una heroína de la profesión galante."[4] She had a questionable reputation and was known by different names in various Chilean towns. The port captain, according to Pérez Rosales, hesitated to let her depart, but Rosa's tears and tender looks brought witnesses from steerage who vouched for the spotless character of this bashful maid. One claimed to be her godfather; another had known her since birth. All affirmed that she was pure and innocent. They even threatened to toss overboard the uniformed maligner of virtuous womanhood—a display of the independent roto at his best! Such men should feel at home in freewheeling California. History would tell! In any event, Rosa was allowed to remain on board and save her charms for wider recognition in San Francisco. Incidentally, contemporary records list her as Doña Rosa Montava and say that she was accompanied by a personal maid,[5] so she may have traveled cabin class rather than with her admirers in steerage.

One passenger, N. Álvarez, was a wealthy Chilean eccentric, according to Pérez R., who said the man traveled steerage because he considered all Frenchmen thieves and believed they would cheat him by serving inferior food to a cabin-class passenger. In steerage, emigrants brought their own victuals for the voyage, and Álvarez preferred to take this precaution. His irascibility would nearly cost him his life before a lynch court in California.

Among the cabin passengers was another eccentric, a man with such bulky hips he had to go sideways through the narrow door from the cabin to the deck. His fellow passengers nicknamed him "Culatus," humorously Latinized Spanish for "Buttocks."

Like all California-bound vessels, the *Staouelí* sailed west, disappeared into the coastal fog curtain, and emerged in the vast ocean beyond. Eventually picking up the southern trade winds, she made good time running on an even keel before the southeasterlies until stalled in the doldrums. There the suffocating heat on deck rasped all tempers. The calm sea reflected ugly storm clouds and the only sound in the stifling air was the occasional flap of a listless sail against a mast. Steerage passengers grumbled; a mutiny threatened and, on investigation, Álvarez seemed to be its instigator. He had consumed his supplies and, hating all Frenchmen, was stirring up trouble.[6] The tension eased when a sporadic shower sprinkled the deck and a puff of wind curved the sails.

One day the sight of an approaching whaleship distracted every man's attention. The rusty American craft lowered a long-boat and with sweeping oars shot toward the *Staouelí*. The French crew rolled Jacob's ladders down their vessel's side and the Americans climbed on board. These New England whalers must have been different from the Puritan who had complained about Lady Katherine's luscious figure and her companions' uncovered "Boosoms,"[7] because Pérez Rosales remembered that on sighting the buxom Rosa they had "almost swooned."[8]

The American captain had come to visit, and the gold seekers learned that his whaleship was headed home with a two and a half years' catch of oil. As she planned to touch next at Talcahuano before going around the Horn, cabin passengers immediately wrote letters to be mailed at that port. During lunch the visiting captain admired the *Staouelí*'s silver, fine china, soft bread, and fresh meat. (The livestock on board was evidently being consumed.) He knew little about the gold discoveries in California and cared less. "I do not envy your luck," he said. "I am on my way to embrace my children."[9]

The whaleship had barely reached the horizon when men on the *Staouelí*'s deck hooked a big shark. Amid much shouting it was gaffed and hauled on board where the lashing tail threatened the curious. When the shark was cut open its stomach revealed a seaman's shoe and two sardine boxes which had just been thrown overboard. The shark's heart, when placed on a dish, quivered with life for three hours, and beat when touched.[10]

Some days later the *Staouelí* picked up the northeasterly trade winds and tacked far to the west, her sails bulging—white and rounded like summer clouds. Cabin passengers had to dine at a listing table edged by a guardrail to hold the dishes. One evening a seaman entered and whispered to Captain Blanco, who rose at once and in a voice full of concern said, "We have a mutiny on board! Álvarez is at the head of it, and if you do not help me we are lost!"[11] The cabin passengers pushed back their chairs and ran to their quarters for arms. Pérez Rosales did not go with them. Instead, he stepped out on deck searching for his servants. Finding them and three of the peons he was taking to California on contract, he urged them to slip below unnoticed among the dissatisfied steerage passengers, capture Álvarez before he organized the mutineers, and deliver him to the captain. The plan succeeded. The mutiny failed and Álvarez finished the voyage in the brig.

On many of these long voyages somebody died, and the *Staoueli's* cruise was no exception. A funeral at sea is always peculiarly impressive, and the ceremony on the *Staoueli* no doubt conformed to the usual practice: the bark hove to, the ensign raised on the spanker gaff, all hands mustered at the lee gangway. There the observers, with heads uncovered and eyes respectfully lowered, heard the captain speak a few formal words, followed by the final plunge.[12] Men who attended such a service never forgot it.

On February 13, after forty-seven days at sea, Captain Blanco learned from his sextant that the *Staoueli*, although far out to sea, was opposite San Francisco. By sailing due east, he told the passengers, they should reach shore in four days. Later, as the breeze increased, he cut the estimated time in half. That afternoon dark clouds threatened rain and the approaching storm kicked up the ocean with increasing fury, but the *Staoueli* sliced the white-capped water, making unprecedented speed.

Toward evening a fog blanked out both sea and sky. The captain realized that the vessel, racing under full sail, might crash against an unseen shore. He did not explain this danger to his passengers, but quietly sent men aloft into the white mist to shorten sail. On the forward deck anchors were readied. Steerage passengers smiled, for surely they were approaching the end of a long, unpleasant voyage. Cabin passengers seemed more skeptical, and to keep them unworried but alert, Captain Blanco proposed a game of whist. Some drew up chairs to play. Others watched, sipping tea. All talked about proposed adventures in California. Bulky Culatus sat on the first step of the companionway calmly enjoying a whiff of fresh air. Suddenly the captain slammed down his cards and rushed to the deck. Passengers heard the terrifying shout, "Rocks ahead! Sandbar to windward!"[13] The card players jumped to their feet, upsetting chairs. Cups and dishes crashed to the floor and rolled to the wall as the ship wheeled suddenly. Fat Culatus forgot, in his fear, to turn sideways at the door and the desperate passengers had to push him through the opening like a cork out of a popgun.[14] Jumping over his sprawled figure, they saw, aft of the careening taffrail, high black rocks encircled by foaming white water.

The ship's escape had been a narrow one and, with no vision ahead, the captain ordered a sounding. From the bulwarks a seaman reported 40 fathoms—an excessive depth surely, but the anchor was dropped. Tethered now in a heavy rolling sea, the *Staouelí* tossed violently. Night came but no one on board dared to try sleeping. At dawn the mist persisted, vivid white, and through it Pérez Rosales heard the confused clamor of seabirds and the bellowing barks of sea lions as they slid heavily from nearby rocks into the seething ocean.[15]

The *Staouelí* tossed all day at anchor. Through the second night the fog continued and in the morning rain deluged the anchored vessel, but a favorable wind convinced Captain Blanco that he could leave this dangerous region. He hoisted anchor and made sail. Catching the wind, his vessel swung around in the downpour and, to everyone's horror, barely missed a fast-sailing brig which passed so close that she scratched the *Staouelí*'s stern. The stranger disappeared so quickly in the storm that Pérez Rosales heard only a shout in a language he did not understand.[16] Then the French vessel was alone again, free of anchor and heaving eastward in a white fog on the inky black sea.

That night Vicente lay fully dressed in his berth. He dozed from exhaustion. At daybreak shouts from steerage brought him to his feet. Out on deck he saw that the fog had lifted and before him, under a bright blue sky, he beheld a magnificent panorama: the looming coast of Alta California with five sailing vessels racing for the shore.[17] Behind the *Staouelí*'s milky wake he could see on the horizon the snaggletoothed Farallones where the ship had almost wrecked.

Late in the afternoon of February 18, 1849, sails were reefed for a cautious passage through the abrupt walls of Golden Gate. Less than an hour later the *Staoueli* rounded Clark's Point and Telegraph Hill. Twilight had come, but eager passengers saw, beyond the forest of anchored ships' masts, the twinkling lights of San Francisco—the city of their dreams—spread out in an amphitheater of hills. In the gathering darkness Pérez R. counted thirty-four commercial vessels* and an American naval squadron of five. The *Staoueli* saluted the warships, and in reply the sailors who were perched on the flagship's yards gave three lusty cheers for the first French vessel to arrive.

This formality was completed in the gloaming. Pérez R., in his memoirs, written in the vigorous style he admired in Sarmiento's work, said that the passengers on the *Staoueli* exclaimed "Mon Dieu" with delight as the captain gave his final order: "Drop the anchor."[18] The rumble of heavy chains through the hawsehole meant the end of a long, dangerous voyage, and few of the passengers heard it without emotion. Pérez Rosales admitted that although he had sailed four times around the Horn this trip to California seemed the most hazardous. It is easy to believe that some of the French disciples of Kossuth felt so much suppressed joy at their safe arrival that they grinned sheepishly at one another and, as pent-up relief weakened their knees, collapsed into one another's sympathetic arms, commingling their revolutionary beards. Not the usual picture of California pioneers, but not one to be ignored!

In the dark a rowboat bumped against the *Staoueli*. Pérez Rosales supposed it to be the port captain's craft, but learned later that in California this officer was often tardy. The visitor was Carlos Robinet, master of a vessel named *Anamakin*, according to Pérez Rosales' memoirs.[19] The ship was, of course, the *Ann McKim*, and her captain had come for the latest news from Chile, but he heard none. Instead, all talked at once, no one waiting for the other to speak—a French custom, it was said. All asked if gold was really as plentiful as had been reported.

Captain Robinet affirmed that the reports were "not a shadow

* *Alta California*, April 12, 1849, noted thirty-eight vessels in the harbor.

of the reality; [here] the most no account hayseed squandered gold like a Croesus."[20] With this assurance of wealth the emotional Frenchmen laughed, swore, raised clenched fists, lifted eyes to the stars; some sank blissfully into coils of rope lost in rapturous meditation. Pérez Rosales, always keenly imaginative, suspected that they were saying to themselves:

"My dream has come true: I shall be a banker in France."

"Amelia is going to die of vexation because she turned me down on account of my poverty."

"What a jolt you are going to get, Julia, if you try to be nice to me now."[21]

Late that night the "candidates for millionaires" went to bed. At dawn the *Staouelí* was surrounded by men in small boats offering goods, sweetmeats, passage to shore. All confirmed the plenitude of gold, even pouring gold dust from leather pokes into their open hands. The passengers' eager eyes saw nuggets large as hazelnuts.

Boatloads of ragged men clambered overside. They spoke Spanish with an unmistakable Chilean accent, called Pérez Rosales by name, and shook his hand. Vicente recognized one of these rough fellows as a former society blade in Santiago. Another had been a well-to-do merchant in Valparaiso. There was also a youthful Chilean socialite operating a landing launch in partnership with a Negro, bunking with him and making big money piloting passengers to shore. Beside him strode Don Samuel Price, still fat and merry, but wearing a muddy, ragged coat and rolled-up pantaloons. His only interest seemed to be the possibility of buying any goods the passengers would sell. Among the tatterdemalions Vicente also recognized Alejandro Cross, supercargo on the *Undine* in charge of goods sent by William Hobson's commission firm.[22] Here, too, was unhappy Dr. Poett who had come on the *Virjinia* and was now trying to be a longshoreman. How different they had all looked wearing dress coats and formal attire in Valparaiso![23]

These men did not come on board for sociability's sake. They were businessmen, eager to buy anything they could resell on shore before the passengers learned its worth. Vicente noticed Cross, standing on the afterdeck, discussing some possible transaction. Another dealer bumped into him, knocking his hat into the bay, but Cross was too intent on business to notice. In California time was money and the niceties of Valparaiso's negotiations were ignored.

As yet no customs or port authorities had boarded the *Staoueli*. Pérez R., familiar with the vulgar antics of Seth Barton in Santiago, may have been prepared for the two men who appeared on the bulwarks at ten o'clock that morning. Certainly he wrote about them with the earthy realism he admired in Sarmiento's work. He described the taller of the men as a corpulent American with one eye purpled from a drunken brawl the night before. The fellow was evidently a man of importance although unused to the mutual ceremonious bows characteristic of democratic society in Chile. Reeking with whisky, he squirted a mouthful of tobacco juice overside, then jumped down on deck announcing in a loud friendly voice, "Welcome to the land of gold."[24]

He was the port captain, a democratic fellow by usual standards but not by Chile's more gentlemanly code of democracy. Captain Blanco, understanding no English, presumed that the man had come for the passengers' passports and handed them to him. The boisterous port captain squinted his open eye at these papers and in disgust replied, "Devil take your licenses to move from one place to another! In these parts we don't stand for imposition on one side or stupid regulations on the other. I only come to congratulate you on arriving in good shape, and to leave on board this customs agent authorized by me to collect the landing permits you get from the office, that's all!"[25]

Revolutions in Chile had replaced one democracy with another but no regime had produced officials so free and easy as this one! Captain Blanco, presuming that the South American *mordida,* or bribe, was practiced here, offered the port captain a glass of wine. The latter replied that he accepted only champagne. After drinking his bottle he departed.

Before long one of San Francisco's afternoon fogs drifted through Golden Gate but it did not dampen the *Staoueli* passengers' eagerness to leave the ship. Among the first to go in the fog, now almost a drizzle, was Rosa in her magnificent silk dress and cape, carrying her parasol which served only to proclaim her professional arrival. She disappeared in the mist surrounded by a boatload of ardent courtiers. Pérez R., with one companion, followed in another boat. The tide was low and they landed in shallow mud, waded to dry land, and walked cautiously through the fog to Montgomery Street.

They had been told that no man should enter the town unarmed, and they noticed that a pistol, which was becoming more common than the dagger, hung from most men's belts. At the first cross street they turned inland. There was no sidewalk, and the houses on both sides of the road were rough structures, some commodious, others mere board shacks. Between them stood rows of tents. Men crowded the center of the street and jostled one another in their haste to go somewhere, anywhere! Heavily loaded porters shouted to clear the way, and the constant clamor of hammering and sawing produced a deafening hubbub. Vicente had seen Valparaiso's miraculous growth, but it never resembled this mushrooming. He estimated San Francisco's population at about 1,500 permanent residents, with as many as 400 newcomers sometimes arriving in a single day[26]—a reasonably conservative figure, because a newspaper, almost three weeks earlier, had boasted a population of 2,000.[27]

To Vicente the appearance of the crowds was unforgettable, their heterogeneous costumes amazing. All seemed to be celebrating at a vast and noisy masquerade ball, and he wrote in his journal that if any women were on the streets they must have been dressed as men, "for, seek as one might through that Babylon, one found never a skirt."[28]

The shops, many of them mere counters under an awning along the street, offered everything imaginable for sale: "store boots" and fancy cheeses, men's clothing and piles of dried pears, Chilean jerked beef and gunpowder, picks, shovels, cutlery. Chilean brandy fetched $70 for a 4-gallon jug, and "the sweetened soda water they called champagne [sold] for eight to twelve dollars a bottle."[29] Sacks of Chilean flour brought their weight in gold.[30] And so eager were customers to buy that little care was taken to retrieve the excess of gold poured on the scales from the purchaser's leather bag, that *escrotos de los carneros.*

Pérez Rosales and his companion had walked only a quarter

of an hour through the gabbling crowds when they heard a deafening din. A former "gentleman," now a waiter, was beating a Chinese gong to announce the serving of dinner. These North Americans ate three times a day, at seven, twelve and six. Inside the "eating house," away from the fog, Pérez R. saw a long table and thirty disheveled diners wielding knives and forks at great speed so they could go outside and make more money. Here were Samuel Price and an effeminate young Chilean standing with others awaiting places at table. The bystanders talked eagerly about gold and where to find it. "Don't go to the Sacramento," one loquacious fellow said, "because there is little gold there; go to the Stanislaus as fast as you can."

"Don't even think about going to the Stanislaus," another blurted, "but go to the Sacramento."[31]

Pérez Rosales realized that neither of these men had been to the diggings and that both were probably as new as he was to California. Price came to his rescue and introduced him to a genuine "old hand" who knew the diggings. After dinner this man showed Vicente some real washed gold, including a nugget he thought weighed almost three pounds. The fellow claimed he found it on a walk before breakfast. Vicente wondered what might lie in store for him on a walk after dinner!

That night Pérez Rosales and his companions went back to the *Staoueli*. They were eager to leave for the diggings but were unable to go until the *Julia* brought their baggage. Captain Blanco's crew had deserted, leaving him helpless in a foreign port. Like many other commanders he was advertising the *Staoueli* for sale,[32] but he begged Vicente and his party to remain on board until she was sold. During the next three days Pérez Rosales, his three brothers, his brother-in-law, their hired men, and three other passengers—one a Valparaiso businessman, another the ex-prompter for the Paris opera—organized themselves as a company of porters to unload the *Staoueli* and other vessels as they arrived. This venture lasted eleven days and netted the participants $1,200,[33] but another two weeks elapsed before the *Julia*, with Pérez Rosales' precious camp equipment, was sighted off the Golden Gate. Vicente had gauged her speed correctly. She sailed only two days after the

Staouelí but was arriving a month behind her. The *Julia's* bad luck did not end there. Coming into port she grounded on Presidio Shoal. Although she was undamaged the accident delayed her arrival until March 19.[34] The *Julia's* crew deserted, like so many others, and Captain Gordot, who was bringing the cargo on his own account, advertised the vessel for sale along with its cargo of Chilean flour, biscuits, preserves, candied fruit, claret, champagne, absinthe, anisette, and cognac in cases, barrels, or demijohns.[35]

The month's delay while awaiting the *Julia's* arrival enabled Pérez Rosales to become acquainted with San Francisco. In the newspapers and from Chilean friends he learned many things. The condemned bark *Undine* was still registered as a United States craft so she had been bid in by Americans at the auction sale, as many suspected. She made the trip to California successfully, kept her crew from deserting, and was now in Oregon fetching lumber for booming San Francisco.[36] The Chilean *Confederación* and *Correo del Pacífico* had both arrived safely.[37] The clumsy *Eleodora*, which had floundered away four days ahead of the *Staouelí*, sailed in only two days after her[38] and was being offered for sale as a lumber carrier. The *Virjinia* had reached this market before the *Mary* brought Larkin's goods from Mazatlán[39] and sold her cargo at a fabulous figure. The expanding demand for supplies, however, absorbed the cargoes of both vessels. The new market impressed merchants. Seafaring men showed more interest in a report that the American bark *Minerva* made a record trip, bringing the Seidlitz powders from Valparaiso in forty-two days.[40]

Pérez Rosales learned, too, that Alejandro Cross, who had lost his hat overboard in his eagerness to close a deal on the *Staouelí*, had established the firm of Cross & Hobson, a San Francisco branch of William Hobson's commission agency in Valparaiso. Also, Pérez R. read an advertisement that must have interested him. The unhappy Enrique Poett, who as a longshoreman had greeted him on arrival of the *Staouelí*, was now Dr. J. H. Poett, physician and surgeon of London and Dublin colleges, and he was seeking a building lot to purchase or a house to rent.[41] A notice more surprising to a Chilean was the announcement in the *Alta California* that the commander of the North American squadron, Commodore Thomas ap Catesby Jones, would pardon all deserters who returned immediately to duty.[42]

In the same paper a reassuring item informed readers that gold was worth $16.00 an ounce and $18.055 at the mint.[43] This news should end the old juggling of prices which had made so large a profit for the supercargo on the *J.R.S.*

A more sinister item disclosed that three men had been lynched at Dry Diggings. Named Pepe, Antoine, and Tehal, they were not identified as Chileans, but they obviously were foreigners,* persons in disfavor with the new Anglo owners of this land. Certainly rotos would have to look out for themselves, or "more better," the Anglos must look out for the rotos. Most astonishing of all, norteamericanos considered Chileans and their ancient enemies, the Peruvians, to be "the same breed of cats"—an odd notion, indeed!

* *Alta California*, Feb. 15, 1849. A different version of this lynching, which caused the Dry Diggings to be called Hangtown, can be found in Leonard Pitt, *The Decline of the Californios* (Berkeley and Los Angeles, 1966), p. 51. Using an eyewitness narrative recorded much later than the newspaper account, he says that two, not three, men were hanged, and that one of them was a Chilean and the other a Frenchman.

PART II
The Reaction of Peru to the Gold Discovery

7

A Vista Filled with Many
Specters of the Past

The boast of heraldry, the pomp of pow'r,
And all that beauty, all that wealth e'er gave,
Awaits alike th' inevitable hour.
The paths of glory lead but to the grave.
—Gray's *Elegy*

Peru and Chile were strikingly different, and although Lima was 1,300 miles closer to San Francisco than Valparaiso, news of the gold discovery in California appeared in Lima newspapers only one day before Valparaiso papers announced it. Yet the first party of Peruvian Argonauts set sail seventy-nine days later than the first Chileans, a delay easily explained by the history of the two nations.

To a visitor at the time of the gold rush the most noticeable difference between Chile and Peru was the number of Negro faces on Peruvian streets.[1] Slaves had been taken into Chile in the early Spanish days, but the plantation system failed to prosper and Indians were available for most of the menial labor. A few slaves may have come from Argentina, acting as esquires for shoddy, self-styled knights who, in the decaying age of Spanish chivalry, found the black fellows brave sword-bearers in battles against infidel Indians. Achieving military equality, these blacks had long since been completely assimilated. The number had always been insignificant, and by the time of the gold rush no sign of color remained.

Unlike Chile, Peru during the 1840s still recognized slavery, and gold seekers from the southern United States noticed that a strong, young black man might be purchased in Lima for $400, a price considerably less than it would have been back home.[2] These slaves had certain rights not recognized in North America. A slave might sell himself to another master, or he might purchase his own freedom at a price set by the court. Under these circumstances some blacks preferred to remain in slavery. In fact one slave amassed a considerable fortune, purchased freedom for his children and two sisters, but remained in bondage himself.[3] Black men, of course, were among the first Old World people to come to Peru. Indeed, blacks arrived with the armies of Pizarro, and in that early day some of them achieved positions of responsibility.[4]

The capitals of Peru and Chile—Lima and Santiago—were quite unlike. The difference between them, which the people of each country seldom forgot, helps to explain their diverse attitudes toward the gold rush. Santiago had risen from an Indian settlement appropriated by Pedro de Valdivia with some five hundred conquistadores who, on their marches, impressed thousands of Indians to carry baggage, the men themselves, and sometimes even the colts of their horses in hammocks.[5] On the other hand, Lima was built on a site carefully selected by Pizarro for his dream Cuidad de los Reyes ("City of the Kings"). Because it was founded at Epiphany, he named it in honor of the Magi.* Conservative religion was never absent from the minds of these Renaissance murderers. In Rome, Michelangelo had finished decorating the ceiling of the Sistine Chapel and would soon begin his gigantic task as architect for the reconstruction of Saint Peter's Church. Pizarro also had great plans for his capital.

Valdivia and Pizarro differed as much as their cities. Pizarro outranked Valdivia from the beginning. He had landed in May, 1532, on what would be the coast of Peru. The Incas (Quechua Indian term meaning "rulers") had just concluded a civil war between two rivals for the throne, a struggle that seems a far

* Clements Robert Markham (A History of Peru [Chicago, 1892], p. 90) says, without stating his authority, that the City of the Kings was named for the sovereigns of Spain, Juana and her son Charles V. The former was certainly never a king. A later writer, John Hemming (The Conquest of the Incas [London, 1970], p. 149), says the Magi were the kings. El Perú, the 1944 tourist guide put out by Banco Popular del Perú, accepts Markham's account.

cry from the California gold rush, but we shall see otherwise. The fighting between the factions had been truly savage, a pattern the conquistadores, like so many "imperialists" since, accepted in their own warfare. Both Inca factions had maintained, near their barbaric palaces, torture pits and scaffolds for hanging political rivals.[6] The legitimate heir, Huascar, finally saw his army defeated. He was captured and held prisoner as a valuable political hostage, while his generals and principal supporters were tortured to death. Their wives and concubines were also killed. Unborn babies were ripped from corpses and placed in the arms of dead mothers along the public roads. Let the people see them and understand that the legitimate line of Inca was to be exterminated! *

Pizarro took no part in the Indians' war but, reinforced by Hernando de Soto, who would fail in attempting to achieve a similar triumph in Florida, he started on his great crusade for God—and gold.[7] After occupying a few lesser Indian villages, he marched south for a conference with the victorious Inca, the illegitimate Atahualpa. The two planned to meet at Cajamarca, a town 9,000 feet high in the valley between the Coast Range and the Andes. The Incas had built a palace at this town, near hot springs which they prized for baths. At this spa Atahualpa, surrounded by his army, was dallying with his concubines in the painted chambers of the royal residence[8] when Pizarro and his bearded men marched into town. Atahualpa had invited them to come and he expected the meeting to be friendly, although he may have planned secretly to capture Pizarro at some future time.[9] On November 16, 1532, Atahualpa was carried to the village plaza in his golden chair to meet the Bearded One who, with a quick movement of his men-at-arms, took him prisoner. The excuse for this aggression was Atahualpa's refusal to accept Christianity in the form of a proffered Bible. The Inca guards were dumbfounded. Horses, matchlock guns, and steel swords

---

* Burr Cartwright Brundage, *Empire of the Inca* (Norman, Okla., 1963), p. 294. William Hickling Prescott (*The History of the Conquest of Peru* [Philadelphia, 1873], I, 349) notes that this attempted massacre of the entire legitimate line may be an exaggeration, as the only record comes from Garcilaso de la Vega, the mixed-blood historian who heard the account from his mother, a member of the dispossessed line.

were unknown to them; perhaps such tools of war cowed Atahualpa's entire army. Perhaps his soldiers lacked leadership in
the crisis.

All these events seem extraneous to the California gold rush,
but at that time William H. Prescott's newly published *The History of the Conquest of Peru* was a best seller, arousing wide-
spread interest in Pizarro's remarkable conquest, an interest
copied by other writers even on the dime-novel level.[10] Such
books were read by gold seekers on the tedious voyage around
the Horn.[11] They learned that an interpreter guilty of seducing
one of Atahualpa's wives saved himself by saying that the imprisoned Inca was using his religious power to incite his tribes-
men to overthrow the Spaniards and celebrate their victory by
drinking out of goblets made from Spanish skulls,[12] an established custom for Peruvian victors in war.[13] Oddly enough, this
gruesome formality, described in these books and read by California gold seekers, was used by propagandists during the American Civil War to engender hatred and revenge. The enemy and
often the enemy's sweethearts, according to these accounts,
celebrated victories by drinking toasts from their slain opponents' skulls.

According to Peruvian history, accepted in the gold-rush era,
the interpreter's story of the plot was believed, and when the
legitimate heir, Huascar, was mysteriously killed, the Spaniards
blamed Atahualpa, maintaining that he had sent a secret message ordering the murder. These partisans said that Atahualpa
feared that his old rival might negotiate with Pizarro to reestablish him instead of Atahualpa as Inca, a natural assumption
in the age of Lucretia Borgia and Lorenzo de' Medici. Although
Atahualpa denied the charge, the Spaniards, according to Prescott's exciting narrative, submitted him to a formal trial before
two judges. After a legal courtroom debate by attorneys for the
prosecution and defense, he was pronounced guilty of murder,
sedition, and idolatry. The penalty for the last of these crimes
was burning at the stake.

Recent scholarship discredits Prescott's account of the trial,
but not the story about drinking toasts from enemy skulls, which
was indelibly impressed on the minds of young American gold

seekers who fought later in the Civil War. Atahualpa, according to modern research, was killed without trial on the order of Pizarro who feared that the Inca's Indian partisans might free him.[14] Pizarro's defenders during the first century after his death manufactured the story of the trial to excuse the murder and glamorize the conquistadores. There was an interpreter named Felipillo, but the story of his philandering was fabricated in the 1550s to justify Pizarro's execution of Atahualpa. Lopez de Gómara in his unreliable *Hispania Victrix* (1552) added the legal trial.[15] Then Garcilaso de la Vega, born in Cuzco, the mixed-blood son of a Spanish governor, embellished the trial with elaborate details of the attorneys' debate in his book published in 1617, eighty-four years after Atahualpa's death. This author, writing in Spain forty years after leaving Peru,[16] accepted without question Pizarro's uprooting of his mother's Inca culture.

To Prescott, translating from the Spanish, all these accounts may have seemed sufficiently ancient to be contemporary with the event, so he accepted them as fact. Undoubtedly Atahualpa, although not formally tried, was formally executed in the plaza. Pizarro, a man probably in his sixties[17] then and turning gray, presided at the execution, with priests and soldiers in formal mourning, as in typical Renaissance procedure. The Inca, also true to his culture, displayed regal calmness as he was bound to the stake and fagots were piled at his feet. During the grisly performance the sun sank behind the mountains and a wide shadow crept toward the village. The witching hour had come for condors—the largest birds that fly—to return to their roosting places,[18] for frogs to croak cheerily in the stream below the Cajamarca baths, for owls to shake their rough feathers, hoot, and begin a night of stealthy killing in the silent valley.

At dusk, executioners and mourners lighted torches so that everybody could see the Inca die.* One of the torches would be applied to the kindling piled at Atahualpa's feet. He was given

---

* Prescott (*op. cit.*, I, 483–485) says the soldiers were called to the plaza at night after the trial; Brundage (*op. cit.*, p. 314) says at dusk. According to Francisco Xeres, Pizarro's secretary, the execution occurred at the same hour as the original seizure of the Inca, which was after sunset, probably at dusk. See also Clements Robert Markham, *The Incas of Peru* (New York, 1910), pp. 52, 105–106.

the choice of death by strangulation instead of by the torture of fire, if he would kiss the cross and consent to baptism. The Inca agreed to this form of conversion, asking only that his embalmed body be sent to Quito for preservation with his ancestors.[19] These last rites concluded, Negro executioners twisted tight the garrote around Atahualpa's neck. His body hung on its stake until dawn, when it received a Christian burial. His women, instead of being mutilated as he is reported to have mutilated those of his rival, Huascar, were distributed among the Spaniards.

Pizarro thus became supreme ruler, and the mighty Inca power had been broken, though not destroyed, for all time. With the fabulous Inca gold at his disposal Pizarro dutifully sent King Carlos in Spain the royal fifth.[20] But the fighting had not ended. Jealous Spanish rivals fought among themselves for the spoils, and the surviving legitimate and illegitimate Inca partisans hoped to reestablish their respective lines. According to reports, the illegitimate faction stole Atahualpa's body from the cemetery and carried it, if not to Quito, at least into the Ecuadorian mountains.[21]

While the shattered Inca groups plotted to regain authority, many of the lower orders welcomed Spanish rule, feeling that the bearded men would be no harder masters than the Incas. Pizarro soon felt sufficiently secure to build his City of the Kings —renamed Lima by the Indians[22]—a city that would play a part in the California gold rush very different from Valparaiso's. Pizarro selected a site for the city, not in the Andes of his conquests, but on the coastal plains where ships from Panama and from Europe might anchor. A small mountain, San Cristóbal, some 2,000 feet high,[23] and the Rimac River at its base promised bounteous water as well as wood for house beams and cooking fires. Eight miles to the west a natural harbor, Callao, was protected from storms by San Lorenzo, an island 7 miles long. Destitute of trees, San Lorenzo resembled a gigantic, humpbacked dinosaur standing more than 1,000 feet tall in the green sea. From the mainland, a finger-like sandbar reached out to within 4 miles of the island, forming an ideal anchorage.[24]

The city of Lima, unlike the settlements built by gold seekers in California, was planned with scientific care. The streets were not laid out north and south with cross streets running east and west, because that arrangement would provide no comfortable shady walls. Instead, city blocks were placed at an angle to the points of the compass, thus guaranteeing shade somewhere throughout the day[25]—a design noticed by Argonauts when they entered Spanish towns in California. In the carefully planned city Pizarro built a church on one side of the Plaza des Armas and his palace on another.[26] For a full decade he gloried in the construction of his city.

On June 26, 1541, Pizarro dined after Mass with friends on the second floor of the palace. A gang of some twenty ruffians strode across the plaza waving their swords and shouting, "Death to the tyrant." The Sunday crowd watched in silence as the assassins forced their way through the massive palace gate, rushed across the yard, and stormed up the stairs.[27] With a clash of steel at the doorway to the dining hall, they cut down a few attendants. The dinner guests grasped their swords. Pizarro, at this time a white-haired man nearing seventy,* had trouble adjusting the fastening on his cuirass. Casting it aside, he wrapped a cloak around his left arm for a shield, drew his sword, and joined his companions. For Pizarro, a fighter all his life, this was the last fight. In the melee he was struck by many sharp blades, but he killed at least one man before he fell among the bodies of his friends and enemies. The dying man traced, with his finger, the sign of the cross in the blood on the floor.[28] No vista in Chile's history is filled with so tragic a specter of the past as this Peruvian event, which haunted the development of both nations.

Lima, after Pizarro's death, became the seat of one of the two great Spanish viceroyalties in the Americas. Peru, which included Chile, Argentina, Colombia, Ecuador, and Bolivia, was second only to New Spain, a vast area comprising Mexico, Central America, the West Indies, and the southern part of present-day United States. In Lima, San Marcos University was established in 1551. Peruvians called it the oldest institution of higher

* The date of Pizarro's birth is uncertain. Contemporary encyclopedias give his age at death as 65 and also 71. Hemming (*op. cit.*, p. 262) says definitely that Pizarro was 63 when he died. Markham, writing at an earlier date (*op. cit.*, p. 109), says Pizarro must have been upward of 70.

learning in the western hemisphere, but the University of Mexico in the rival viceroyalty of the north, disputed that claim.

The next century of Peruvian history was one of great development. Immigrants were carefully selected. All had to be Spanish and Catholic. Some were impoverished nobles, while others of low social origin, who had been nobodies in Spain, suddenly found themselves men of authority over servile Indians. These newcomers often had the unpleasant manner of such persons everywhere,[29] but they possessed religious fervor and the dogged energy to build and become rich. Imitating the Spanish Inquisition, they determined to convert the heathens to a life everlasting. With dedicated zeal they burned fifty-nine convicts at the stake, a lenient record compared with Spain's.[30] Most of the victims were blasphemers, heretics, Jews, witches, or forgers, and while engaged in these intrepid acts of faith, Peru flourished intellectually, publishing belles lettres, history, and geography,[31] just as Massachusetts had flourished in the days of witchcraft executions.

The Peruvian renaissance is peculiarly related to the California gold rush, for it was during these years that the name El Dorado ("The Gilded Place") came into common use. According to an Indian legend, a young chief in Colombia was annually anointed with gum and rolled in gold dust which was later ceremoniously washed off in a nearby lake.[32] For half a century conquistadores looked for the lake, and the name El Dorado became a synonym for a place of gold. Cabeza de Vaca and Coronado sought "places of gold" in Arizona and New Mexico, but eventually California proved to be the real Dorado. The legend did not end there, however. At the time of the California gold rush many workers in Peru would moisten their bodies and roll in silver *polvorilla* in order to steal the precious dust.[33] In California this idea grew into a tall story which described a prospector as anointing his body with "Gold Grease," then rolling down a California hill and becoming wealthy, a story so fantastic that it was copied by newspapers in lands as far away as Australia.[34] At Sonora, California, Gold Gulch was allegedly discovered by a man rolling down a hill.

While adventurous Peruvian conquistadores were still seeking El Dorado in the steamy jungles at the headwaters of the Amazon, others practiced old and new mining skills at Potosí, the richest mountain of minerals ever discovered. Although some 900 miles away, Lima controlled the shipping of the ore and supplies, and Lima bankers collected 100 to 120 percent interest on loans to promoters of this gigantic development.[35] Tunneling, stoping, shoring, and ventilating were practiced at Potosí, as was amalgamation with mercury; these skills were all known to seventeenth-century Latin Americans whose descendants later went to California.

With Lima booming, a cathedral was built on the site of the old church. Travelers said it exceeded in splendor the churches of Rome. The sacramental robes worn by priests in processions equaled in magnificence any in Europe.[36] The fragrant gloom under vaulted arches, the tapers burning before saints on altars decorated with gold and silver ornaments, the devout whispering through the green curtain of a confessional—all were impressively Catholic.

Pizarro, dead now for more than half a century, was no longer the hated tyrant, and his body, or one thought to be his, was found in the old church. These remains were entombed in a special chapel built inside the cathedral and decorated with a profusion of virgin gold.[37] Outside, in the old Plaza des Armas, a magnificent fountain, with bronze basins cast in Europe, served water boys and their donkeys. A short distance away the new Plaza de la Inquisición was established beside a formal building to house the ecclesiastical court, an ornate structure with artistically tiled window casings and a beautifully carved beam ceiling. Sinners were brought there from the entire South Pacific coast for trial, and prelates seated in the splendid chamber ordered some of them burned at a stake in the nearby plaza.[38]

Success and leisure finally sapped the zealous faith that had built the viceroyalty of Peru. Young men educated in philosophy at San Marcos became thinkers, not doers, and distributors of strange new ideas. Radical members of the second and third generations, born into a prosperous society, began to scoff at the materialism of their forebears, and the sun began to set on great days of physical accomplishments coupled with orthodox religious fanaticism.

During the late seventeenth- and early eighteenth-century years of inherited affluence—some call them years of decadence —even the Church became lax; the priests grew fatter and were less concerned about the sins of humanity. In Lima, Jews were no longer burned at the stake. Instead they became both wealthy and gross. Books banned in Spain sold readily in Peru.[39] The looming liberalism sent shivers up and down the rigid spines of old-school aristocrats. Having traveled in Spain and studied art and music abroad, they had imported conventional paintings by Murillo, and they gloried in the venerated music of the Italian Palestrina and his Spanish disciple, Tomás Luis de Victoria. Although laughing politely at the antics of Harlequin and Columbine, they looked back with nostalgia at the culture of the past. With jeweled fingers they turned the exquisitely printed pages of Pierre Corneille's *Le Cid*, discussing in learned language the author's debt to Guillén de Castro y Bellvís. They cited the romantic chivalry these writers had reconstructed from the twelfth-century Spanish classic, an age "more better," yes, than the permissive utopia demanded by modern youths. Surely the morals of that early day might still be accepted in Lima if the new radicals would "shut the mouth."

Erudite conservatives enjoyed another book that contained a name important to all gold seekers. This fictional romance of the cherished chivalric age had been written by Garcí Ordóñez de Montalvo in 1510.[40] It described an island laden with gold and jewels called "California," an amusing name to early eighteenth-century Peruvians. To them California was the name of the lower west coast of North America, a barren region unworthy of even a single mission.

True conservatives clung to memories of the good life destroyed by radicals. Meanwhile the younger generation perused the dangerous pages of Roger Bacon, Descartes, Newton, and even Cervantes who mocked books about the chivalry which, with the Inquisition, might have preserved the fine established values. Most distressing of all to an old-school *limeño* was the

realization that a half-dozen dangerous liberal writers had been
born in Peru. Among them was Diego Martínez de Ribera (died
1600), a poet praised by the notorious Cervantes.[41] Another
rhymster of this age of affluence and moral laxity was Luis de
Góngora y Argote (1561–1627),[42] whose extravagant verse
would be read for 300 years[43] by persons bred to the impres-
sionistic manner few could understand. Still another was Juan
del Valle y Caviedes (1653–1694),[44] the reprobate son of respect-
able parents. His wife died young, probably because she acquired venereal diseases from him. Drunk most of the time, he
sold cheap literature from one of the bookstalls that lined the
outer wall of the viceroy's palace. His own picaresque novels—
for adults only—probably had a larger popular sale than the
works of any other Peruvian author.[45] Affluent Lima had indeed
become sophisticated—and soft.

The Lima of this worldly age is described with compelling
charm in Thornton Wilder's *The Bridge of San Luis Rey*, whose
climax is the collapse of the bridge which kills five people, including the illegitimate son of La Perichole, the sobriquet of a
popular actress and mistress to the viceroy. Unfortunately for
historians, there was no bridge in Peru named San Luis Rey,
although the Inca built several vine and fiber suspension cause-
ways across rivers. One, the Punte de Rumi-chake, in the province of Ayacucho, resembled Wilder's bridge, being a 100-yard
span across a deep gulf.[46] In Wilder's novel, the San Luis Rey
bridge on which La Perichole's son plunged to his death collapsed on July 20, 1714, a date that actually preceded by more
than fifty years the date on which the son was born. The famous
actress may have been as irresistibly beautiful as Wilder describes her, but her sobriquet, "La Perichole," is Peruvian Spanish for "The Half-Breed Bitch." Her power over the viceroy is
unquestioned. He deeded her a special palace equipped with a
marble bathtub and gave her a golden coach, which she, to ex-
piate her sins, bequeathed to the Church. This coach, in the era
of the California gold rush, was still being used to carry the
Sacrament to dying sinners.[47] North Americans who stopped at
Lima after rounding the Horn on their way to San Francisco
admired the vehicle.

In the early eighteenth century Lima rivaled Europe in architecture. The elegant residences displayed intricately carved mahogany balconies[48] and magnificently studded portals through which a coach could drive. Small entry doors on the portals admitted pedestrians into cobbled patios. The chambers in the houses were furnished elaborately with carved cabinets, massive tables, delicate settees, and beds with high headboards.[49] This was the Lima of merchant millionaires, of ladies wearing elaborate combs, flirting behind satin fans hand painted with pictures of romantic chivalry,[50] the Lima of 40,000 Negroes, mostly slaves, the Lima of forty shops selling fine goods from all parts of the world,[51] the Lima of the days when to be "worth a Peru" meant to be rich indeed. This Lima of high-ceilinged splendor came to a sudden end in 1746 when a tremendous earthquake struck the city.

Such quakes were not new to Peru. Roadways had trembled and houses had shuddered in the quakes of 1586, 1630, 1687, and 1713,[52] but none was remembered with so much horror as the earthquake of 1746. The first shock struck shortly before midnight. Walls crumbled, ceilings crashed. Of 3,000 houses in Lima only twenty-one remained standing.[53] A tidal wave submerged Callao, sweeping one vessel as far inland as half a mile. Tradition says the quake thrust the island of San Lorenzo up from the bottom of the sea; believers pointed to fossil shells on the island to prove the legend, but it is obviously false since the map prepared by Francisco de Ulloa in 1742 shows the island in existence at that time.[54]

The 1746 earthquake killed some 5,000 persons.[55] Crazed survivors fled across the Rimac River to San Cristóbal Mountain.[56] When the earth ceased trembling they draped themselves in purple, girding themselves with strands of rope as a symbol of piety, and erected a cross on the crest overlooking the dusty ruins of the city.

The next bad quake, in 1806,[57] shook down a different city in a different age. The era of revolution had dawned. France had overthrown the ancient Bourbon kings. England's colonies in North America had become the United States, and Boston ships by the dozen were sailing the Pacific as whalers and as merchants in the China trade. The captains of these vessels were continually annoyed with Spain's restrictions at her South American ports, which were sometimes of vital interest to wrecked or disabled craft. To help stranded mariners, as well as the United States interests they served, two North Americans appeared in Chile. One, well known to history, came in 1809. The other, who may have come earlier and traveled on to Peru, remains a shadowy figure, although he is the probable founder of a shipping agency destined to be important in the gold rush from Peru to California.

Joel Poinsett, who imported from Mexico the brilliant poinsettia, was sent to Chile by the United States to foment a revolution for independence.[58] A free nation, it was hoped, would open its ports to North American ships and liberate crews imprisoned for trespass, many of them coming from Nantucket.*

The other prominent North American who came to South America during the last days of Spain's Peruvian viceroyalty is more obscure. Richard Alsop was a New England millionaire. Inheriting a fortune from his father, he amassed additional wealth by engaging in coastwise and West Indian shipping.[59] He, or his family, is credited with pioneering the South American trade and establishing A. Alsop y Cía, one of the first commission firms in Peru and Chile. A search has failed to reveal Richard Alsop's relations with this firm, but his interest in the South American Pacific trade is evident. He wrote a burlesque concerning the Nootka Sound affair of 1790 and a more serious history of Chile. In New England he is remembered as a bookish man and as one of the Connecticut Wits.

A genial conservative, Richard Alsop was—or his men were—probably earlier in the South American field than Poinsett, and certainly his influence would be more important at the beginning of the California gold rush. Unlike Poinsett, the Alsops took no part in encouraging South American revolutions. Instead, A. Alsop y Cía. favored the Establishment, and the royalists in power gave special privileges to Alsop vessels. Richard Alsop was known in New England as a member of the tiewig school of

---

* The Nantucket Inquirer, Aug. 27, 1924, notes that seven captains being held prisoners by the Spaniards are listed in the Southern Patriot.

politicians who had opposed the American Revolution, approved the status quo, and disliked political or economic change. He used his literary ability humorously to describe a democratic Massachusetts town meeting. During the Revolution he had poked fun at vain, wealthy John Hancock's eagerness to be idolized by the mob. In addition, Alsop's sharp quill pen had exposed the unreliability of debt-ridden Sam Adams who, having failed to manage the wealth he had inherited, insisted on telling the government how to manage its wealth. Richard Alsop even enjoyed analyzing the democratic pronouncements of Thomas Jefferson:[60] Was it true that all men were created equal? Upper-class Peruvians, in the days of the viceroyalty, must have understood Richard Alsop, and he certainly understood them. This mutuality may account for the survival of the Alsop firm during a later generation of Peruvian turmoil and its final importance at the beginning of the gold rush.

The old order, which had maintained Lima as the headquarters of a vast viceroyalty, suited the well-to-do, established residents. Only a minority, like all minorities, fretted for change and favored independence from Spain. Indeed the Liberator, José de San Martín, had to bring an army from Chile to expel the Spaniards from Peru, and Lord Cochrane, as noted above, brought the Chilean navy to clear the Peruvian seas of Spanish ships. The Liberator, having surrounded Lima with his army, offered freedom to all Negroes who would join his forces. To emphasize the idealism of the revolution, he proclaimed all men free who were born after Independence Day, July 15, 1821,[61] but the blacks failed to respond. Perhaps, as household servants, they could not assemble in large numbers, or they may have felt genuine loyalty to their masters. Clearly, during San Martín's invasion to liberate Peru, the residents of Lima feared his army of free blacks and Indians more than a rebellion of their own slaves.[62] Men, women, children, and slaves fled to convents and monasteries for protection. Four thousand took refuge in the fort at Callao, where two towers, round but not high, stood within a wall enclosing some 20 acres surrounded by a moat easily flooded from the sea.[63]

San Martín's forces besieged the fort, but life in Lima resumed normalcy. Once more hawkers cried their wares and donkey boys peddled water. Beggars crept from their lairs on crippled legs to shake empty cups for alms. Theaters opened, but instead of Spanish grandees in the audience the galleries and pit were filled with Chilean officers, many from Cochrane's fleet, and English sailors of fortune from his ships. American and English merchants, who no doubt looked forward to freer trade, sat in the boxes with smiling Lima women,[64] those ubiquitous females, strangers to the best families, who appeared in fine clothes to welcome a conquering army. Whether or not Alsop's agent sat among them the records fail to disclose, but the old firm remained prominent for the next twenty-seven years. Then it unwittingly caused a tragic event in the California gold rush.

The defeated royalists, with remnants of the Spanish army, remained under siege in the fort at Callao for a year and a half. As supplies began to diminish, 400 women marched out and surrendered to the liberators. Later, groups of men sallied forth to take their chances, but 200 remained, eating their horses, asses, rats, dogs, and cats. On February 19, 1826, they surrendered,[65] and the last Spanish flag in South America came down, but Spain refused to recognize Peru's independence. Their situation boded trouble during the days when hundreds of ships carrying gold seekers rounded the Horn on their way to California.

In the meantime, the tempo of life for refined Peruvians had changed completely; the problems of an unwanted independence created situations that few understood. The old economy had been based on inherited wealth and position, on regulated mining, merchandising, and transportation. How would generations disciplined to the viceroyal complex respond to an experimental democracy agitated by a gold rush to California?

8

Lima Learns about
the Gold Discovery

The adjustment to vulgar, democratic politics proved difficult for aristocratic Peruvians. The intelligent elite had read sufficient history to know that a government of all the people could be only a government of mediocrity, that a fight for home rule meant only a fight to determine what clique should rule at home. The idealistic San Martín, a conservative, self-effacing liberator,[1] failed as a ruler in Peru. He was followed by that other revolutionary idealist, the flamboyant Bolívar whose histrionic statements many Latin Americans wanted to hear, but he, too, was considered a meddlesome foreigner unacceptable to the best people of Lima.[2]

Yet Peru, or certain classes in Peru, prospered after independence from Spain was forced upon them in 1821. The Alsop commission firm readily adapted itself to the change and several merchants became wealthy, although many old families believed that life should have values of more importance than trade. True, Lima prospered temporarily, owing largely to the unrestrained importation of British goods,[3] but was that preferable to the established Peruvian culture? To make matters worse, Mexico was now independent. She had opened her ports, and several Englishmen, with offices in Lima, had engaged in buying and selling smelly hides and tallow.[4] Peru, in spite of herself, had become part of the free-trade world, a world of competition in which she had had no experience. To raise operating expenses the Peruvian government issued 6 percent debentures in 1824 which sold in Europe at figures so low that the interest climbed to almost 40 percent on the sales price.⁵ Hopelessly in debt, the once proud and powerful viceroyalty experienced continual civil and national wars. Mestizo caudillos appealed for mixed-blood followers while pure-blood Spanish leaders promised a return to the old days of peace, prestige, and prosperity.

The continual revolutions might have been disastrous for North American gold seekers who, after sailing around the Horn, needed tropical fruit from Peruvian ports to prevent or cure scurvy. Fortunately, a gifted Peruvian soldier maintained peace in his country during the gold rush. Ramón Castilla was a mestizo with a face to remember. He had thin, sharp features with tight lips and dark, lively, penetrating eyes which had watched many battles. This horseman's bullethead was full of deals with revolutionists as tricky as he was.⁶ He had grown to manhood * during Spanish rule, fought in the Spanish army, later joined the rebels, and received a lance wound in a cavalry charge on the plains of Ayacucho in the battle that defeated the last Spanish army in South America.† Famous for this everlasting mark of heroism, he participated in numerous revolutions during two decades, sometimes helping gain a victory and once serving a term in jail. These military campaigns for political power resembled a game, and the oligarchy of commanding generals was popularly called La Rosca ("the circle of card players").

During the years prior to the gold rush, Ramón Castilla watched president after president try again and again to reestablish Peru's national importance by fighting the neighboring countries Peru had ruled before they all gained independence from Spain. In a famous battle General Agustín Gamarra achieved immortality by losing his life. Castilla, a true member of the circle of card players, had fought against Gamarra in one revolution and as his cavalry commander in another.⁷

Wars and revolutions, together with Peru's bankruptcy,

---

* Jorge Basadre (*Historia de la República del Perú* [Lima, 1961–1968], II, 727) gives Castilla's date of birth as August 31, 1797. So does Pedro Pablo Figueroa (*Diccionario Biografico de Estranjeros en Chile* [Santiago de Chile, 1900] p. 60). Frederick B. Pike (*The Modern History of Peru* [New York, 1967], p. 91) says the date was 1799.

† Basadre, *op. cit.*, II, 730. The last royalists in Chile were driven from the island of Chiloé in 1826.

caused the United States and several European nations to propose joint occupation of Peruvian ports in order to collect customs, pay off the national debt, and protect foreigners.[8] In this predicament Castilla engineered a brilliant military coup, became president, and with a firm hand maintained peace in Peru for five years, during which the gold rush began. He claimed to represent Peru's three worlds, the Spanish, mestizo, and Indian worlds that had warred continually since independence. With Indian and European blood in his own veins,[9] he married a black-eyed Creole beauty from Peru's socially elite. She was being courted by an officer of the United States navy patrol assigned to the Pacific[10] but, as the Spanish say, "the black in her eyes did not prevent her from seeing a more advantageous marriage" with the new ruler of Peru.

Castilla faced two immediate issues at the beginning of his administration: first, to prevent *insurrectos* from capturing and recapturing Peruvian ports and, second, to reestablish Peru's national credit. He solved both problems adroitly. He strengthened the army by freeing all slaves who would enlist,[11] and he began liquidating the national debt by selling rights to dig guano on the Chincha Islands.[12] The guano had great value since many Europeans feared that the population explosion of that day doomed mankind to death by starvation. A fertilizer like guano might produce more food and thus save the world.

Guano, the solidified droppings from seabirds, had accumulated for centuries in banks often 150 feet deep.[13] To dig it some 2,000 coolies were imported, thus setting a precedent for Chinese immigration into California. During the gold rush as many as sixty American and British vessels congregated at one time beside the islands, awaiting their turn to be loaded.[14] The guano was dug with pick and shovel. When exposed to the air it became dusty, and Argonauts sailing north to California often met southbound ships with white decks, masts, and rigging—ghost ships on the dark blue sea. A knowing captain could explain, "She's from the Chinchas. After the first rain, guano dust turns white as snow on yards, trucks and halyards." [15] Later, when the Argonauts sailed farther north, they sometimes saw a golden column of guano dust rising from the distant islands.[16]

This ammonia-smelling "gold" enabled President Castilla to engage in extravagant spending which helped keep him in power. To compensate for Peru's repeated defeats he purchased ships for his navy, naming one of them *Jeneral Gamarra*. This ship became notable in California history when she sailed to San Francisco in 1849 to protect Peruvian gold seekers. Castilla also modernized the shipbuilding equipment at Paita (a tiny Peruvian port on the most westerly tip of South America), making it one of the best naval bases in the Pacific. He purchased, in New York, the first steam warship to cruise the Pacific.[17] His official press published, with national pride, a detailed account of the *Rimac's* cruise around the Horn.

An announcement concerning the armistice between the United States and Mexico was duly printed in the Lima newspapers,[18] but it failed to specify that California would be ceded to the United States, although that seemed evident. Nobody, of course, was suggesting that gold might be found in California. Indeed, Peruvians did not learn about the gold discoveries until two and a half months after Captain Andrews brought the exciting news to Valparaiso. The delay seems strange, for the Chilean Guillermo Wheelwright had established a monthly mail service[19] on two paddle-wheel steamships, thereby shortening the Valparaiso–Lima trip to eight days. Chilean newspapers came regularly but, as we have seen, they delayed printing any word concerning the discovery.

The news finally reached Peru through an involved series of events which began when the Peruvian schooner *Lambayeque* sailed from Monterey, California, on August 24, 1848, with mail for Valparaiso.* On board, Lieutenant Lucien Loeser, of the 3d United States Artillery, carried a tea caddy containing gold dust and nuggets worth more than $3,000.[20] He was being sent posthaste on a special mission to Washington with a letter from Governor Richard B. Mason, later quoted by President Polk in the

* Hubert Howe Bancroft (*History of California* [San Francisco, 1884–1890], VI, 155) says the *Lambayeque* sailed from Monterey on August 30. The *Californian* of Sept. 2, 1848, says she left San Francisco on July 7 and Monterey on the 24th. The latter dates have been accepted. According to the *California Star* of Dec. 9, 1848, the trip to Paita consumed forty days, which would mean that the vessel arrived there on October 3.

annual message that started the gold rush. The *Lambayeque* also carried copies of the newspaper, *Californian*, dated August 14, 1848. It was the first San Francisco paper published since May when the typesetters had deserted to join the rush. The editor described in detail the discovery of gold by Marshall and Bennett in the millrace on the American River, as well as the marvelous development of placers elsewhere.

On October 3, 1848, the *Lambayeque* called at Paita, Peru, the site of President Castilla's new naval base. Many New England whalers were anchored there. What, if anything, Lieutenant Loeser may have told the people he met, the records fail to disclose. All we know is that he left the *Lambayeque* and boarded a steamer for Panama with his famous letter and tea caddy of gold, while the *Lambayeque* continued her voyage to Valparaiso with the mail. A copy of the *Californian* must have been left in Paita because an account of the discovery printed in that paper was reprinted on October 17 in Spanish by *Del Tridente*, a newspaper in the town of Piura, 35 miles inland.[21] A copy of this Spanish paper containing the startling news was carried five days later aboard *El Callao*, a little two-masted, 156-ton schooner bound for Callao some 600 miles down the coast. Callao was Lima's port of entry and the news would not be known in the Peruvian capital until the schooner arrived there.

In the meantime, on October 30, only eight days after *El Callao* had left, the first gold seekers from Peru sailed from Paita for California in the schooner *El Peruano*, but they were not Peruvians. The local newspaper described them as "electos estranjeros." Certainly, "selected foreigners" must have been North American, English, and possibly French adventurers, the kind of men who loitered in every South American Pacific harbor. Deserters from the whaleships at Paita would have lacked the money to buy passage. These gold seekers had been at sea only four days when *El Callao*, carrying the copy of *Del Tridente*, dropped anchor at Callao. She brought a "cargo of the country" including rice and "sacks of superior California tallow," which she offered for sale on board, on the beach, or at the office of the shipping agent in Lima.[22]

The editor of Lima's *El Comercio* read about the gold dis-

covery in *Del Tridente*, which arrived on Saturday, November
4. The Lima paper for that day was already made up, but on page
3 the editor found room for an announcement, headed NOTICIA
EXTRAORDINARIA, which described how the exciting news had
come from California to Paita. He also suggested goods for shipment to the new market—clothes, shoes, picks, shovels, and
knives—saying that all could be purchased in Lima on credit.[23]
The next day, Sunday, November 5, 1848, no paper was issued,
but on Monday, November 6, two columns under the heading
ORO DE CALIFORNIA reprinted *Del Tridente*'s account of the discovery by Marshall and Bennett. People in Lima were told that
Indians in California built their huts out of gold, believing it to
be yellow dirt. California was said to have changed from a barren
country ruled by a few wealthy traders to a place where laborers
had become capitalists! About 4,000 of them were already at the
placers. Their average daily income ranged from $75 to $150.
Many had earned, in a single day, from $300 to $800, and only
a sheath knife was needed to pick gold from the rocks. Readers
also learned that a reporter from the town of Sonoma—wherever
that might be—said the laborers there had quit and gone to the
placers. One of them had averaged $100 a day and was now
worth $1,500.

This news was exciting for readers of *El Comercio*, but the
editor had not yet squeezed all the sweet copy out of *Del Tridente*'s excerpts from the *Californian*. In the next issue he
printed a translation of Governor Mason's proclamation of July
25 stating that gold could be dug "on government land, without
charge and without hindrance," provided certain laws and regulations were respected. The editor also reprinted, in Spanish, a
petition to Mason begging for the acceptance of gold dust as
currency at the customhouse and Mason's reply, agreeing to
take the dust as collateral if half the due payment was made in
coin within ninety days and the balance ninety days later. The
governor concluded by saying that he hoped to establish a mint
in California.

These enticing accounts came to Callao, whose dominant activity was shipping guano. On November 6, the day of the first
big announcement, four vessels left the port city. Three of them

were British, loaded with supplies purchased in Callao before sailing to the Chincha Islands for guano. The fourth was a Peruvian coastal trader. That same day five vessels arrived in the Callao port. One was British and four were American. All were seeking guano except one, which was carrying a cargo from New York consigned to A. Alsop y Cía.[24] Compared with Valparaiso, Callao had insignificant trade, which would have been almost entirely local save for President Castilla's guano business. This moneymaking activity, however, was so successful that the news from California failed to excite many speculators, even though *El Comercio* urged them to send supplies to San Francisco.[25] Owners of the Peruvian *Concordia*, which was anchored in the harbor, advertised on November 10 for freight and passengers to the gold fields,[26] but few shippers responded. Nevertheless, President Castilla, proud of the Peruvian navy and eager to display his country's new importance in South America, ordered the new 415-ton warship, *Jeneral Gamarra*, to prepare for a cruise, but he specified no destination.[27]

A North American sea captain in the harbor, Edward Waterman, had sailed his two-masted tramp schooner, *Glyde*, into Callao two months earlier[28] with a cargo including linen handkerchiefs, cotton cloth, thread, clocks, and hemp-backed chairs he had purchased in China. Finding the cargo unsalable in Callao, he decided to remain in port no longer; perhaps he would find purchasers in San Francisco. On November 14 he weighed anchor and sailed away without a single passenger.[29] His was the second ship to leave Peru for California since news of the gold discovery.

On the day after the *Glyde* sailed, a Peruvian brigantine, the *Susana*, advertised for California passengers and freight. To compete with the *Concordia*, her owners promised to sail within eight days, a better offer than the *Concordia's* uncertain sailing date.[30] Next day the *Neptune*, a tramp frigate of Danish registry, arrived from Valparaiso. Her captain saw an opportunity to make money in the gold rush. His craft was small and fast and could transport gold seekers rapidly. He began unloading as quickly as possible.

No rush from Peru to California had started yet, but interest in transporting freight, not passengers, seemed to be growing. The Peruvian schooner, *Bello Angelito*, was advertised by J. Tavara, who tried to outdo the *Concordia's* indefinite date of departure by promising to sail "dentro de pocos días."[31] On November 22, a fourth vessel, the Peruvian brigantine *Venus*, was added to the ships in the harbor available for transporting cargo and passengers to California.

These four vessels were of minor importance in the harbor's shipping trade. An equal number of ships were advertised for other ports, and the guano trade was still the major maritime activity. Certainly no rush like the one from Chile had yet developed. Instead, on November 23, owners of the *Concordia* canceled her California cruise.[32] The *Susana's* owners claimed to have sold all her accommodations, but she had booked only nine passengers, perhaps all a freighter could carry. Owners of the *Venus* maintained that their craft was also fully booked, but this may have been a trick to attract passengers, because a public announcement warned all ticket holders to make full payment within the next four days or forfeit their accommodations to tentative passengers on the waiting list. Instead of sailing, however, the *Venus* continued, along with the *Angelito*, to advertise berths. With the number of vessels offering transportation now reduced from four to two, a demand for passage was obviously not developing.

On November 28 Juan de Dios Calderón assumed the management of the *Bello Angelito's* affairs. Did he see an opportunity others had overlooked? Don Juan was a wealthy shipbuilder, perhaps the wealthiest in Lima, and his entry into the gold rush is significant. He had already dispatched one of his freighters to San Francisco from Paita,[33] and now he was assuring speculators and passengers that the *Angelito* would leave Callao between December 12 and 15[34]—a period in which a startling piece of news would upset all shipping plans but he, of course, could not foresee this.

On November 30 the *Susana* sailed from Callao. She was the first craft to leave for California with Peruvian passengers, and their names are revealing. The nine emigrants on board differed sharply from the first gold seekers leaving Chile. Unlike those

from cosmopolitan Valparaiso, most of the passengers on the
Susana had Spanish names. Only two, Don José Macgregor and
Don Guillermo Gibson, could have been Anglos or of Anglo
descent. Gibson took his wife and son.[35] By the time the *Susana*
sailed, the Danish *Neptune's* hold was cleared and her captain
began advertising for freight and passengers. Another brigantine, the Peruvian *Mazeppa*, was also laid on for California although space was still available on the *Bello Angelito*, which
seemed unpopular.

Passengers were apparently reluctant to book on any of these
four vessels. After ten days the *Venus'* owners resorted to their
old trick, if it was indeed a trick. Claiming to have filled the
brigantine's berths again, they announced that the *Venus* would
sail December 18 and all passengers must pay their full fares by
the 15th,[36] but again the ship failed to sail. In fact the *Venus*,
like the *Concordia*, was soon withdrawn from the California
voyage.

Accommodations on these four vessels were still available on
December 14 when the upsetting advertisement that changed
all shipping plans appeared in *El Comercio*. On the front page,
A. Alsop y Cía. announced that the North American steamship
California, due to arrive in a few days, would sail immediately
for California, stopping at Panama and other Central and South
American ports. According to the advertisement, space was
available for freight and for 60 cabin-class and 150 steerage passengers,[37] thus providing an excellent opportunity for gold seekers. A reader may wonder why the Alsops in Lima could make
this attractive offer before the steamer arrived when the Alsops
in Valparaiso, who could have charged more for a longer voyage,
had failed to get permission from Captain Forbes to take a single
passenger.

Perhaps it was a coincidence that on the day the Alsops' announcement was printed three British ships arrived in Callao.
They brought newspapers from England which contained accounts of the California discoveries. Although dated three
months earlier than the stories taken from *Del Tridente*, the
stale news was translated by the editor of *El Comercio* and
printed in a column under the old heading ORO DE CALIFORNIA.

This publicity, along with the offer of tickets for the *California*, stimulated interest in the gold rush. To cap the good news, the Valparaiso mail steamer arrived with copies of that city's newspapers, and the Lima editor reprinted a long report from *El Mercurio*. He also reprinted a circular released by the American consul in Valparaiso. Indeed, Valparaiso papers, from now on, seemed to be the chief source of information concerning the gold rush, even though Lima was 1,300 miles closer to San Francisco.

The flood of favorable publicity fails to explain the Alsops' offer of passenger space on the *California*. The firm could have received word from Panama to sell tickets but that, as we shall see, seems unlikely. It could not have learned about the captain's refusal to take passengers from Chile because the advertisement appeared in Lima before the *California* had anchored in Valparaiso. Perhaps the Peruvian Alsops, eager for commissions, decided to act without authority, believing that they could negotiate with the captain when he arrived. In any event, they sold a large number of tickets to San Francisco[38] ten days before the *California* arrived and at a time when four local vessels were unable to fill their berths. These sales had far-reaching effects on race relations in California during 1849.

The reason that gold seekers in Peru seemed so eager to sail on the *California* instead of on the local vessels may have been the poor quality of passenger accommodations on small Latin-American craft. One rhymester described sailors and conditions on shipboard as follows:

Pícaros sin ninguna consider-
    ación
	Rogues without any consider-
	    ation

Pasajeros ser nunca contentos	Passengers never contented
Pésimas son nuestras comidas	Very bad are our meals
Peor sería no comerlas.[39]	Worse it would be to not eat them.

Evidently these lines did not describe conditions on a big North American craft like the *California*, and emigrants were eager to board her. In fact the announcement of her proposed stop in Callao marked the apex of gold-rush excitement in Peru, which, as we have seen, lacked the keen aggressiveness displayed in

Valparaiso. To take advantage of the enthusiasm a Peruvian promoter organized the Sociedad Filantrópica de California. Membership, according to a newspaper advertisement,[40] was available for twenty-five or thirty qualified individuals willing to pay 500 pesos and work at any job voted upon by their fellow members. All would share equally in the work and at the end of one year all gold and other profits would be divided equally. Men wishing to join this Latin-American imitation of the Mayflower Compact were asked to consult D. Pedro Osorío in Barroza's bakery across the street from the post office.

The success of the society is difficult to determine, but all shipowners except Juan de Dios Calderón stopped appealing for passengers, although some vessels did sail for California with a few people on board. Freight to California, not gold seekers, had become the established business, and Don Juan presented a petition signed by the commanders of various merchant ships. He was a power in Lima, and when he spoke even President Castilla listened. He had known Sonorans and Californios during the Mexican War and probably distrusted North Americans more than any other man in Peru. The petition he presented stated that Peruvian crews would desert as soon as their vessels arrived in California, thus leaving the owners helpless. In addition, all Peruvians, both laborers and merchants, would be ill treated by adventurous Yankees in San Francisco. Therefore, would President Castilla be good enough to send a warship to protect his people's interests? [41]

On December 21 President Castilla agreed to honor the request. It gave him a splendid opportunity to impress the Latin-American world, especially Chile, that Peru had become a naval power in the Pacific. He did not name the vessel he would send, but the *Jeneral Gamarra* had been under orders for almost six weeks to prepare for some voyage, and on December 27 Castilla published in the official newspaper, *El Peruano*, an editorial on the gold discoveries, lauding the advantages for trade in California.

On December 28, while the people were reading the president's descriptions of commercial opportunities in California, the boom of cannon echoed from the 1,300-foot bluffs of San Lorenzo,[42] setting off a shower of screaming gulls. The salvo was fired by the S.S. *California* as she rounded the island. Waves from her paddle wheels splashed against rocks where seals basked, and they barked at the steamship. The ailing Captain Forbes, standing on the quarterdeck, had no forewarning of the sale of passenger tickets for his ship by A. Alsop y Cía. Looking ahead as the vessel entered the Mediterranean-blue waters behind the island, he could see across Callao Bay what appeared to be a thick white line some 3 miles away. This line was the surf and the sandy beach in front of the port town. Beyond Callao, 8 miles of desert reached to another thinner white line at the foot of ocher mountains. That was Lima. Between the ocean and the mountains stood three brown, sugar-loaf hills. The largest, San Cristóbal, had a cross on top.

At 9:00 A.M. the *California* dropped anchor in the roadstead. She had made the trip from Valparaiso in five and a half days. Steamers did, indeed, cut the usual sailing time almost in half.[43] From the quarterdeck Captain Forbes must have noticed Callao's fort wall enclosing two round towers,[44] the area where loyalists had been besieged for a year and a half. The sandbar that protruded into the bay at right angles to the coast had been converted into a mole by filling grounded vessels with rocks and surrounding them with piles. Along the top, derricks lifted cargo from lighters into small railway cars which ran to the shore.[45] The captain, very ill with a sore throat and almost voiceless, rested on his ship until afternoon.[46] Then he was rowed in a small boat to the mole. He climbed the stairs and walked to shore along the narrow-gauge tracks,[47] passing the usual swarm of ragged Indians and tatterdemalion Negroes who peddled fruit and *dulces* to incoming sailors. A crowd of excited emigrants begged for passage to California,[48] but the captain ignored them as he had ignored the hopeful gold seekers in Valparaiso.

No representative of A. Alsop y Cía. greeted Captain Forbes. Did they all hesitate to tell what they had done? At the foot of the mole he boarded an omnibus[49] (manufactured in Newark, New Jersey)[50] which hauled passengers to Lima every hour; the fare of 4 reales was later increased to a dollar as the gold rush developed.[51] The ill captain sat down among men and women smoking strong cigars.[52] His impression of Callao from the lurching conveyance could not have been favorable. Many houses were constructed of reeds plastered with mud. Rain never fell here. The only moisture came from occasional heavy mists, and straw mats served as roofs.[53] The two principal streets, paved with cobblestones,[54] were intersected by countless winding lanes between dull adobe buildings.

Low-grade Americans, usually deserters who had married Latin wives, kept rooming houses for transients on shore leave. At one place some old chairs on the street in front of a ship's chandlery were usually occupied by dowdily dressed sea captains—probably Nantucket whalemen—talking earnestly, spitting, whittling, making deals for rope and canvas.[55]

Shops, usually run by Englishmen, often had no front wall to protect goods from the dust of the streets. Huge overhead shutters were pulled down at night. Not far beyond them elaborate bedrooms, presided over by gaily dressed prostitutes, also opened onto the street, and sailors, half-drunk on Pisco brandy, gaped at the "gals" or picked fights with strangers to determine who was the better man.[56] The captain, beset with premonitions of his own doom, may have noticed as he passed the Callao cemetery that most of the headstones marking graves bore English and American names,[57] a dreary reminder for a man in his condition. In Lima, Catholics buried their dead in a gay garden, emphasizing that death was not somber, except for suicides whose bodies were denied interment there.[58]

The road to Lima crossed a plain as level as the ocean. The highway, well paved by the viceroys, had been neglected during the revolutions. Robbers might hold up the omnibus anywhere.[59] Many of these rascals were discharged soldiers from Castilla's army or the Negro slaves he had emancipated, but one gang was said to be led by a North American clerk who had gone native.[60]

Captain Forbes must have noticed that from a distance Lima appeared magnificent, almost Moorish with its domes and spires.[61] As the omnibus drew nearer, he could see that the city was enclosed by a 20-foot adobe wall. A mile from town a dilapidated sidewalk along both sides of the roadway reminded visitors of Spain's vanished glory. Cypress trees, oddly distorted by the prevailing southerly winds, shaded broken-down stone benches which once tempted pedestrians to rest every 150 yards. Indeed, the viceroys in colonial days had built a beautiful approach to the City of the Kings.[62]

The highway ended at an elaborate city gate surmounted by an embellished clock tower, built in 1800[63] by an Irishman named Ambrose Higgins, who had once operated a small shop in Lima. He became the captain of Peruvian cavalry, then captain general of the Peruvian army. Changing his name to Ambrosio O'Higgins, the king of Spain created him marquis and finally viceroy of Peru. His illegitimate son, Bernardo O'Higgins,[64] better known as the Liberator of Chile, had been educated in Europe by his father. He became a leader in revolutions for democracy which destroyed, by neglect, all the former magnificence his father had maintained.

Inside the great gate, Lima disappointed travelers. The church spires that seemed so attractive from a distance proved to be made of wood, daubed with mud.[65] The residences in Lima, built of adobe, usually stood two stories high with windows on the second floor.[66] The elaborately carved mahogany balconies of colonial days were still fashionable. From them women could watch through a lattice the incoming omnibus from Callao and see the passengers without being seen. During fiestas, young ladies played pranks from the safety of these balconies. A passerby in the street, presumably a good-looking young man, might be surprised by a crash of breaking glass and porcelain above his head. Looking up, he would see that the shattering sound had come from a bag full of crockery at the end of a 7-foot rope, which prevented it from hitting him.[67] The bag had evidently been dropped from one of the balconies, and the man might hear suppressed giggles and glimpse a fleeting view of sparkling black eyes.

A small stream flowed down the central streets of Lima, and garbage was thrown into it. Vultures, tame as barnyard fowl, skipped away from the omnibus and ran among the legs of men

and beasts,[68] snatching morsels of food. They were protected
by law, and as many as sixty or eighty of these big, sooty birds
might roost in a row on some houses, their wrinkled, red heads
watching for garbage.[69] Occasional fine residences reminded
observers of Lima's prosperous days before the earthquakes and
the revolutions. Such houses were still entered through a high-
arched portal which, when open, disclosed an attractively fres-
coed patio surrounded on four sides by two tiers of galleries.

The omnibus was one of the few wheeled vehicles in Lima.
Most delieveries were made from the backs of mules or burros.[70]
In this foreign, well-nigh Oriental city, Captain Forbes, "almost
exhausted & very sick"[71] called at the counting room of his owners' agents. These gentlemen, undoubtedly aware of the unpleasant situation they had created for the ailing captain, displayed typical American salesmanship by greeting him with
cordiality and sympathy. One of them took him home and en-
sconced him in what Forbes remembered as "a neat & pleasant
Bed Room," where he was treated "with great kindness & attention."[72] The records fail to disclose the name of the doctor they
recommended, but Lima boasted several English and North
American physicians. A dentist advertised that he filled teeth
with gold for 5 pesos, or with a "metal to take its place" (*con
mineral seccedaneum*) for $2.40[73] (he or the typesetter mis-
spelled the Latin word *succedaneum*).

As Captain Forbes, surrounded by these luxuries, improved
in health, he must have pondered the sly trick his benefactors
had played on him. Regardless of his orders to take no passengers from South America, these men, as agents for his owners,
had already accepted money for the fares. His protests were
overridden by suave assurances that the ticket holders had
agreed not to interfere with passengers booked in Panama.[74] If
necessary they would sleep on the empty, unsheltered deck,
though they had paid $300 for cabin-class accommodations or
$150 for steerage. In addition, freight, netting the company
$15,000, had also been accepted,[75] earning unexpected profits
for the owners, not to mention the agents' commissions.

The Alsops' argument was persuasive, and Captain Forbes,

having accepted their hospitality, acquiesced. The exact number of passengers foisted on him is questionable, but certainly less than 100 went aboard.* Their nationality is also difficult to determine. Of the fifty on one list,[76] almost half had non-Spanish names. Of the sixty-two listed in a contemporary newspaper, only thirteen had Spanish names.[77] Obviously the later complaint that the *California* brought too many South American "foreigners" was an exaggeration of the facts. The record shows a Frank Ward and lady, a Mr. A. M. Hindman from Connecticut, and "an elderly gentleman from Maryland."[78] These four were described as having lived a long time in Peru. Such individuals were not Peruvian gold seekers, but a certain Don A. M. Villanul did board the ship with twelve or thirteen men. He was one of South America's large mining operators, and reports said he planned to bring forty more workers to California later.[79]

On January 10, 1849, the *California* steamed off, carrying the passengers forced upon Captain Forbes, passengers who would form the basis of the opposition to South Americans in California. They were the foreigners a United States general would condemn and thus justify, in some men's minds, the riots that disgraced California in the year ahead. President Castilla, in his palace on the plaza where Pizarro had been assassinated, could hardly predict these events, but he ordered Captain José Silva Rodríguez, commander of the *Jeneral Gamarra*, to muster a large crew[80] for a cruise to California. Castilla sent a consul, a vice-consul, and two secretaries aboard the *Gamarra*. She sailed on January 25.[81] By that time the *California* had anchored at Panama and Captain Forbes was in trouble for bringing South American passengers, a fact unknown to Captain Silva Rodríguez until he arrived in San Francisco on March 28.[82]

In the meantime the steamer *Oregon* had arrived in Lima on February 12, after only five days from Valparaiso.[83] She was the second of the three Pacific Mail Steamship Company vessels due to operate north from Panama. Her arrival revealed the

* Victor M. Berthold (*The Pioneer Steamer* [Boston, 1932], pp. 34, 39) says fifty or seventy-five passengers were taken aboard. Berthold cites other records (p. 35) which indicate that the ship carried seventeen cabin passengers and eighty "forward."

great change that had come to Callao. Alsop y Cía. offered passage on her, as they had on her sister ship *California*, but only five passengers bought tickets.[84] The rush to California from Lima had ended. Never again would there be the demand for passage which had annoyed Captain Forbes. The Danish *Neptune* and the Peruvian *Mazeppa* both sailed with cargoes but no passengers. Don Juan's *Bello Angelito*, which had tried so hard to attract emigrants, stopped on her cruise north at Paita and finally arrived in San Francisco with only thirty-four passengers, picked up God knows where.

The S.S. California Sails to Panama and San Francisco

The *California*, after refilling her coal bunkers in Callao, paddled away with a crew of forty-five and an undetermined number of passengers, who would cause much trouble for the ship's owners when she stopped in Panama. As she steamed across Callao Bay, native boys probably navigated their clumsy 4-by-8-foot balsas[1] into the steamer's wake to enjoy riding the swells. The *California* soon chugged around the northern bluff of San Lorenzo. Passengers who looked back saw that Callao and the old fortress had already shrunk to the well-known brown line above a white thread of surf and sand on the horizon. Out in the ocean the weather was fine; it was never too hot, thanks to the Humboldt Current, although this area was as close to the equator as sweltering Nicaragua. Marine life flourished, and passengers often pointed to *malaguas* ("sea nettles") which looked like big striped umbrellas.[2] Some passenger was sure to remark in Spanish, "Like to me is said, *las malaguas*, when half dried by the fishermen in the village coastal of Peru, bait irresistible make for fish. Si, Señor?"

Such a statement might be challenged by a man from the mining districts east of the Andes who would embellish the account with, "Seguro, amigo, and in my country it no dispute is that the Indians, the poison of *las malaguas* use, to shrink the heads of enemies dead. No bone extracted is. Only the heads shrink. En verdad, si?" Listeners who accepted this information could expect the narrator to continue, "y si, Señor, much truer is that in days before the Pizarro, a vial of this poison when poured on the hills smooth of the Andes, cut deep the canyons red that today one sees. No?"

Many such bits of Peruvian folklore must have been repeated by deck passengers long before the *California* stopped at Paita to disembark an American consul and his clerk. From that point northward the ocean suddenly became discolored by the brackish water seeping from the alligator-infested Guayaquil Delta,[3] and passengers felt the first real equatorial heat, so different from the cool, moist air of Lima. Looking over the starboard bow, they could see the rugged island of Puná at the mouth of the estuary where Pizarro landed before invading the mainland.[4]

Farther on, in the doldrums, passengers on the *California* laughed as they steamed past sailing ships stalled for lack of wind, though they themselves had to scamper to their cabins when rain squalls swept across the deck. Whales, apparently enjoying these equatorial waters, congregated in such large numbers that the fetid smell of their blowing annoyed many travelers.[5]

In Panama, some 1,500 impatient men awaited transportation to California.[6] Among them was General Persifor Smith, accompanied by his wife and his staff, bound for California to take command of the army. The group also included John McDougal, destined to become the second governor of California. He and his wife and child, along with the general and his suite, had come to the isthmus aboard the *Falcon*, one of the steamships carrying mail to Chagres. From that port mail would be transported overland to Panama City, and the *California*, the *Oregon*, and the *Panama* would carry it on to California and Oregon.

The *Falcon* had left New York with no anticipation of a gold rush. Carrying ninety-five passengers, she had been at sea when President Polk announced the "extraordinary" discovery of gold which "would scarcely command belief." The *Falcon* docked at New Orleans after the rush had commenced, and there some 100 additional passengers[7] swarmed aboard with tickets to San Francisco, or at least with the understanding that they could get passage in Panama on the S.S. *California* when she came north. Several other vessels loaded with gold seekers raced with the *Falcon* to Chagres. The passengers had to cross the muddy isthmus on foot, on muleback, and by canoe to Panama City, which became overcrowded with travelers who claimed to have reservations aboard the *California* on the northbound trip.

The days of waiting in the steamy, tropical city caused continual anxiety. Cholera was sweeping across the United States, and travelers in Panama were fearful that an epidemic might start in the isolated, sultry city.[8] Many persons became ill and some died,[9] but not from cholera. Finally, on January 17, 1849, at eleven o'clock in the morning,[10] a shout, "Steamer coming! Steamer coming!" started men running in a mad rush down the winding street between the two-story adobe and stone houses.[11]

Along the quay an excited crowd watched a dark speck under a murky smudge on the horizon. The speck changed to an approaching steamship, the *California*. Here at last was an escape from dreaded cholera and an opportunity to reach California and find gold. Desperate emigrants offered bonuses of $1,000 for passage on her.[12] Two miles from shore the *California* cast anchor and a flock of the inevitable, fork-tailed frigate birds, which meet all vessels, zoomed menacingly around her. Vicious as these birds seemed to be, they were less threatening than the 300 prospective passengers on shore who learned that a vessel with accommodations for only 200 had already taken on board some seventy-five South Americans.[13]

The gold seekers had been told, during their restless waiting in sultry Panama, that many Latin Americans had gone to California ahead of them. There the foreigners were said to have skimmed the cream from placers, having already taken out $4 million in gold, and they might get all of it before the North American owners of the land could reach El Dorado. Now this injustice was being supported by a North American steamship in the harbor at Panama City which was carrying these greedy "greasers" in preference to "citizens" on the way to their own new country. To forestall such unfairness, protesters congregated in front of the shipping agents' office, at the American Hotel, and in the plaza.[14] No one noted that at least half of the hated greasers on the *California* had Anglo names and were probably New England Yankees! The disaffection became so ugly, with threats of violence, that General Persifor Smith wrote a notorious letter to United States Consul William Nelson in Panama, who happened also to be a partner in the firm that handled the *California*'s affairs.[15] The letter reads, in part:

Sir:
The laws of the United States inflict the penalty of fine and imprisonment on trespassers on the public lands. —As nothing can be more unreasonable or unjust, than the conduct pursued by persons not citizens of the United States, who are flocking from all parts to search for and carry off gold belonging to the United States in California; and as such conduct is in direct violation of law, it will become my duty, immediately on my arrival there, to put these laws in force, to prevent their infraction in future, by punishing with the penalties prescribed by law, on those who offend.[16]

General Smith asked that copies of his statement be transmitted to all United States consuls "on the coast of South America,"[17] for the information of prospective emigrants. The letter seemed to contradict Governor Mason's earlier statement that gold could be dug "on government land, without charge and without hindrance." This statement had been translated into Spanish and published in both Chile and Peru, so the general's tardy counterstatement was sure to cause consternation in Latin America and incite racial conflict in California.

The irate gold seekers waiting in Panama read General Smith's letter and called a public meeting to be held on January 19, at 8:00 P.M., in the American Hotel. Three hundred men assembled, including the United States consul. After the group formally elected officers, a committee was appointed "to consider and report upon the course pursued by Capt. Forbes, in bringing passengers from the Pacific Coast to the exclusion of Atlantic passengers."[18] The committee called on Captain Forbes and found him to be a very ill man. He explained that, contrary to his wishes, Alsop y Cía. had booked the Peruvians who agreed to sleep on deck, thus occupying no space reserved for Panama ticket holders. He said, also, that illness had forced him to yield the command to John Marshall, who would be master from Panama to San Francisco while he, himself, would become a passenger.[19]

This information quieted some of the complainers, though a few radicals still threatened violent action.[20] While the *Cali-*

fornia was being loaded with coal from lighters, another meeting of potential passengers was called for January 22, ostensibly to hear the committee's formal report. This assembly passed seven elaborately written resolutions protesting the immigration of lawbreaking Peruvians, asserting "the people's" right to passage on the *California*, and censuring Alsop & Co. for compelling Captain Forbes to accept passengers against his will.[21] With this business concluded, the committee reported that the company had agreed to give preference to all holders of through tickets. Others would be booked on the *California* in the order of application until the vessel was filled. The rest would be given passage on slower sailing vessels. A noisy minority still objected, but the men who held tickets assuring them passage on the *California* became conservatives determined to uphold the status quo and quell further disturbances. Had not General Persifor Smith's circular letter assured North Americans that Peruvians would not be allowed to dig all the gold in California?

During these tense hours of threats and argument the new skipper, Captain John Marshall, constructed bunks in steerage and ordered the Peruvians to the unsheltered upper deck.[22] He also loaded the ship with supplies to feed the throng of passengers. Beef cattle, hogs, sheep, and coops of chickens were hoisted aboard. Four crates of Panama hats[23] indicated that somebody, perhaps a ship official, was speculating on the San Francisco market. The speculator may have been the new captain, who later proved to be an untrustworthy character, as the passengers would learn.

Finally, on February 1, 1849, with sails unfurled before a favorable wind and paddle wheels churning, the *California* splashed away.[24] Captain Forbes recorded in his diary that 400 souls were aboard—twice the ship's normal capacity.[25] The rabble on the *California*'s decks could not be fed at table. Instead, these passengers were divided into messes which elected officers to receive supplies from the purser and the cook.[26] Each mess chief carried his allotment of food to an appointed spot on deck where his company consumed it from their own plates and kettles.[27] That night the passengers who had to sleep on deck found the planks wet and, in desperation, cut up all the ship's cushions they could find. Some of the vandals may have been the Peruvians quartered there but Captain Forbes, after inspecting the cluttered deck, made no mention of that nationality, and the number of them on board was undoubtedly small. The captain did wonder whether the unruly passengers were a sample of future California gold seekers, and he wrote in his journal: "I am heartily sick & tired of this life of vulgar deportment. . . . One cannot handle pitch without soiling his hands."[28]

Somebody in the turbulent crowd reported a stowaway, smuggled on board by a fireman. Captain Marshall put the offending stoker in irons for punishment—a great mistake, as all the passengers soon discovered. This voyage of the *California* was no routine cruise. Even the crew had become gold seekers, contemptuous of the traditional law of the sea. They called a sympathy strike for the guilty man and stalled the vessel until he was released.[29]

Such incidents caused more amusement than concern, but one day a monster from the sea frightened everyone. Ten feet long, it was believed to be a swordfish intent on piercing the *California's* hull. The detailed description, however, which fortunately has been preserved, classifies it as a sailfish which swam directly toward the vessel but, instead of attacking, dived underneath and disappeared.[30]

The passengers, packed closely together on the ship and out of sight of land, tried desperately to amuse themselves. At first many persons fed and petted the animals penned on deck, gave them names of friends or of conspicuous passengers on board,[31] and may have squared accounts with old enemies by giving their names to beasts about to be butchered. Boredom spread even to the cabin passengers who claimed that the preacher, while all heads were bowed for him to say grace, slipped the bowl of peas to his place and with the "Amen" took them all.[32]

Eight days out of Panama, on February 9, 1849, the *California* paddled through narrow headlands into the 5-mile long, 2-mile wide Bay of Acapulco. Passengers said it looked like a blue lake in the mountains[33] until they saw the dorsal fin of a white-bellied shark rising and sinking along the surface as the big fish leisurely circled the vessel. Opposite the bay's entrance, on the mountain-

Ho, for California! Chilean mode of travel at time of gold rush.
From J. M. Gilliss, *Chile: Its Geography, Climate, Earthquakes* . . .
(Washington, 1855)

Deep canyons in the Andes made passage difficult for gold seekers. Some forty-niners, however, preferred this crossing to the hazardous cruise around the Horn, and mail service was established between Argentina and Chile.

From Charles Wilkes, *Narrative of the United States Exploring Expedition* . . . (Philadelphia, 1845)

Ancient suspension bridge at time of gold rush.
From Sir Clements Markham, *The Incas of Peru* (New York, 1910)

Lima, Peru, at time of gold rush. The entire history of Lima, almost a hundred years older than Boston, was linked with the discovery of precious metals.

From Jorge Basadre, *Historia de la República del Perú* (Lima, 1961–1968)

The main gate to Lima, Peru.
From Charles Wilkes, *Narrative of the United States Exploring Expedition* . . . (Philadelphia, 1845)

Veiled ladies in Lima. The custom of ladies veiling their faces
on the public streets of Lima intrigued North American gold seekers.
From Jorge Basadre, *Historia de la República del Perú* (Lima, 1961–1968)

A modest residence in Lima. It has the usual enclosed balconies and the vultures on the roof and at the gutter.
From Charles Wilkes, *Narrative of the United States Exploring Expedition* . . . (Philadelphia, 1845)

One of Lima's many churches in gold-rush days.

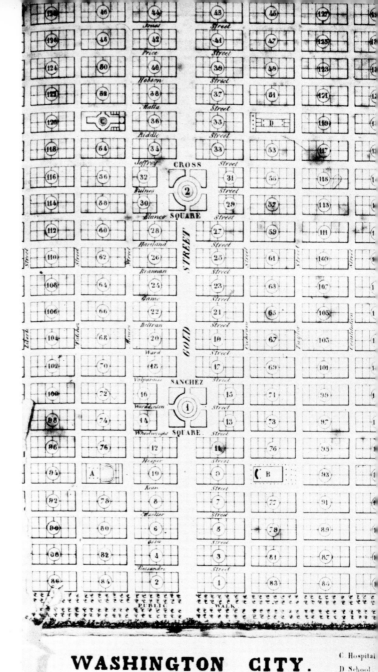

WASHINGTON CITY.

Alta California.

C. Hospital

D. School

2 Garden

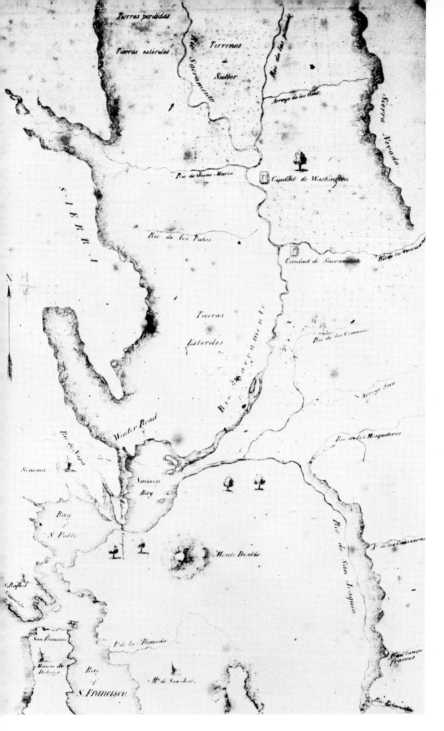

Map of proposed Washington City in California. The map, showing the layout of the streets and the location of the city to be built by Chileans on the Sacramento River above Sacramento, was published in *El Mercurio* (Valparaiso), December 31, 1849.

Anti-Chilean riot in San Francisco in 1849. The artist has incorrectly dressed the Chilean in the costume of a Mexican *charro*.
From *Century Magazine* (February, 1892)

The Chilean *arrastra* used in California during the gold rush. The
wheel, pulled by two blindfolded mules, crushed the ore from
the barrow carried by the two men.
From Thomas Archer Rickard, *Journeys of Observation*
(San Francisco, 1907)

---o---

CALIFORNIA
¡ORO!

Un Sueco ó Aleman que posee unas tierras al interior del punto de Monte-rey ha descubierto este venero de riqueza al hacer cortar una acequia para regar sus campos. Se cree que el oro ha sido depositado allí desde tiempos primitivos por varios rios auriferos que hoy corren en esas inmediaciones y que antes han tenido sus cauces en algunos puntos de la comprehension de las treinta leguas en que aparece manando el oro: hoy mismo sucede que en tiempo de afluencia en los rios, saliendo las aguas de sus propios alveos, bañan aquellas tierras dejandolas tan marabillosamente abonadas.

El Coronel Mason gobernador de la California calcula que hay cien millones de pesos por año y para quinientos años.

Hemos dicho al principio que el oro se encontraba en pepita de media onza de peso y ahora sabemos que las hay del peso de 16 onzas: que el valor del jornal de un peon, cualquiera que sea, es de 18 pesos diarios y que aun asi no se encontraban trabajadores.

Habia once buques abandonados por la desercion de su jente y la corbeta de guerra de los Estados Unidos "warren" quedaba con treinta hombres, pues la otra parte de su tripulacion habia ido á recojer oro.

Los articulos de mas necesidad como ropa hecha, barretas, cuchillos, zapatos &. habian subido extraordinariamente en sus precios.

First announcement of the California gold discovery in *La Aurora* (Cajamarca, Peru), November 18, 1848. In Cajamarca, Pizarro had been given a roomful of gold for the promised release of Atahualpa, the Inca he had captured.

CALIFORNIA.

Del Comercio.

Por la Fragata N. A. "Isaac Walton' que recien ha fondeado, se ha recibido las noticias siguientes.

Que la abundancia de oro en las Californias es positiva, y que por mas que se diga á este respecto nada será suficiente para encarecer una maravilla, que ninguna historia antigua ni moderna rejistra. Que 7,000 y mas individuos trabajaban en los zanjones ó minerales, cada uno para sí. Que por el correo llegado á Monte-rey de San Francisco, se habia sabido que en este puerto quedaban como 20 buques sin ningun individuo de tripulacion por haber desertado toda en el acto de legar. Que el barril de tocino se vendia á 100 pesos, el de carne salada á 60 pesos, botella coñac a 8 pesos, y asi proporcionalmente se realizaba, y al contado, todo lo demas.

El capitan del antedicho buque, refiere, que hallandose él sin ningun individuo de tripulacion, ocurrio á un buque de guerra N. A. (cuyo nombre no recuerda), para que lo auxiliase con alguna jente, buque conseguida en numero de 5 personas, con la condicion de ganar cada uno 50 pesos mensuales, se vino á Paita, en donde tomó 10 marineros mas para el completo de su tripulacion, y ha venido á este puerto con los 15 individuos. Dicho capitan ha traido una cantidad pequeña de oro, de veinte y dos quilates. Ademas comunica que el capitan Stevens de la barca nacional "Callao", habia ganado mas de 40,000 pesos en solo 3 lanchadas de mercaderias que habia desembarcado.

Que de Norte-America se reciben infinitas mercaderias, pero que no obstante tardará algun tiempo la baja de précios, segun opinion jeneral, de los moradores de esos lugares. Que no hay periodicos ni se piensa en ninguna otra cosa, que en la de sacar oro, el que es tomado por cuantas personas ingresan, sin que nadie moleste ó trate de prohibir su esportacion, ni tenga la menor contribucion in ningun otro gravamen.

Verification of the magnitude of the California gold discovery, in *La Aurora*, February 7, 1849.

OCHOCIENTAS TONELADAS
DE MUJERES.

Los Americanos son todavia mas mercaderes y mas positivos que los mismos Ingleses; es una jus. ticia que es preciso tributarles.

A los Estados Unidos corresponde el honor de haber tenido la idea de medir las mujeres por to. neladas.

Todos los periódicos de Nueva York han publi. cado que se ha hecho á la vela, de esto puerto pa. ra la California, un buque conduciendo "ochcien. tas toneladas de mujeres."

Apresuremos á esplicar que esto no quiere de. cir que cada mujer habia sido considerada como una tonelada en su gravitacion: no señor: los pe. riodistas americanos quieren buenamente espresar que el arquéo de aquel buque ascendia á ochcien. tas toneladas, y que su cargamento se componia por entero de pasajeras que iban á buscar á San Fran. cisco, caudal y marido.

Caudal no sé si todas lo hallarán, pero en cuanto á marido, la mas fea de todas ellas puede estar segura de encontrarlo inmediatamente.

Parece, segun las últimas noticias, que el ren. glon "mujer" está cada vez mas solicitado. Es muy natural asi sea; la mujer es renglon de grave lujo; todos aquellos colonos, que son ó millonarios ó próximo á llegar á serlo, desean pavonearse y poder alabarse de tener una "esposa."

El anuncio de la próxima llegada á San Francis. co de esas "ochocientas toneladas de mujeres," ha debido exitar en toda la California una alegria ficil de comprender en los demas paises, donde t to abunda el consabido renglon.

No estrañaremos que el dia en que se po en tierra el cargamento de este buque, sea decla do por los Californianos, dia de regocijo natu "á perpetuidad."

Una cosa tan solo nos ha molestado en el tículo del periódico de Nueva York, y es, que redactor no ha pensado en darnos á conocer nombres y paises de las pasajeras, para que que semos impuestos de las clases de naciones á pertenecen esas ochocientas futuras Californian

Al observar ciertos vacios que se advierten este momento en algunos parajes de la ciud podriamos quizá adivinarlos en gran parte. C tentémonos con manifestar que se llevan cons nuestras simpatias, y que les damos nuestra b dicion.

Por separado hemos sabido que el capitan buque tiene intencion de utilizar, los ocios de travesia de Nueva York á San Francisco, dando á e ochocientas señoras algunas nociones que no p den menos de serles muy útiles en sus nuevos d tinos de buenas madres de familia.

Mañana y tarde, las ochocientas mujeres ben sobre cubierta, y toman una leccion segun método lancasteriano.

Se les enseña particularmente á tener un pecto lleno de modestia, aprender igualmente á p parar el té y hacer medias, que son las dos cuali des de ornato que los maridos americanos estim mas en sus mujeres.

Report in *La Alforja* (Ayacucho, Peru) that 500 tons of women were being shipped to California.

(facing page, bottom) Trailing cattle on the pampas, sketched by Tito Saubidet Gauche. At the time of the gold rush large herds of Argentine cattle were often smuggled into Chile. The risky business once tempted Vicente Pérez Rosales, the only South American who wrote a book about his experiences in the California gold rush.

From José Hernández, *El Gaucho Martín Fierro y la Vuelta de Martín Fierro* (Buenos Aires, 1937)

(*left*) A South American cowboy, sketched by Tito Saubidet Gauche. South American cowboys felt at home in the Wild West. Chileans claim that Joaquín Murieta, the California outlaw, was one of their men.

> From José Hernández, *El Gaucho Martín Fierro y la Vuelta de Martín Fierro* (Buenos Aires, 1937)

(*below, middle*) A gaucho and his *mujer*, sketched by Tito Saubidet Gauche. Contemporary records reveal that 72 percent of the women who came on ships to San Francisco at the beginning of the gold rush were Latins, most of them from Chile.

> From José Hernández, *El Gaucho Martín Fierro y la Vuelta de Martín Fierro* (Buenos Aires, 1937)

Frederic Remington's conception of an early-day Spanish-speaking
gold seeker. Documents show that colts were taken along
by conquistadores.

side, a gray fort bristled with cannon. North of the fort a small town nestled on the shore. Many of the adobe houses were in various stages of decay. This town had been a prosperous out-fitting port for galleons from the Philippines in the days of Spanish rule. Indeed the port was once so prosperous that a plan had been made to cut a tunnel or gap in the mountains to create a draft of refreshing sea breezes.

With the gold rush, Acapulco promised to return to its ancient importance. A coaling station had already been established and, as the number of steamships increased, the port would become a necessary stop between Panama and San Francisco. Month after month 1,000 to 1,500 people disembarked at Acapulco, and, since they had money to spend, the town boomed. A new Hotel Americano offered good accommodations.[34] When Benjamín Vicuña Mackenna, a Chilean historian, stopped at Acapulco in 1853, he marveled at two things: the sumptuous vegetation, including tangerines and bananas, on a coast very different from that of barren Chile, and the noise made by American Argonauts while eating. He called Acapulco the city of sugar-cane, cotton cloth, and unbelievable laziness. A few naked boys in canoes, he said, met incoming vessels to dive for pennies, but the adults lay in the shade remembering the bygone days of the golden galleons from Manila. Strong men showed no interest in earning money by loading vessels with coal.[35]

An unexpected delay held the *California's* impatient gold seekers in Acapulco. The crew pumped dry all the wells in town and the steamship had to wait for more water to seep in before her tanks could be filled.[36] When this was finally accomplished, on February 11, the *California* paddled northward again across the endlessly empty ocean until the helmsman sighted Las Tres Marías, three islands like mountain peaks sticking up through the water. The Three Marys, according to men of the sea, are the Virgin Mary, Mary Magdalene, and María Cleofás, though some say "Cleófas" or "Cleóbis." Cleofás was a Spanish name for one of Christ's apostles.[37] Cleófas was a picaresque personality in seventeenth-century fiction, popular in decadent Peru, who explored the sins of Madrid. The legendary Cleóbis was the son of a devout mother who prayed for him to receive the greatest blessing on earth, and an obliging God gave him a swift and painless death. None of these three "Cleos" are Marys, but all of them are revealing keys to an understanding of Hispanic-American folk character.*

South of Las Tres Marías the *California* steamed to starboard and within 50 miles dropped anchor on the Mexican mainland at San Blas to get coal.[38] Passengers who went ashore came back with discouraging stories. Southbound vessels had brought word that San Francisco was overcrowded, with 15,000 jobless gold seekers waiting for the snow to melt in the mountains. Drifts were reported to be from 6 to 16 feet deep.[39]

The *California*'s next scheduled stop was Mazatlán and on February 13, 1849, the vessel anchored among rocky islands two miles out from the harbor. Hundreds of flying ducks laced the eastern sky with quivering geometric patterns. Evidently wild rice swamps lay beyond the bare coastal peaks, and the harbor must be there. General Smith and several others climbed down into small boats to be rowed toward a gap in the wall of hills. Many passengers who could no longer tolerate the crowded *California* followed him, resolved to find better passage somehow to San Francisco. Dozens who remained on the steamship sent letters with them to be mailed in the port.

The disgruntled passengers who went ashore learned before they landed why the *California* had anchored out in the ocean. The harbor was packed with vessels from many nations, all bound for California, and every available anchorage was occupied.[40] Many of the ships were small coastal craft from Chile and Peru whose owners had given up local trading to make quick profits transporting Argonauts from Mexico to California. This would confuse observers in San Francisco who took it for granted that a Peruvian craft brought Peruvians while as a matter of fact many of the gold seekers on board had been picked up in Panama, Acapulco, San Blas, and Mazatlán. Evidently dozens of Argonauts, traveling north by ship, broke the unpleasant voyage by stopping at one of these ports. Then, after a rest, they sailed

---

* Gauchos also called a constellation in the southern sky Las Tres Marías (Tito Saubidet Gauche, *Vocabulario y Refranero criollo* [Buenos Aires 1943], p. 393).

on board any ship available.[41] Many other gold seekers from the United States came overland across Mexico from the gulf and embarked at Mazatlán. In spite of the large number of vessels available there, the demand for passage exceeded the supply.

Before the gold rush, Mazatlán supported 10,000 people,[42] many of them well-to-do foreign residents engaged in importing. Aside from the large warehouses along the docks, most of the buildings in town were miserable one-story adobe structures whose roofs of broken tiles were patched with palm leaves. The squalid village was hardly a pleasant place to await transportation, but passengers who had escaped from the disagreeable deck accommodations on the *California* did not return to that steamer.[43]

General Persifor Smith and the crewmen came back to the *California* with the bad news that trouble was brewing for American gold seekers in California. Hundreds of Mexicans who resented their country's recent defeat by the United States had organized a volunteer army and were marching north, shouting "California's recovery or death!"[44] But passengers on the *California* soon forgot the dire prospect of this invasion as their ship paddled out from Mazatlán. After it rounded the tip of Lower California and met the prevailing westerlies, the temperature changed quickly. All sails were furled and the *California* headed straight into the wind. Big swells rolled against her bow and struck with resounding thuds, covering the stormy black water with foam as delicate as lace. The paddle wheels churned this discolored surface until a great V of milky billows surged away in the ship's wake.

Far to the east the summits of Baja California's mountains seemed to be floating in the pale blue sky, their peaks more distinct than their hazy bases. Plainly capped with snowfields, they reminded passengers of the dismaying reports of huge drifts holding gold seekers back from the diggings. Could that really be so? Now the prospect of a North American winter seemed very real, and sailors on the ship donned their warm pea jackets.

Steaming northward against the wind, the *California* rounded Monterey's rockbound headland on February 23, 1849.[45] California at last! The passengers cheered and were answered by friendly shouts from a small Peruvian brig in the harbor. On shore, cannon boomed a welcome from the capital of California. General Persifor Smith, dressed in full uniform, was rowed ashore with his wife and suite.[46] He came with full military authority to assume command* and enforce, if he could, his hasty and unwarranted circular prohibiting foreigners from digging gold on the public domain.

The *California* needed coal again but, finding none available in Monterey,[47] purchased wood to fire the boilers. While it was being loaded some passengers, eager to end a tiresome voyage, disembarked with bags and sea chests to travel overland the hundred miles to San Francisco. Then, by chance, some bags of coal were discovered "under the floor of the cabin,"[48] and the *California* made steam once more. One passenger, Edward E. Dunbar, wrote *The Romance of the Age*, a book about his experiences, which was published in 1867. On page 85 he said the *California* ran out of coal when 300 miles south of Monterey and all the wood on board—spars, railings, frames for bunks—was chopped up to fire the boilers and make steam for the trip to port. When this fuel was exhausted, the last planks flooring the lower hold were taken up and a hundred bags of coal were discovered lying as ballast along the keel.

This story is hard to believe. Two other passengers reported the fuel shortage as occurring in Monterey, and a contemporary newspaper discloses that the *California* on her return trip to Panama did run out of coal 300 miles south of Monterey and was forced to burn spars, berths, bulkheads, and boats. Finally she had to wait at an island for a supply of coal.[49] Mr. Dunbar had evidently read this account and then wrote in his book that it happened while he was on the ship's northbound voyage.

The *California*, on her original trip, arrived at San Francisco on February 28, just three days after leaving Monterey. She was one of three vessels passing through the Golden Gate that day. The other two were the English brig *El Progreso* and the Ameri-

---

* Two days after landing General Smith's wife learned that she lacked authority to hold her Irish maid, who accepted a marriage proposal from a wealthy gold seeker (Joseph Warren Revere, *Keel and Saddle: A Retrospect of Forty Years of Military and Naval Service* [Boston, 1872], p. 156).

can bark *Tasso*, both from Valparaiso. *El Progreso* had left that Chilean port a day before the *California*, and the *Tasso*, having sailed seventeen days after the steamer, arrived on the same day, making the trip in the notable time of fifty days.[50] The *Tasso* brought forty-two passengers, among them one woman, Doña Juana Davis, and her son. Also on board were Don Pastor Ovalle and his eleven peons. Almost half of the passengers bore non-Spanish names, including Edwards, Gobler, Haynemann, Lewis, Page, Peterson, Pritchard, Schrader, Spence, Story, and Thompson.[51]

When the *California* rounded Clark's Point, the passengers saw a small squadron of United States warships. Soon a great cloud of white smoke hid them from view and a moment later the boom of cannon came across the bay. The navy had saluted the *California* for being the first steamship to arrive in San Francisco.[52] Beyond the fleet passengers could see some thirty commercial vessels, many of them deserted.

The *California* dropped anchor, but no landing boats with porters came alongside and she lacked sufficient small boats to disembark her many passengers. Captain Marshall, with a few favored individuals, rowed to shore.[53] Next morning the passengers realized that the captain had deserted and the remainder of his crew were leaving as fast as they could get away. In this predicament Captain Forbes reassumed command and appealed to Commodore Thomas ap Catesby Jones, commander of the fleet, for marines to man the steamer and hold what was left of the crew. The commodore replied that any marines assigned to such duty would probably join the deserters,[54] but he did send a trusted officer who held one fireman under ship arrest and thus prevented the *California* from being completely abandoned.[55]

A list of passengers compiled before landing at San Francisco identifies 364 by name, 54 of whom had embarked at Callao.[56] If, as has been estimated, 75 were taken on board at that port,[57] 21 must have left ship, probably at Mazatlán, to continue the trip—perhaps overland—with people speaking their own language. Moreover, less than 10 of the 54 Callao passengers who finished the trip had Spanish names, so only a handful of Peruvians occupied space to California claimed by North Ameri-

can gold seekers in Panama. Thus General Persifor Smith's unfortunate circular was based on immediate hysteria instead of
justifiable fears.

The *California*'s passengers, after landing at Clark's Point,
carried their own luggage around the flat tideland to the miserable collection of tents and small houses known as San Francisco. The "city," as explained in an earlier chapter, was crowded
with many foreigners, including Vicente Pérez Rosales and his
Spanish-speaking kith and kin. Such Chileans, frontiersmen in
their own country, might be resolute individualists determined
to pan gold "without charge, and without hindrance." Persifor
Smith, when he tried to enforce his circular letter, would find
out!

PART III
Experiences of Chileans and Peruvians in California before the Riot against Them

My Patron Saint Is San Joaquín

> *"Ride, boldly ride,"*
> *The shade replied—*
> *"If you seek for Eldorado!"*
> —Edgar Allan Poe (1849)

Trouble greeted most South Americans in San Francisco as soon as they stepped ashore. A Chilean physician, who will remain anonymous, arrived on January 24, 1849, aboard the *Ann Mc-Kim.* He hoped to acquire gold, not from the placers but from Spanish-speaking workers who without his aid in this hazardous climate might join the spirit world. He came more than a month ahead of General Persifor Smith, author of the threat to "fine and imprison" all foreign trespassers on the public domain. For two days the doctor remained on board, shivering in the cold January fog with three of his Chilean companions and their servants. Men who ventured ashore came back stamping muddy boots and reporting that only eight days ago a foot of snow had covered San Francisco—and the doctor believed it![1] Everyone admitted that in this weather a man on shore would "get his fingernails pulled," South American slang for "be tortured," a phrase that had survived since the Inquisition when victims were tortured by having their nails pulled.

Finally, waiting until noon on the third day, the doctor bundled himself up in warm clothes and climbed down a wet Jacob's ladder into a landing boat. The tent city he entered differed greatly in size from the burgeoning metropolis Pérez Rosales would see only twenty-five days later. Jostling his way through the muffled crowds the doctor estimated that 6,000 souls were seeking accommodations in 200 flimsy houses—thirty men to the house—inadequate structures built of boards instead of Chile's heat-holding adobe bricks. He marveled at another oddity: glass windows in poor folks' houses! Moreover, the price asked for miserable accommodations was *muy caro* ("more dear").[2]

At 5:00 P.M. clammy twilight settled over the dreary encampment. Waterlogged clouds shrouded Telegraph Hill and sagged to the roofs of San Francisco's ramshackle buildings. The doctor, chilled to the bone and thoroughly discouraged, gave up his search for lodgings and trudged back to the shoreline, seeking a launch to the *Ann McKim*. On the way he met a fellow Chilean who had come from Valparaiso on another vessel. This man said he had found a room which he offered to share with the doctor, and he led the way to a barnlike structure where twenty men were packed into a room so small that all of them could not lie down at the same time. For this shelter they had paid $100 for a month's rent.

Outside, the night was pitch black and drizzling rain. The doctor could do nothing but remain and tolerate the fetid surroundings. There was no heat in the room but the rotos, being Chilean frontiersmen, brought in a box full of dirt and built a little fire in it exactly as peons might do in Valparaiso. The small blaze failed to satisfy twenty men, and some of them tried to keep warm by drinking a gallon of brandy. Soon they were fighting drunk, quarreling and shouting. "Chingado cabrón" were favorite dirty words and a roto might safely call the smoky fire "an oversexed cuckold," but when he dared apply that insulting phrase to another man he should *smile*, or draw his knife for a fight.

The weary doctor left his foul associates at dawn and returned to the *Ann McKim* where his three friends awaited his report on accommodations in town, but instead of listening to his tale of woe they greeted him with bad news of their own: Captain Robinet insisted that they leave his vessel at once. So the doctor, his three companions, and their four servants returned to the bare room that already housed twenty men. New buildings, however, were being constructed daily and within a week the doctor's little party rented a room approximately 7 by 14 feet for $40 a month. The quarters seemed luxurious,[3] and the four men and four servants planned to wait here until snow had melted from the mother lode. Then they would "ride, boldly ride," to El Dorado.

On the second day after disembarking the doctor applied for a license to practice medicine. He encountered some difficulty but eventually succeeded. The alcalde, he learned, was a physician who resented competition, and a monopoly of the practice of medicine could be extremely remunerative. A doctor received $5 to $10 a visit during the day and twice that at night.[4]

In spite of these attractive fees the Chilean doctor received no calls. He complained that California was a healthy country. Few people became ill, and even fewer seemed to fear death. With no income, the price the doctor had to pay for supplies seemed exorbitant. Only coffee, beans, and meat were cheap, the latter selling for 25 cents a pound. Cheese, raisins, figs, if obtainable, cost $1.00 a pound, butter $1.25. The doctor was delighted when his friends bought wheat flour and their servants made "tortillas a la Chilena," which were very different from the Mexican maize variety.[5] The price of this flour, imported from Chile, fluctuated daily. The flour on one ship might sell for $30 a barrel, and, while it was being unloaded, another ship might arrive from Chile causing the price to drop as low as $9.[6] Supercargoes complained that North American businessmen would bid eagerly against one another for a ship's entire cargo and repudiate the agreement when another shipload of flour arrived.[7]

Many patrónes who had brought gangs of peons to mine for them lacked the money to support the workers in idleness during the month or two before they could be sent to the diggings. These entrepreneurs became bankrupt and their companies dissolved.[8] Other groups broke up when the workers, having had their passage paid to California, decided to take advantage of the fabulous daily wages offered in San Francisco—$5 to $6 for unskilled and $8 to $10 for skilled workmen. Employers said the wages would double come spring when many laborers left for the diggings.[9]

Few Chileans were carpenters, but they did know how to lay adobe blocks and soon got jobs as bricklayers. Most of the workmen had, since childhood, watched their mothers bake bread in outdoor beehive ovens and, in San Francisco they quickly found employment as bakers.[10] Chilean sailors accepted $150 to $200 a month for a short cruise to Oregon, Monterey, or Mazatlán,[11] but refused to sign on for a long voyage at any price.

The doctor, possessing none of these skills and having no income, began to meet living expenses by selling his clothes. His black satin vest, which cost 6 pesos in Santiago, brought $20. Two warm but badly worn woolen vests fetched $10 each. These three articles paid a month's rent for the room he occupied with his companions and servants. The doctor's frock coat, valued at $64, was kept in reserve. Extra money in hand was dangerous property but clothes on a man's back seemed safe. A band of city thieves dared to steal food, money, or anything that caught their fancy. The doctor was told that the authorities knew all the members of the gang but lacked the power to apprehend or punish them. These rascals, he wrote friends in Chile, were called the "Sociedad de los 42,"[12] an odd name for the famous Hounds which had been organized in February, 1849,[13] at about the time the doctor wrote. There is no Spanish word for "hound," and Spanish-speaking people soon called the Hounds Los Galgos,[14] literally "the greyhounds." Could the doctor, accustomed to a broad Chilean accent, have confused *Los Galgos* with *cuarenta-dos,* Spanish for 42? It seems unlikely, but *quién sabe?*

For exercise the doctor and his small party, after dining on the little they could afford to eat, usually took a walk. When they returned to their lodgings the servants had cleaned the room, built a good fire in the stove, and prepared hot water for coffee or good Chilean maté. One Sunday the four "gentlemen" walked to the San Francisco Mission. They did not ride because they found horses to be "more dear." A skinny nag, worth $6 in Chile, here fetched from $150 to $200, while a mule, valued at $300 to $400,[15] was really an extravagance. The doctor found the mission priest to be a Mexican, "but of adequate capacity, and very friendly." The doctor's condescension is reminiscent of the attitude of Chilean Argonauts in Acapulco.

To the doctor the most remarkable aspect of San Francisco's bare slopes was the daily appearance of new houses. He also marveled, as Pérez Rosales did, at the abundance of gold in so many persons' hands. Workmen in the street would pour a sparkling little stream of gold from a dirty leather poke into a friend's callused palm. In shops the precious dust was poured on scales in payment for a few groceries, or a pinch was bestowed as a tip for some minor service. Everyone seemed to have gold and everyone talked constantly about the certainty of getting more gold as soon as the snow melted from the sluices. The doctor heard that the vast goldfields could not be exhausted by 10,000 miners in fifty years.[16]

Three ways led to El Dorado, two of them by boat, one by "footback." The northern placers could be reached by sailing up the Sacramento; the southern region, by either sailing up the San Joaquin River or walking via Santa Clara. Boat fare varied from $15 to $80, but many said that after the snow had melted as much as $200 might be charged. This estimate was an exaggeration,[17] for a month or two later, in June, the four-day trip to Sacramento cost only $20 to $30.

No matter where the boat stopped a man must expect to walk with a knapsack on his back another 30 to 60 miles to the placers; and the farther he walked, gossips said, the more gold he would find. Indeed, if he walked 600 miles the abundance of gold would be prodigious, and the full extent of the gold-bearing land had not yet been discovered. Such news could only delight a doctor selling his clothes to meet current expenses.

The journey to El Dorado, the doctor soon learned, was one that no man would consider taking alone. At least twenty-five bold men must join together for protection from Indians, wild beasts, and wild "Americans of the North." The animals included bears, tigers, and lions, all of extraordinary size and all eager to attack man. Gold seekers also had to be prepared for such illnesses as yellow fever, typhoid, and anemia. Prospectors who stood for hours in icy water lost their resistance and often became seriously ill.

The doctor had come to California to practice medicine, not to dig for gold, and he was told that at the diggings he might earn as much as $100 for a single medical call within four city blocks of his office. In addition he could charge $15 to $20 for a dose of any kind of medicine.[18] This sum was what he had received for his vest! A doctor in California did have to adjust to new values. His funds were diminishing daily, and with the prospect of riches elsewhere, he decided to depart for the placers, snow or no snow, and the sooner the better.

Many Chileans planned to go to the northern or Sacramento country where Jim Marshall had first discovered gold. The doctor decided otherwise. He was told that more gold could be found on the Stanislaus River, a tributary of the San Joaquin. The doctor's best friend, who wanted to go with him, said his patron saint was San Joaquín, father of the Virgin.[19] Good fortune would follow them to a river with that name. The doctor agreed, and they set off.

There would be no snow on their route. The road down to Santa Clara was easy to follow. The two men encountered no lions or tigers and found camping every night much cheaper than living in San Francisco. Their roundabout course might be long, but spring would surely come before they reached the mother lode. The Santa Clara Mission proved to be a dismal ruin, although a fine avenue of poplar trees indicated former prosperity. Such decay, since the grand old Spanish days, was familiar to Chileans.

Tramping east from Santa Clara, the travelers learned from experience that wagon roads in California, like those in Chile, had been neglected since independence,[20] but like true Chileans they felt at home in vast distances. The harsh landscape was a world they had always known, and they felt self-sufficient with food and bedding on their backs. Ranch houses were often 20 miles apart. Built of adobe blocks, occasionally whitewashed, seldom having windows, these habitations resembled the huaso huts in Chile's backcountry. The door in daytime was usually open. Outside, a straw mat or a stiff beef hide on the ground served as a table. In the cool of the morning it was placed on the hut's sunny side and then was moved to the shady side in the heat of the day. Busy, gossiping women crouched on the ground around this table.[21] The young ones were often very pretty, with hair so black that its highlights looked deep blue. On the ground beside the women a heavy granite *metate* showed where maize was ground for tortillas, and little gray towhees, tame as chickens, scratched in the nearby dirt. They had learned that the first grain ground each day was thrown away because it might contain grit from the grinding stones.

Near the mountains the vegetation became more luxuriant.[22] Spring had come while the doctor and his companion were plodding across "the Valley," and they finally saw a wall of willows ahead of them. It marked the western bank of the San Joaquin—the name so important to the doctor's friend. Across the river they could see tent tops above the willows where the Stanislaus flowed in from the east. A dozen craft of various sizes were moored along the river bank, and a rowboat ferried travelers across to the foot of a wide pathway over trampled grass between two lines of tents. The usual flapping signs announced the services of real estate agents and assayers. The smell of frying bacon indicated the location of a restaurant, and Sam Brannan had opened a store.[23] The doctor heard from eager townsmen that this "city" would be the outfitting place for the great goldfields beyond. True, oceangoing vessels had to stop at Stockton, 20 miles downstream, but smaller sailboats brought supplies here and received much higher prices. All good promotional talk for Stanislaus City!

Among the crowd of weary, unkempt gold seekers the doctor must have seen many Spanish-speaking men, not Mexicans in steeple hats and embroidered *charro* jackets, but South Americans who were easily recognized by their ponchos—white cotton on Peruvians, heavy gray wool on Chileans. All wore leather belts 6 inches wide for money, tobacco, flint, and steel.[24] Many of these men were bonded laborers whose patrónes had paid for the trip from San Francisco by boat, believing it to be faster than walking overland. The patrónes had learned to their sorrow that a passage normally requiring five or six days to go only as far as Stockton sometimes consumed fourteen. Sailing up San Francisco Bay and through the long channel to Benicia was easy, but from there on, through the tule swamps, boats often stuck in the mud, two or three times in a single day. After entering the San Joaquin, travelers expected the passage to be better but it usually proved worse for a patrón who was paying the last of his money to feed a score of rotos. Independent norteamericanos with guns entertained themselves by landing to hunt the antelope they saw on the dry flats or to shoot at tule elk in the swamps, although they usually failed to bring back any meat. Wild geese, flying overhead, also made tempting marks, but they were too high for the boatmen's guns. Redwing blackbirds in flocks of a thousand or more sang constantly in the reeds. When disturbed they rose into the air, their wings roaring like derisive laughter at patrónes losing money every day on the tiresome voyage.

It is easy to believe that these disgruntled patrónes, after arriving in Stanislaus City, told the doctor in mournful language about the inexperienced boatmen they had engaged, men who failed to find the deep channels through the tules and often ran aground. Then anchors had to be floated downstream and all hands, even paying passengers, would pull the craft back into deep water. When the channel became narrow, sails could not be used unless the wind blew in the right direction.[25] Such tales were bound to end with, "Yes, amigo. Was better to walk, like you!"

Talkative fellows in Stanislaus City, as in San Francisco, peddled advice to anyone who would listen. Standing at a saloon bar, which might be only a plank supported by two kegs, some man was sure to say that the Stanislaus was overrated; be wise, go on to the Merced! A Latin, eager to practice his English and be heard by everyone on the rutty street between the tents, might reply, "No! Go more far. Coronel Free-mont and hees party, being *científico*, they go Mariposa. Must know more better. Yes?"

The doctor decided that the upper tributaries of the Stanislaus would be the best place for him to practice medicine. The diggings there had been panned less than a year and were far from being worked out; many prospectors believed that area to be the country of the future. Only last summer a few gold seekers had crossed the low divide to Wood's Creek, which flowed into the Tuolumne. Some of them were "Americans of the North," and some were Spanish-speaking Californians from Los Angeles.[26] When winter came all these men had returned to the settlements, bringing gold and wondrous tales. One man claimed to have filled the crown of his hat with the precious dust in a few hours' work. Another said he spread a towel on the ground and, with no tool but his knife, filled it so full of nuggets that when picked up by the four corners it failed to hold them all.[27]

Eager to reach El Dorado, a long line of hopeful men trudged away daily from Stanislaus City. Each bent forward slightly under his heavy pack, and the doctor, accustomed now to this method of traveling, went with them. The flat river-bottom country was beautiful in early spring, brilliant with yellow poppies, purple lupines, and mariposa lilies. At the end of the first day's march the men entered foothills dotted with oaks. This was the beginning of wild Indian country.[28] On the hillsides, chaparral sparkled with blossoms among the smooth red trunks of manzanita. Bees by the thousands warned prospectors that they were seeking golden honey.[29]

The country seemed free of dangerous Indians in the spring of 1849, although travelers were cautioned never to go alone. The Stanislaus River bore the name of a good Indian, "Estanislao," who became bad. He ran away from the San José Mission, joined the wild red men in the mountains, and harried white rancheros until stopped by the Mexican army a quarter of a century earlier.[30] The doctor learned that grizzly bears, not Indians, were now a constant menace. These monsters prowled along the open hillsides and several men had been killed by them.[31]

Gold seekers trudging up the river trail came to stunted pines and hemlocks scattered among the gnarled oaks. Here was a new kind of chewing gum which helped tired and hungry travelers. Pine resin, sticky and bitter at first taste, could be chewed into a yielding substance, slightly fragrant and stimulating.

Among the stunted trees, even on the steepest slopes, small excavations revealed where human woodpeckers with beards and picks had left their hopes and empty bottles in prospect holes before moving on in the endless search for gold. Now and again the travelers passed through a cluster of tents[32] erected only the night before, but already proclaimed by the occupants as the site of a future city.

"Keep going," old-timers whispered as they spat thoughtfully while chewing resin gum. "The biggest settlement up this-a-way is Campo de Sonora on Wood's Crick head of Tuolumne,[33] heart of the gold country only twenty-five mile from the San Joaquin. All Spanish-speaking people there. You bet!"

With such assurances gold seekers expected Sonora to be finer than the miserable clusters of tents and brush shelters they had passed, but they were not prepared for what they saw when they rounded the rim of Table Mountain and beheld a line of houses under the trees ahead. Gay flags, banners, and curtains, all as festive as an Oriental bazaar, were waving in the wilderness and, what was most unusual, dozens of women in brightly colored dresses were tripping merrily along the street. Men saw nothing like this in San Francisco, where females seemed extinct. And even more important, Anglos admitted later that these Latin ladies were far more attractive than the angular, ill-dressed North American women who came with the first gold seekers. The Mexican beauties had been coming north all winter along with pack loads of merchandise.[34]

Campo de Sonora, when the travelers finally reached it, proved to be less imposing than from a distance. Many of the residences were built of brush with brilliant sarapes in the doorways. In fact the first adobe house, built by Chileans, was not finished until July.[35] Many other homes were soon constructed. The population that summer of 1849 has been estimated at 5,000, with 10,000 on trade days—almost as many as our Chilean doctor had calculated for San Francisco in January. An accurate reckoning is impossible.* Many of the men left town every Monday morning to work mining claims, some as far

* William Perkins (*Three Years in California* [Berkeley and Los Angeles 1964], p. 100) estimated the population of Sonora at some 5,000 in July, 1849. This figure is corroborated by Thomas Robertson Stoddart (*Annals of Tuolumne County* [Sonora, Calif., 1963], p. 101). Perkins (p. 27) cites a correspondent writing on June 30, 1849, who estimated that 8,000 Mexicans and South Americans were there. Perkins (p. 33) also quotes Thomas Butler King as reporting to the secretary of state that more than 10,000 "Mexicans" were in Sonora in July.

away as 10 miles. They would camp close to their work and return on Saturday to wives and families in Campo de Sonora for a grand weekend spree.

Merchants in Sonora reaped a harvest importing from Mexico brilliant sarapes, fancy saddles, neatly braided riatas, warm blankets, lace mantillas, cashmere shawls, bolts of gay cotton cloth, silk stockings, satin slippers, and even rolls of velvet, along with cornmeal, raw and crystallized sugar, chili peppers, and beans.[36] Restaurants served venison and bear meat, spicy tamales, coffee in pewter cups, or wine imported on muleback from south of the border.[37] On Sundays bullfights attracted crowds, the Chileans ignoring their national objection to the spectacle. Dances became magnificent affairs for those with "dust," while the have-nots, with sadness and envy in their faces, watched wistfully through open doors and windows.[38] Mexicans, defeated in the late war, derived esoteric satisfaction from singing as they danced:

> Que diremos de Taylor!
>   Que es un monstruo, eñjie de hombre
> Inhumane, cruel, infamé,
> Detestado sea tu nombre![39]

Another song beginning "Donde vas, bueno caballero," had a repetitious phrase in the melody which was easily remembered. Spanish-speaking miners sang this ditty so persistently that the North Americans, in spite of themselves, began humming the tune. Finally they improvised for it the familiar lyrics of "Clementine,"[40] which were copyrighted in 1883 and again in 1885.[41]

In Sonora the favorite gambling game was monte. Men played and drank all night by the light of sperm candles on tables made of hand-hewed logs covered with rich cloth. A player bought silver dollars or gold doubloons with the "dust" he had washed during the week and paid a discount of 10, 15, or sometimes 20 percent for these coins.[42] No scales had arrived in Sonora and a pinch of gold was reckoned worth a dollar. A teaspoonful was called an ounce, worth $16 in trade or $8 in exchange for gambling coins.[43] At dawn on Monday the men, usually penniless

and certainly drunk, staggered away to distant camps. Now and
then some drunken fellow stumbled into a prospect hole half
full of water and drowned,[44] but most miners toiled for five days
at their distant claims and then returned to carouse again in
Sonora.

It would be a mistake, however, to believe that all Latin
Americans squandered their money in this fashion. During the
summer many Chileans, having made a fortune, left town quietly
and returned to South America. Reports said they took as much
as $15 million out of California by September, 1849.[45] Such
figures cannot be verified, and the percentage of Peruvians and
Chileans among the Latin Americans in California is also impossible to determine. Not counting the Chilean soldiers in the
Mexican War who remained in California and the dozens of
Chilean sailors who deserted from merchant vessels, the records
show that by the last of June, 1849, only 1,350 had come from
Chile by sea. During this same period only 227 of record came
from Peru. Certainly not all these South Americans went to
Campo de Sonora, and those who did must have made up a
small minority of the Spanish-speaking people there. The percentage becomes even smaller when we remember that many
of the gold seekers leaving South American ports were North
Americans. On the other hand, since some South Americans
came overland from Mexico, any figures become dubious. It may
be pertinent to note, however, that of the 205 females recorded
as arriving in San Francisco by ship during this time, 72 percent
were Latins, 70 of them coming from Chile, 57 from Mexico,
and 21 from Peru.[46] This is a relatively small number, and the
exaggerated stories published in Australia concerning the large
number of South American women in California may have been
part of that country's program to discourage emigration of
husband-hunting females.[47]

All statistics become doubly apocryphal because any person
who spoke Spanish during the gold rush was apt to be called a
Mexican. William Perkins, the storekeeper in Sonora, wrote in
his journal that "Mexican" cooks served very popular tortillas
made of "wheaten flour,"[48] a Chilean delicacy. He also described
the way "Mexican" women covered their heads with shawls.

Peruvian women covered their faces as well as their heads with shawls, exposing only one eye which might be sparklingly beautiful when the rest of the face, to the disappointment of many North American youths, was unattractive. Perkins also described the steps of what he called "a Mexican dance" in which the girl, instead of stamping around in the brim of her escort's steeple hat, retreated with an occasional enticing pirouette before an eager partner.[49] Perkins certainly was describing the Peruvian *cueca* which, although disapproved by upper-class limeños, was performed openly by working people and in secret by daring young members of the elite.[50] Also, the billowing white pantaloons which some North Americans considered the mark of a Mexican[51] were typical of Chilean laborers.

Around Sonora, gold in the sand of the streams was soon exhausted, but Chileans who understood mining found large quantities of gold in granite veins on the hillsides. Processing this rock disclosed another Chilean skill. Mexicans crushed gold-bearing quartz with what they called an *arrastra*, or drag mill, in which the granite was spread between two large millstones. A mule dragged the upper stone in a circular motion over the lower one. The Chilean arrastra substituted a heavy circular wheel for the upper, or Mexican, drag stone[52] because it was easier to pull and it crushed more rock in a shorter time. The crushed quartz, after being sprinkled with mercury from nearby cinnabar mines, was reground until slimy and then spooned into pots for distillation,[53] in the old process known so well to many South Americans. By the middle of 1849 these mechanisms had made Sonora one of the leading gold-producing areas of the mother lode,[54] and the southern diggings attracted gold seekers of all races. Some accounts claim as many as 20,000 men worked there.[55]

The Chileans' superiority in mining antagonized the less intelligent North Americans. Soon the so-called Sonorans were accused of keeping cribs and bawdy houses which became hiding places for shady characters, such as sluice-box robbers and horse and cattle thieves.[56] The ugly sound of drunken brawls, or the scream of a stabbed victim, came too often from "Sonora town."

The better-class Latins built houses in another part of the village,[57] but all Spanish-speaking persons had earned a bad name; friction developed between them and the Anglos, although Persifor Smith's order against foreigners on the public domain was still ignored in Sonora. Yankees did feel a national contempt for "greasers" and exulted over the North American victory in the late war. Mexicans resented this attitude, and the Chileans who originally camped in separate communities soon joined them,[58] sharing their resentment. Rotos were always ready to fight at the drop of an insult.

Incidents frequently occurred when no offense was intended. A Mexican dog might bark at a Yankee's horse and cause a runaway. A Spanish burro might enter a Yankee's tent and devour a precious sack of white flour,[59] expressing delight over the feast by switching its shaved tail. The pony express rider, employed to carry the mail, claimed that a robber had tried to lasso him in the dark. To defend himself the rider fired his pistol at his unseen assailant and raced away, but he was followed. He heard the oncoming horse's hooves plainly. Arriving in town he saw that the horse behind him was riderless. Had the saddle been emptied by the mail carrier's bullet? A body was never found but people said the robber must have been a Mexican.[60]

The North Americans' prejudice against Latins may have been augmented by the realization that in Sonora those greasers formed a majority of the population. The town was not Americanized until 1850,[61] when an apprentice printer from West Chester, Pennsylvania, became editor of the *Sonora Herald*.[62] After becoming acquainted in town he wrote in his diary that he felt more respect for the Spanish-speaking people than for the coarse Anglo Argonauts.

Early in 1849 a rough, illiterate North American, R. S. Ham, proclaimed himself alcalde.[63] Since he was a former teamster in the army that defeated Mexico, he exacerbated the town's sensitive race problems. Perhaps he was not typical of many hard-working North Americans in the camp, but another odd North American proclaimed himself a judge. Tall and straight-backed, he wore a gray flannel shirt and brown denim jeans held up by a strand of hemp rope. An incessant talker, he had married a squaw and panned gold only as needed for his daily bread. In his shack a volume of Shakespeare, the Bible, and box above box of old magazines awaited his perusal.[64]

More objectionable North Americans also flocked to Sonora, not to pan for gold, but to live by their wits in the get-rich-quick community. Amber-haired Samuel Brown and exquisitely dressed William Anderson both hated Latin Americans and, when "likkered up," engaged in rough-and-tumble fights, stabbing, gouging, and kicking as viciously as any Chilean roto. Indeed, a serious clash between Anglos and Latins seemed inevitable, but oddly enough, the first violence of consequence came, not at the southern diggings, but up north where Pérez Rosales had led his companions.

11

The Northern Diggings

On March 19, 1849, Vicente Pérez Rosales was in a predicament. His mining tools, tents, camping equipment, clothing, two-wheeled cart, and barrels of toasted flour,[1] wine, and brandy had finally arrived from Valparaiso on the slow-sailing *Julia*,[2] but the cost of freighting the supplies more than 100 miles back to the diggings seemed prohibitive. His party could raise only $1,000, and twice that amount was necessary for the trip. They finally borrowed the additional sum from a Jewish moneylender who charged 5 percent interest per month.

Time was money now, big money, and Vicente negotiated with the ubiquitous Sam Brannan who, in addition to his stores, real estate offices, auction rooms, and mining claims, owned a leaky old sloop in the harbor. This 20-ton craft,[3] named the *Dice mi Naña*, or *Dysy my Nana*,[4] as the Yankees called her, could carry all the Chileans' freight, and Brannan offered to transport Vicente, his party, and their equipment for a moderate fee if he might also take additional paying passengers. Vicente agreed to the proposal—a great mistake!

The *Dysy* was manned by Captain Robinson, a small, irascible Yankee, and three sailors, one a Scotsman with a nose that, according to Vicente, resembled a ripe tomato. The other two were North Americans who took the job in order to get free transportation to the diggings. In addition, Sam Brannan booked seventeen rough Yankee passengers wearing huge spiked boots and armed with rifles, pistols, and daggers.[5] Pérez Rosales' party consisted of twelve men. One was a North American named Clackston who had lived for years in Chile. Three were peons from a Chilean estate. The vessel's hold, when crammed with the Chileans' tents, sacks and boxes, shovels, baskets of provisions, and other goods, left no place for the passengers to sit except on the narrow decks and gunwales.

The *Dysy* cast off at four o'clock in the afternoon.* Captain Robinson had already spied the Chileans' demijohn of whiskey and, being master of his craft, began sampling the liquor. As soon as the *Dysy* was officially waterborne, a rowboat brought out five more passengers the captain was taking on board without Brannan's knowledge.

The usual afternoon fog soon crept through the Golden Gate, veiling from view the fleet of vessels stranded in the harbor. The *Dysy* dared not make sail lest she crash into that hidden wall of ships, but Captain Robinson, aided by a strong current and the contents of the demijohn, succeeded in running the vessel aground near shore. Some of the passengers jumped into the water and endeavored to shove the old sloop free, but failed. The captain, taking another consoling swig from the jug, announced that everything was fine. The incoming tide would float the *Dysy* free in a few hours and then, although it would be dark, they could make sail, cruise out through the anchored vessels, and be on their way. In the meantime, the demijohn would alleviate the delay.[6]

The Chileans regretted the loss of their whiskey and, even more, the dangerous prospect of losing all their possessions— and perhaps their lives—by crashing blindly into those anchored vessels after dark. They protested, but the captain, emboldened now by strong drink, insisted that he would sail, dark or no dark. This ultimatum dismayed the Chileans and they discussed among themselves different ways to thwart it. Clackston, being a norteamericano, offered to wade ashore and see Brannan. All agreed to his proposal and he left, but his trip failed. He found Brannan asleep in bed and aroused him but all he could get from the *Dysy*'s owner was a note telling the captain not to sail until the next morning. The note infuriated Captain Robinson. Really

---

* Vicente Pérez Rosales (*California Adventure*, trans. Edwin S. Morby and Arturo Torres-Rioseco [San Francisco, 1947], p. 27) says the *Dysy* cast off on March 6, 1849, but the *Julia* did not arrive with his equipment until March 19. Inconsistencies of this kind are common in Pérez Rosales' journal.

drunk now, he threw it overboard without trying to read it in the dark. His act might have intimidated a foreigner unused to North American ways, but Clackston felt himself as much an independent-minded Anglo as the captain. "That note," Clackston told the befuddled captain, "ordered you to hold this sloop here. It's an order from your boss!"[7]

Pérez Rosales knew Chilean cattle thieves and rotos but he was unprepared for the Yankee captain's reply, and he remembered it to the letter. The word "boss," Vicente said, set Robinson on fire. "What's that you say about boss?" the drunken captain muttered with a curse. "I got no boss, and there's no bosses around here, and if I had my say, there's nobody I'd sooner hang for a thief than that devil Brannan!"[8] This drunken outburst exhausted Captain Robinson and he pitched forward, face down, on a heap of bundles. By this time the rest of the crew and all the North American passengers were also drunk on the Chileans' whiskey, so Vicente and his party stood guard with cocked firearms until the eastern sky paled for another day.

The morning dawned clear and cold. On shore, columns of fresh smoke rose from the chimneys of shacks where early risers were building fires. Out in the harbor, now clear of fog, the line of abandoned ships stood in plain view and the incoming tide floated the *Dysy* free again. The captain and his crew still snored lustily, and the Chileans, eager to go, took command and steered the sailless sloop through the anchored craft. The vessel bumped harmlessly against some of them and was warned off from others by the men's outstretched arms. At last the sloop reached the open bay.[9]

By this time the bleary seamen awoke from their drunken sleep. Captain Robinson, watery-eyed and with swollen tongue, ordered the lateen sail set and the clumsy *Dysy* spashed away at last. The passengers, being young men, laughed now at one another's miserable appearance and the Scotsman's tomato-nose. They even laughed about the vessel's hold which was so full of cargo that no man dared stand erect lest the rigging of the lateen sail sweep him overboard on every tack. They also joked about the prospect of other hardships they must endure for days, perhaps for a week, on this decrepit craft.

Sailing north, Pérez R. noted Alcatraz, Angel Island, and San Quentin. The channel ahead became "more narrow" with every mile, like the entrance to a great river. He was surprised when the sloop rounded a point of land and entered San Pablo Bay, a large lake surrounded by towering mountains. The water ahead was calm but along the shore he saw fringes of dirty foam left by falling tides.

At the upper end of San Pablo Bay the sloop sailed into a slender channel, narrow as the Golden Gate and with equally steep walls. Through this miniature fjord the *Dysy* tacked for 10 miles while the passengers ducked their heads constantly as the lateen rigging swept back and forth across the gunwales. Finally, to everyone's relief, they spied a warship at anchor ahead,[10] and on the nearby shore they saw a flagstaff surrounded by busy people building houses, a church, two schools, a large restaurant, a theater, and a mint. At least this is what the town's promoter, who rowed out in a boat, told the Chileans the buildings were to be. He also urged them to stop and trade at what he called the future capital of California. "Our town," he said, "is called Benicia, named for the wife of Governor Vallejo."

Beyond Benicia the sloop entered a third large bay, a navigable lake called Suisun. Unlike the first two, Suisun Bay was not walled in by towering mountains. Instead, the surrounding country was flat, and long tongues of tules reached out from shore. The main channel could float seagoing craft, but woe to the navigator who mistook a gap in the tules for that channel. In no time he would stick fast in the mud and might have to wait twelve hours for the tide to float him free.

The Chileans, sprawling along the gunwales to escape the *Dysy*'s annoying rigging, dipped their hands in the water and discovered that they could drink it,[11] although it was a bit brackish. They also discovered that the mosquitoes were almost unbearable. Somewhere in the maze of channels through the tules, they knew that two great rivers from the north and south flowed into this gigantic marsh. The Sacramento came from the north and they had planned to sail up that stream to the northern diggings but, strangely enough, Captain Robinson steered for the mouth of a river on the southern shore. Was the man still drunk?

Fortunately, another budding town, named Montezuma, appeared at the mouth of this stream. Its citizens reassured Vicente that the Sacramento did flow in from the south, but that it soon circled in a huge arch through the tules, thus draining a valley to the north. He was also told that eager norteamericanos planned to build another town at the neighboring mouth of the San Joaquin, to be called New York.[12] *En verdad*, the *yanquis* were what people called "go-getters," yes!

After miles of marshy tules the travelers finally emerged on the broad, gently flowing Sacramento, and the *Dysy* sailed easily upstream. The calm surface sometimes mirrored magnificent sycamores on the river's bank. The branches of these gigantic trees occasionally caught the rigging of unwary vessels that ventured too close to shore. During the heat of the day the men washed their faces in river water poured from a drawn bucket. Toward evening, as the sun slid down behind the trees on the west bank, a fresh breeze wrinkled the river surface and sent the *Dysy* ahead with a rush. The Chileans, nipped by the cold air, thanked God for the warmth of their woolen ponchos. Finally, after seven days and seven nights, Vicente sighted the mouth of the American River.[13] This was their destination.

Vicente knew that Captain Sutter had built his famous fort above the junction of the American and Sacramento rivers. Below the fort, along both streams, stood a few shacks which formed the much talked about city of the future, to be named Sacramento. The location failed to impress Vicente, for it seemed too low, too flat, too subject to floods and illnesses from putrid fever.[14] His Chilean comrades rejoiced, however, when the *Dysy* was moored to the muddy bank. At last the tedious voyage had ended, and the men eagerly unloaded their equipment. Any place seemed better than another hour on the infirm *Dysy*.

The Sacramento settlement, where the Chileans landed, boasted four buildings of rough boards, each with a canvas roof. There were a few tents and many brush shelters made from the branches of trees.[15] The Chileans pitched their own big tent and noticed the envious glances of bystanders who admired its size and the quantity and quality of their supplies and mining equipment, including the cart. A man representing himself as

the city's promoter offered to give them a lot in the future metropolis if they would erect that magnificent tent on it. The offer
seemed generous but the Chileans were too tired to trade. Instead, they closed the tent flaps, tied the fastenings, spread out
their blankets, and lay down for the first night of solid sleep
since leaving San Francisco.

At dawn the Chileans were awakened by shouts on all sides
of their canvas walls. They heard men cursing, calling everything they owned, even pack mules, the sons of female dogs.
Others sang, "Oh Susanna." This odd hubbub, the Chileans
learned, was typical of North Americans packing for a day's
march. Time was always too precious for good manners. Vicente
stepped out of the tent and gaped at the activity around him.
Many of the tents pitched there the night before were gone,
leaving only stray odds and ends of torn garments and broken
bottles, but new vessels were already unloading along the river
and more men staggered under heavy loads into town. New
tents soon took the places of those that had gone.[16]

The Chileans were as eager as anyone to reach the diggings.
They planned going first to the famous Sutter's mill, reckoned
to be some 55 miles up the American River.[17] Their small cart
could carry their little tents and some of their mining equipment,
but it was not large enough for the big tent, their cooking stoves,
their heavy sacks of flour, and the wine that had escaped the
Dysy's crew. Here was a transportation problem they had not
anticipated, but Vicente met an American in the tent city who
offered to haul a ton of their goods to the mill for $700. This
price seemed muy caro, and their goods weighed considerably
more than a ton. Vicente contrived a solution: load the cart,
hire the American to haul a ton of the equipment in his wagon,
and sell the remainder here in Sacramento.

The Chileans agreed to this proposal and organized themselves into a company for the trip, electing Pérez Rosales the caudillo or leader. He promptly appointed committees, one to select the ton of goods for the wagon and a smaller load for the
cart. Another committee was to put wheels, shafts, a singletree,
and sideboards on the cart and affix a proper tug for the extra
horse to pull it birlocho fashion. A third committee of two,

headed by the American Clackston, was commissioned to purchase two horses. These men set off at once to visit a rancho up
the American River where horses were said to be available.

Vicente headed another committee to select the goods for
trade in town. They employed a friendly North American, named
Gillespie, to negotiate sales. Clothing and tools brought un-
expectedly high prices. Toasted Chilean flour fetched 40 cents
a pound. The wine was sold for $18 a gallon, the brandy for $10.
The cash the Chileans received offset the high rental they had
to pay for the team and wagon.

By nightfall the extra supplies had either been sold or were
left in Gillespie's charge. The little cart was put together. Everybody was ready to start in the morning, but the horse-buying
committee had not returned. After dark they stumbled in, tired,
hungry, and with no horses. The sleepy Chileans assembled to
hear bad news. Their committee had found the rancho where
horses could be purchased, yes, but Clackston, the chairman,
frankly confessed that a very pretty girl had taken his attention
from negotiations until other buyers purchased all the horses
but one, and that was a miserable nag the owner priced at $250.
Clackston said that he might have paid $150[18] for the condor
bait, but he could not bring himself to make so paltry an offer to
the charming siren's father. After all, she was the first female he
had seen since Rosario Améstica had been rowed ashore from
the *Staoulí* in San Francisco.

Vicente admitted that the mention of a beautiful woman
made his own ears tingle, and he lectured his company about
the danger of feminine attractions, the gullibility of man, and
the temptation to pay exorbitant prices when a charming woman
is concerned. Vicente concluded the lecture by saying that he,
as a man of the world with business acumen, would therefore
appoint himself as a committee of one to go in the morning and
trade with the owner of the horse.

At dawn he set off, but not alone. The entire party, being *muy
macho* ("girl crazy"), decided to accompany him on the hazardous undertaking.[19] The way led up the river under scattered
groves of live oaks. They soon came to Sutter's Fort, an enormous

building with thick, cracked walls which stood behind a moat filled with debris and tangled weeds. A few grass-covered cannon lay on the ground. The men also saw a cabin, a few huts built of the inevitable branches of trees, and a large store. A huge sign announced that it was operated by Brannan & Co.[20] The store was also a *cantina*,[21] but the Chileans, being accustomed to strong drink, felt no temptation. They also felt good-natured contempt for "Bishop" Brannan. Gossips said that this professed "man of God" had taken advantage of his parishioners by filing mining claims in their names for his exclusive profit.[22] In addition, the Chileans may or may not have heard that Brannan collected tithes from his workers, and when asked by Brigham Young to send the Lord's money to the church in Salt Lake City, Brannan replied that he would do so if Brigham Young sent him a receipt signed by the Lord.[23]

Leaving Sutter's Fort, Pérez R. and his party walked on up the American River for two hours. They came to the edge of a desert stretching eastward to hazy mountains. Ahead of them they saw the adobe buildings where Clackston had sought the horses—certainly unattractive surroundings for a beautiful woman. Vicente could see nothing but shapeless blocks of mud called houses; not a flower, not a tree, not a bird relieved the drabness. The landscape resembled the Chilean foothills where he had rustled cattle. On the pampas he had stopped many times at a similar rancho to change horses.[24]

In the corral Vicente found the owner dickering with an American over the price of the miserable steed which Clackston had failed to buy. In Chile the animal would be sold for grease,[25] Vicente thought, but here time was money and his men were desperate to move on to the diggings. Therefore he outbid the American buyer by offering to pay $300, $50 more than Clackston had refused to pay the day before. But more disturbing to the Chileans was the disappointment of not getting even a glimpse of the beautiful woman. In due time, however, they all beheld her.

To weigh the gold dust payable for the horse, the owner led his customers to the storehouse, and there the fair one stood behind the scales. Indeed, she was as beautiful as Clackston had described—or was it because none of them had seen a female for so long? In any event, after weighing their dust she served them milk to drink, a great treat. Then, leading the decrepit horse, the Chileans returned to Sacramento.

Arriving in camp after dark, they were all eager to be off at dawn and would not consider sleep. Instead, they devoured a full pot of beans, prepared a makeshift harness for the nag to haul the little cart, and then lay down on the ground to rest. Before daybreak three strange Chileans appeared, probably shouting "Hola" in native fashion. They wanted to join the company and Vicente accepted them. Everyone was up now and they breakfasted on a bowl of hot gruel. The Chilean *harina tostada* ("toasted flour"), when boiled in water, made a satisfying mush and with full stomachs they all set off on the long hike to the diggings.

Two men led with the loaded wagon. Behind them five men accompanied the cart. Clackston and Pérez R. marched behind as a rear guard.[26] They followed a road of sorts, passed Sutter's Fort, the fair one's rancho, and went on across the desert to the misty mountains, a rolling country beautiful now with lush vegetation and brilliant flowers. But the succulent grass failed to improve the cart horse's disposition; he kicked at times and finally balked. No amount of beating persuaded him to move a single step. North Americans might have built a fire under the stubborn brute, which certainly would have incited him to move forward if only far enough to burn the cart. The Chileans, with disgusted laughter, unloaded the cart onto their own shoulders. Time was money, so they marched on. That night they wasted no time in pitching a tent, but camped instead under a gigantic live oak. The umbrella-like foliage protected them from the evening dew, and a sack of toasted Chilean flour served each man for a pillow.[27]

Next day the little party stopped where the road forked. Here was a perplexing situation. Each road led up a different valley. Which should they follow? Finally they decided to travel the most easterly one, a mistake they soon regretted. Vicente had learned the mysteries of trailing in the Chilean Andes and, as his party plodded along, he soon became suspicious of the new route. North Americans, he had learned, always left a trail of empty bottles and he saw none here, so he ordered a halt. The men gathered around him discussing what to do next, when a mixed-blood Indian rode up. He told them that they were indeed on the wrong road. In fact they had already entered dangerous Indian country. The red men in this area had been abused by North American gold seekers and, in revenge, were murdering every unarmed prospector they found.

Pérez Rosales immediately hired the mixed-blood as a guide and ordered his men to ready their arms, pitch camp, and cook some beans. Then, with a few followers, he strolled off to explore the neighborhood. He had acted this way many times during the life he had lived in the dangerous Araucanian Indian country of Chile. His companions carried scoops and troughs—Chilean gold pans—and planned to prospect the nearest stream, but before they were out of sight of the camp a peon came running to them. He had slipped away from the party ahead of everyone and, being familiar since childhood[28] with panning gold, had already collected in his little trough a brilliant string of "colors."[29] Gold at last! Plenty of it in dangerous Indian country! What more could be wished for by true descendants of the conquistadores?

The whole party, back at the wagon, dropped their guns and tools. Forgetting the Indian danger, they scampered to the creek. In the stampede one man stumbled over a squaw hiding with her papoose in a thicket. She jumped up, ran, tripped, and fell, shrieking for help. Her cries were immediately answered from afar by what sounded to Vicente like the barking of many wild animals. In no time a gang of angry Indians appeared, half-naked fellows dressed in rags and tatters. One wore a cast-off coat and nothing else. Another was clad in a knitted shirt that barely covered his middle. Most of the savages had only breechclouts. These primitive men surrounded the unarmed Chileans, fixed arrows in their bows, and menacingly pulled back the bowstrings.

The situation was extremely dangerous. Ferocious grimaces distorted the Indians' faces, and the chance of survival for any

of the Chileans seemed doubtful, but at that critical moment
the mixed-blood's voice rang out. He shouted to the Indians
that these men were not North Americans but Spanish-speaking
friends of their friend, John Sutter. That name quieted the red
men, for Sutter had been good to them. They hated only the
invading North Americans. The mixed-blood explained, also,
that these white men had come into this country by mistake and
planned to leave in the morning.[30]

The Indians lowered their bows and arrows and stepped forward suspiciously. When friendship was established, an assortment of dusky females joined the group. Some were dressed in
knee-length woolen skirts, others in a peculiar cloth made from
esparto grass. All were barefoot and naked above the waist. To
Pérez Rosales these Indians seemed darker-skinned and less
strongly built than the Araucanians[31] he had known so well in
his cattle-rustling days. The South American Indians had resisted Europeans since the first conquistadores failed to subju-
gate them, and they still controlled a vast tract of land from Concepción to Valdivia and eastward to the Andes. Some Chileans
liked to claim that these Indians' fighting ability was due to an
admixture of good Spanish blood. Generation after generation
of Araucanians had captured the wives and daughters of settlers
who edged into their domain. The Indian country, back in the
lake region near Villarrica, was reported to be rich in gold,[32]
available only to white prospectors who dared visit it.

Belligerent Indians in a gold country were meat and drink to
Chileans. Their parents and grandparents told stories about
pioneer encounters. To fight or trade with red men was part of
their heritage and they soon began to exchange goods with the
savages. A squaw offered a neat little packet of gold dust worth
$5 or $6 for a cheap cotton handkerchief. Others paid larger
amounts of gold for a few ounces of Chilean toasted flour. Finally the Indians led the Chileans to the place where they washed
gold, showing them how to dig into the dry ground with fire-
hardened sticks until they came to the gold-bearing sand. The
sand was scooped up into woven-grass baskets which children
carried down to the stream; there the women, using grass trays,

washed out the gold and wrapped it in small packages for trading at Sutter's Fort.[33]

Next morning the Chileans repacked their camp, retraced their steps, found the main road, and by sunset that night reached the famous Sutter's mill which had been uppermost in all their minds since they left Valparaiso. El Dorado at last! Or was it?

12

The July Fourth Thundercloud

The fabled Sutter's mill failed to impress Pérez Rosales. Built of roughhewn logs, it stood a scant two stories high, and many of its best timbers had been stolen by gold-seeking campers. The mill was in a basin traversed by the American River, a small stream at this point. Vicente, standing on the deserted mill's second floor, could see a nearby store, two wooden shacks, and many tents and brush shelters.[1] This was Coloma, where seventy official ballots had been cast in February for delegates to the territorial convention in San Jose.[2] Beyond Coloma lay a waste of sun-bleached gravel, scarred with ditches, broken dams, flumes, sluice boxes, rockers, and Long Toms. Men, small and busy as ants, worked among the primitive mining machinery. Above them the encircling mountains were black with a forest of pines, the timber Sutter had planned to saw into boards.

North Americans had worked this basin for more than a year but Vicente knew that Chileans could find gold in country abandoned by less skilled workmen. He ordered the men to pitch their tents, the large circular one and the smaller canvas shelters for beds and tools. In no time a crowd assembled, admiring the outfit but asking if the expense of bringing such equipment so far inland was justified, especially since the nearby store had accumulated a surplus that was for sale cheap.[3] Again and again men said that this country had been worked out and that more gold could be found farther upstream.

Every evening heavily packed prospectors from Sacramento stumbled into camp. They often rested a day, then tramped on deeper into the mountains. Perhaps they acted wisely but the Chileans, experienced miners, decided that Americans were both ignorant and lazy. Plenty of gold could probably be found right here by skilled men who were willing to work. Confident of this, the Chileans established their camp. Then, with scoop, spade, and pick they worked the tailings abandoned by gringos, and within two hours had panned out an ounce and a half of gold,[4] which certainly was good wages. Yes, they would remain. In high spirits they returned to camp, feasted on boiled beans, and began to build gold-washing rockers.* These finished, they worked for a month swinging the handles like violinists, while they sang the aria concerning the sin of slander from *The Barber of Seville*, a song then popular in Chile,[5] or the equally rhythmic "Donde vas, bueno caballero" ("Dreadful sorry, Clementine!").

Early in April their busy life was interrupted by an Indian scare, a foreboding of trouble that might cost all of them their lives. It began one morning when they observed several columns of white smoke, rising straight as ships' masts, on the western slope of the encircling mountains. This sight was not remarkable, but that night the row of smoky pillars became little lights that did not flicker in spite of a wind that began blowing at sunset. The unblinking phenomenon interested the Chileans, who were outdoorsmen trained to read nature in all its moods. After some discussion a small party of Chileans and North Americans decided to investigate. They climbed the mountain and returned with the information that Indians had built fires in a line of holes where the wind could not disturb them. These were evidently signals, but for what?[6]

Next morning an Indian appeared in camp. A traitor to his village, he came to explain the fires as signals to all red men for a massacre of the whites. Vicente marveled at the immediate reaction of the norteamericanos. Instead of awaiting the slow remedy of the law, as Chileans in an older civilization might have done, these Americans held a mass meeting and organized a corps of 170 riflemen and 18 horsemen to march at once against the Indians.

Vicente did not attend the meeting and a committee, noting his absence, called to ask why he, a Frenchman,[7] had failed to

---

* In July the Chilean commission firm, Cross, Hobson y Cia., announced that they were importing hand-operated gold-washers of a long established design. *Alta California,* July 12, 1849.

volunteer to save the country so dear to Lafayette. Vicente did
not deny his French nationality. He knew that Chileans were in
disfavor in California, being blamed for coming to the diggings
ahead of the norteamericano owners of the land. To excuse himself for not attending the mass meeting, he pleaded illness, and
he promised to join the military force if given ten minutes to
arrange his affairs. If his illness might delay the column's march,
however, he would gladly contribute powder and lead to the
war effort.

His second offer was accepted and the column marched away.
Two days later it returned with 114 captive Indians, including
men, women, and children. The hostile village had been surprised, and those who resisted had been killed. The wretched
survivors were driven like sheep to the encampment and herded
in a bend of the river which, with the spring freshets, ran bank
full and was rough, rapid, and impassable. White men who had
not joined the expedition assembled to inspect the captives.
Vicente noticed that aspiring American politicos spent the next
two hours selecting a judge, jurors, and attorneys. Then, after
a mock trial in which the lawyers displayed their talents for
oratory, the red men were adjudged guilty, and fifteen of them
were drafted from the huddled prisoners. These men were lined
up in a separate group, and a miner who could speak Spanish
announced to those who were left: "If you behave yourselves
from now on you have nothing to fear; but if not, the same thing
will happen to you that you are now going to witness before we
let you go home to tell about it."[8] With these words riflemen
fired at the fifteen Indians, killing all of them. The abject survivors standing in the bend of the river were then released and,
with bowed heads, they left the camp, trudged up the bare slope
of the mountains, and, wailing with grief, disappeared into the
black forest. Did Valdivia, in his hunger for gold, ever act with
more precipitancy?

The gold seekers had scarcely recovered from this ghastly
scene when an excited prospector came to camp, reporting a new
gold strike across the river. Although not far away, the area was
difficult to reach because the stream, at the ford, flowed chest

deep with a current no man could stand against. Fortunately a cable had been stretched across for any daring man who cared to clutch it and risk his life in the icy water. There was also a rowboat, but in mid channel a comb of tossing white water warned boatmen to beware of navigating so fragile a craft. Yet both methods of crossing tempted some bold individuals to go at once. They crossed safely and that night their campfires on the mountainside indicated successful digging over there.

Vicente watched the fires and, as chief cook, caudillo, and banker for the Chileans, decided to represent his people at the new discovery. So, on the following day, April 11, 1849, he walked to the ford. Looking downstream, he saw the rapid white water tossing over the cable that spanned the stream. To row a small boat packed with men across such a torrent seemed foolhardy, but before he realized what he was doing he found himself, crowded with fifteen others, in the rowboat.

Friends shoved them off and as soon as the little craft reached the comb of white water it tipped over, spilling all on board into the churning flood. Vicente was a good swimmer but the frightened men clung to him and they all went under. He thought first of drawing the dagger a Chilean always wore and freeing himself from the clutching hands. Then he decided to dive for the bottom and escape. Down he went, tumbling over and over in the rough current. His breath gave out. His lungs filled with water, and he said later, "I remember the furious rolling of a thousand drums that made me lose consciousness."[9] By good luck Pérez Rosales lodged against the cable spanning the river and was rescued by his countrymen. They understood rolling a man face down over a barrel to expel the water from his lungs and Vicente, gasping for breath, finally came back to life.

Two weeks later, on April 25,[10] Vicente was chosen by his company to go to San Francisco, get the mail, and settle his debt with the Jewish moneylender. He also planned to collect the money due him in Sacramento from Gillespie, who had helped sell the Chileans' wine and brandy. For the trip Vicente carried a 16-pound bag of toasted Chilean flour, a tin bowl for mixing it, a Mexican sarape, and a Chilean *ruana*. He strapped two pistols and a dagger to his waist and in his broad belt stowed 17 pounds of gold dust worth some $4,000. He also carried a rifle in a sling over his left shoulder.

Vicente found the road to Sacramento crowded with men and heavily packed mules coming to the diggings. Often, before he could see the travelers, he heard snatches of song, sullen curses, the rattle of hobble chains, the tinkle of horse bells—all sounds he had learned to associate with a North American gold rush. Sometimes he had to stand aside for a pack train to pass, much as he had often done for mule trains on narrow Andean trails. Delayed by these interruptions, he spent four days walking the 55 miles to Sacramento.[11] At night he smoothed a place for his blankets beneath a giant live oak and built a fire to frighten away the howling coyotes, which he believed dangerous, and the bears that might have been.

Arriving in Sacramento on April 30, Pérez Rosales remembered years later that the city had changed completely during his short absence. Town lots, instead of being given away, were now selling for high prices. The river banks were crowded with deserted hulks; he counted thirty brigs in addition to scores of lesser craft. He also remembered that he saw twenty seagoing vessels of more than 300 tons each.[12] He did not notice that one of them must have been the Luco brothers' Chilean bark, *Natalia*, said to be the first seagoing vessel to reach Sacramento.[13] Vicente also recalled that on this visit he found that the city contained "many buildings erected at great expense."[14] He was guilty of a slight exaggeration, for another traveler, who visited Sacramento the next day, reported only thirteen houses and many tents. Most business, this man said, was still being transacted at Sutter's Fort 2 miles away.[15] But the entire area was crowded, and Vicente did not meet his fellow countrymen, Leandro and Manuel Luco, who had brought a cargo of goods from Chile to sell here. Their father, a prominent attorney, had served Chilean shipping houses in Valparaiso since 1835. Their first cousin would later be president of Chile,[16] while Pérez Rosales himself was destined to be a prominent government executive in his own country.

In the milling crowds Vicente failed to find his old friend Gillespie, but by chance met him leaving his tent to inspect a piece of land he contemplated purchasing. He urged Pérez R. to leave his pack and artillery inside the tent and come with him. They could talk on the way. Indeed, in California time was money. Neither of the men suspected that this trip would be one of the most horrifying experiences in Vicente's California sojourn.

After inspecting the land the two men rested in the shade of a pine tree a short distance above Sutter's Fort. They were disturbed by a shrill cry: "Socorro! Socorro!"

Vicente thought he recognized the agonized voice. Jumping to his feet he cried to Gillespie, "They are killing one of our friends."[17] The two men ran toward the sound and saw a crowd of miners standing around a man on a wagon with a rope from a tree limb tied around his neck. The miners evidently planned to pull the wagon away and leave the condemned man suspended in the air. Vicente recognized the wretch as Álvarez, that troublesome passenger who had tried to lead a mutiny on board the *Staoueli*.

Vicente asked, in broken English, the man's crime and learned that someone had stolen a spade. Therefore Álvarez, the "Chilean son-of-a-nigger," must have been the thief![18] This seemed questionable proof, and Vicente resolved to save him. Pérez R. was still new to North American characteristics but he had a plan he believed would work. At Sutter's mill he had learned that North Americans considered Lafayette a great hero who had helped them win independence. He also remembered that his party had been mistaken for Frenchmen. As a boy he had attended school in France, so now, in his best French manner, Vicente pleaded for the condemned man's life. In halting English, which he knew sounded French, he told the crowd that he had known the condemned man in South America, where Chileans abused and sometimes killed Frenchmen. But the Chilean standing on yonder wagon, Vicente said, admired Frenchmen because they were fellow countrymen of Lafayette. Yes, the doomed man over there, with the hangman's rope around his neck, had once risked his life to save a Frenchman from being beaten to death by a Chilean mob, and he performed the brave act on account of his admiration for the noble Lafayette.

Gillespie nodded agreement to all Vicente's lies, and the name of Lafayette calmed the lynchers. They freed Álvarez, and the three men hurried away to Sacramento without further mishap. No wonder that Pérez Rosales was destined to be a great political administrator in democratic Chile!

In town, Gillespie loaned Pérez R. a sailboat for his trip to San Francisco. All alone, but with blankets and food, Vicente sailed down the broad expanse of the Sacramento River. Out on the still waters he admired the reflections of northbound vessels and the trees behind them. The entire scene reminded him of his own Valdivia River[19] which flowed out of the blue Chilean lakes at the foot of the Andes. The only difference, he noted, was the unusual aspect of the oaks and sycamores along the distant shores. Their branches were clouded by strange streamers of waving moss called "old man's beard" by norteamericanos.

When Vicente reached the junction of the Sacramento and San Joaquin rivers he scarcely recognized the area. Two months ago when he had been there the tide was high and Suisun Bay appeared to be a huge lake with tules protruding through the water. Now at low tide, the lake had become a myriad of channels meandering through mudbanks capped with the same tules. To his amusement, Vicente counted nine launches, seven sloops, and one two-masted schooner, all stuck fast. Behind them groups of men stood knee deep in the mud. They held long ropes and pulled lustily every time one of them shouted, "All together now!"[20] It was good to watch them from a small boat and pleasant, indeed, to sail past them.

In spite of the mosquitoes, Vicente found boat travel so easy that he decided to steer up the San Joaquin River and visit the much talked about Stockton. The money he and his companions had borrowed was drawing interest every day, but the diversion might be worth the cost. His small boat navigated the river with ease and he soon tied up at the growing city's shore. Here he counted sixty wooden buildings—many more than in Sacramento—and in addition he saw dozens of tents and brush shelters. In all, he estimated that there were 180 dwellings. As in so many other inland gold-rush cities, the first person he met was an extravagantly dressed promoter eager to buy his goods or sell him town lots. On the street along the river many men, armed to the teeth, swaggered by, shouting arrogant curses above the orchestra of saws and hammers that kept most of the population dancing in lively step. Indeed, everybody seemed to be in such a hurry they threw empty bottles from doors and windows, littering the street until passing feet crushed them into the ground. Women were nowhere to be seen, but pictures of their naked bodies adorned the walls of restaurants. Pérez Rosales reckoned the permanent population at about 1,000, with sometimes twice that number coming and going every day.[21]

After resting in this fleshpot for forty-eight hours, Vicente shoved off in his sailboat for San Francisco. Arriving in due time at the bay city, he realized that he would have made more money investing in cheap town lots there than in panning for gold on the American River. He saw at once that the men getting rich in California were not the men who found the precious metal, but those who served the gold seekers. These middlemen were building a great city, whose population he now judged to be near 30,000. Long, half-finished wharfs already ran out from streets that terminated at the bay. To extend these streets, deserted ships had been floated in at high tide, grounded side by side in long rows, and ballasted until they stuck permanently in the mud. From the beam-ends of these vessels, joists were laid for the construction of stores between them. A young Chilean, Wenceslao Ubistondo, had beached his ship at the foot of Vallejo Street, felled its masts, and planked them over, thus making a causeway to his vessel and its stores.[22]

As yet none of the North American forty-niners had arrived overland and only a few had come to Panama. Indeed, San Francisco seemed to Pérez Rosales as Spanish as Valparaiso.[23] The steamship *California* had chugged in late in February with some North Americans, and her sister ship, the *Oregon*, came in April. The *Panama* followed on June 4,[24] but the large crowd of emigrants from the eastern United States, coming around Cape Horn, were still at sea. Indeed, some 200 vessels had already left

New York[25] and many more were coming from a half-dozen other big eastern ports. New vessels arrived every day, bringing gold seekers. Most of them came from Mexico or Central and South America, and half of the immigrants they carried were said to be Chileans.[26] In fact, the harbor was full of Chilean vessels,[27] and Castilla's Peruvian warship, *Gamarra*, stood among them ready to help Spanish-speaking captains and prevent their sailors from deserting.[28]

Vicente walked along the city's streets, noting that all names prominent in Chile could be found in some kind of business here.[29] The bold letters ABOGADO CONSULTOR on a sign over the tent belonging to a well-known Valparaiso insurance agent proclaimed him to be a counselor-at-law. The shack of a former Santiago barber was labeled FRENCH HOTEL.[30] The shipping agents and commission merchants all seemed to be South Americans. In the plaza on feast days native Californios, in embroidered jackets and jingling spurs, frolicked on their spirited horses.[31]

Law and order were administered by an alcalde—certainly sufficiently Spanish—but Pérez Rosales noticed a wide difference between this exalted office in California and in Chile. In South America an alcalde's orders, just or unjust, were obeyed. At a San Francisco trial he saw a gang of rough North Americans terminate a trial. One of them shouted: "Hear, hear! Citizens! In as much as the Alcalde is in favor of the immediate application of fifty strokes to this *citizen of the United States*, I propose that ten of us escort the Alcalde for a distance of one mile with kicks in the————!"[32]

Obviously the same laws did not apply to Spanish-speaking people as to a "citizen of the United States," and Chileans prided themselves on being fighters equal to any men on earth. Their number in relation to the Anglos, however, was diminishing rapidly. San Francisco would soon cease to be a North American Valparaiso, but the Chileans were not intimidated. They had been the victors during a generation of wars with their South American neighbors and were proud of the record. They looked on the submissive Californios[33] in their embroidered clothes with tolerant contempt, on the Mexicans as lazy and shiftless, and on the rough Oregonians as cowardly bullies who always fought in gangs.

Chileans at the diggings were not to be intimidated by Persifor Smith's proclamation against "foreigners," and as it circulated among the placers, resentment between Anglos and Latins grew.[34] An explosion seemed bound to occur come July the Fourth, when North American "patriots" delivered orations about the heroic days of old, describing how redcoats, Hessians, and all other "furriners" had been driven back across the sea. In fact, the lightning struck before the Fourth, probably as the outcome of meetings held to plan the patriotic celebrations. There was no apparent concerted action. Armed Yankees raided Chilean encampments on both the "Tagualamo" (Tuolumne)[35] and American rivers. Some Chileans fought back stubbornly. Rotos told one another that the Virgin was on their side, yes! Gringos, Lutherans, and heretics were all the same breed of *mapurito* ("hog-nosed skunk"). At one mining claim, according to reports received in Chile, rotos maintained their rights to the location by forming a circle for defense and erecting a Chilean flag in the center. This act, as *El Comercio* in Valparaiso later admitted, was a great mistake since it gave the United States government proper authority for expelling them from the country.[36]

Pérez Rosales was never deluded about the ultimate ascendancy of the Anglos. He saw hundreds of Chileans streaming into San Francisco from the diggings with small fortunes they were eager to take home.* The number leaving for South America was larger now than the number arriving. While Pérez R. was in town the Chilean *Virjinia* sailed for Valparaiso on July 4 and the French *Chateaubriand* on July 8.[37] Both vessels were fully loaded and lucky to get away before the impending storm, but their departure made little difference in San Francisco's congested Chilean population.

The refugees flocking in from the diggings brought bad news to Vicente. They reported that all foreigners at Sutter's mill had been driven off by raiders who sold their property at auction to

* Susanna Bryant Dakin (*A Scotch Paisano: Hugo Reid's Life in California, 1832–1852* [Berkeley, 1939], p. 175) quotes a contemporary letter of July 18, 1849, which says that "upwards of one thousand persons came down last week to San Francisco and embarked, chiefly Chileans."

the mob. Vicente was told that one North American who employed foreign workers had defied the raiders by fortifying himself in the mill. Others who fought for their claims had been overpowered and killed; some of these, according to reports, were Frenchmen.* The news shocked Pérez Rosales. His party at the mill had been called Frenchmen. Had his brothers survived? In desperation he paid $200 for a boat to take him to Sacramento. Almost overwhelmed with fear when he landed at the American River, he went first to Gillespie's tent, and there, to his delight, he found his brothers. They had been robbed by the raiders and had lost everything except the gold dust concealed in their broad leather belts, but they were safe,[38] sassy and eager as any roto for more adventures.

* *Ibid.*, p. 174. Leonard Pitt ("The Beginnings of Nativism in California," *Pacific Historical Review*, XXX [Feb., 1961], 25–26) says the fight at Sutter's mill occurred in April. Vicente Pérez Rosales (*California Adventure*, trans. Edwin S. Morby and Arturo Torres-Rioseco [San Francisco, 1947], p. 57) says he left the mill on April 25 and was in Sacramento until the end of the month, but he mentions no fight.

13

The Anti-Chilean Riot
in San Francisco

Pérez Rosales and his brothers, on their return to San Francisco, learned that many Chileans in town had suffered during their absence.* Here, in a city named for the most virtuous of saints, men and women repeated harrowing accounts of a riot on July 15, 1849. Blackened ground and charred furniture showed where their friends' tents had stood. The catastrophe had evidently been triggered by the overwhelming influx of Chileans driven from their placer claims[1] by Persifor Smith's pernicious proclamation. More than 1,000 had streamed into San Francisco,[2] but the riot was not exclusively one of Anglos against Chileans. Some individuals were renewing old grudges which originated in South America.

In the plaza a tent saloon called Tammany Hall had become the loafing place for deserting sailors, discharged soldiers, and roustabouts. The alcalde, having no funds to employ constables, had once engaged two men from the Tammany tent to flog a sailor he had sentenced for threatening the captain of his vessel with a knife. The alcalde had no money to pay these servants of his court, so they collected what was due them by paying for the meals they ate in restaurants with orders on the alcalde. A novel solution, surely!

Soon these loafers and their acquaintances found other easy

* Vicente Pérez Rosales (*California Adventure*, trans. Edwin S. Morby and Arturo Torres-Rioseco [San Francisco, 1947], p. 69) says he left San Francisco three days after the riot, but news of the raid on the American River was published in *Alta California* on July 12, three days before the riot. If Pérez R. left as early as he says, he must have left before July 15.

ways to make a dollar. Some of them became claim agents and bill collectors for merchants. Once, three of them insisted that a storekeeper, who happened to be a Chilean, pay a debt of which there was no record. When he refused to pay, these self-styled agents threatened, they would return with "forty men." The number suggests that they might be members of the Sociedad de los 42, or perhaps the Hounds, the Galgos,[3] or Perros de Presa[4]—all names for semiorganized dockside gangsters.

Many of the Chileans in town were men of property who had come to San Francisco with goods to sell, and one of them who established a shop in his tent had trouble on June 21, 1849. That day, while the shopkeeper was serving a customer, two men entered and quarreled about an alleged payment. In apparent fright the shopkeeper drew a pistol. One of the gangsters grappled with him and the other one fled. As he ran out the door the handgun fired. Who pulled the trigger was never known, but the bullet hit the running man and he died the next day.[5] His name was Benjamin B. Bailey, a private in the recently disbanded New York regiment. The sound of the shot attracted a crowd, and by the time the sheriff arrived with a warrant the Chilean shopkeeper had disappeared. His tent and goods were auctioned off to the crowd, and the self-righteous Hounds, several of whom had served in the regiment with Bailey, maintained that his death justified them in organizing themselves as the city's Regulators. The editor of *Alta California* protested, upholding the Chilean shopkeeper's right to protect his property with a gun.[6] Obviously two points of view were beginning to polarize in San Francisco, and at this time businessmen who happened to be Chileans were respected by the best citizens.

The sudden influx of displaced Chileans from the placers during the last weeks of June gave the city a real problem. The refugees came in an ugly mood and rotos were known to be dangerous characters. Policemen were needed, but the city had no money to pay them. Perhaps the self-styled Regulators might serve in this capacity. They claimed to be upholders of law and order. Some persons welcomed them and lauded the grotesque costumes they wore while marching, two by two,[7] through the streets. Tradesmen smiled indulgently when the Regulators (or

Hounds) ended their march at a saloon, where the drinks were "charged to the dust so the rain could settle it."

These young men crossed the bay to Contra Costa on Sunday, July 15, to parade there, and Sam Roberts, who would be convicted for leading the Hounds in the notorious riot, entered upon the scene. He was an odd ruffian from Valparaiso. Unable to read or write, he had served on a Chilean man-of-war[8] and had probably deserted to come to California with a United States regiment.[9] He may have been a member of the New York volunteers to which Ben Bailey belonged. Certainly he marched with the Hounds wearing a lieutenant's uniform.* Between parades he had operated a boat for landing incoming passengers, and no doubt he resented the necessity of competing in this occupation with newly arrived Chileans who supported themselves temporarily as boatmen the way Pérez Rosales' companions had done.

Nevertheless, Sam did have friendly relations with some Chileans, and, knowing Spanish, he was naturally attracted to Washington Hall on the plaza. This Chilean house of prostitution later became famous when the beautiful spitfire, Mariquita, stabbed the equally fair Camille La Reine. Her crime was considered totally inexcusable because the death of her victim would have left only one buyable female for every hundred males in the community.[10] Spanish-speaking Sam, the watchful owner of a boat for landing passengers, quickly appropriated a Chilean courtesan, Felice Álvarez, when she arrived from Valparaiso, and he established her in the Chilean house of ill fame. He also appropriated the 10 ounces of gold she had brought from South America. Felice admitted later that she was afraid of Roberts, but in this foreign country she dared not lock him out of her room.

On July 15, when the Hounds were known to be parading across the bay, Felice dared to admit three Germans she may have known in Chile. One of them, Leopold Bleckschmidt, was

---

* Dominguez Cruz, in testimony printed in *Alta California*, Aug. 2, 1849, says that the Hounds' leader was known as "Captain George." Sam Roberts had made his headquarters at the saloon operated by Cruz, who may have been reluctant to identify him.

well known in Valparaiso and another, named Koch, may have been the Mr. Krafft described in John W. Palmer's book of fiction, *The New and the Old; or, California . . . in Romantic Aspects* (1859). According to Palmer, Krafft was an adventurer who arrived in Chile in 1839 or thereabouts. He brought many letters of introduction, probably forged, from distinguished men in Europe. With these and his pleasing personality, he became a confidential clerk for an Italian merchant in Valparaiso, married his daughter, bankrupted the firm with speculations, and on the death of his father-in-law joined the California gold rush. His wife and three children were left to the bounty of her late father's friends. In San Francisco, Krafft became cashier in the customhouse.[11] A handsome man with a classic nose, soft blue eyes, and aristocratically drooping eyelids, his face was habitually flushed "as though by refined intemperance." When in his cups Krafft invariably sang an aria from *Lucia di Lammermoor*, an opera very popular in Chile at that time. He dressed immaculately in a brass-buttoned, claret-colored coat with a velvet collar and, according to Palmer, distinguished himself in a minor way during the forthcoming riot.[12]

However that may be, of the three Germans who visited Felice on the tragic day, it was Leopold Bleckschmidt, not Mr. Koch alias Krafft, who was sitting on Felice's bed when Sam Roberts rode up in his lieutenant's uniform, dismounted, and strode into the room. Koch, who was nearby, saw Sam drag Bleckschmidt out of the house, knock him unconscious with a club or his riding whip, take off one of his spurs, and rake the prostrate man's face until the blood streamed from the wounds.

"For shame! That is not manly," shouted someone in the crowd outside. Sam retorted that he would kill the fellow if he caught him again with his woman.[13]

No doubt smarting from becoming a Chilean woman's cuckold, Sam Roberts returned to the Tammany Hall saloon where he urged drinking companions to parade again with fife and drum. Many assembled, but not all of them around Sam. Instead, independent parties with self-appointed leaders began carousing from saloon to saloon singing, bragging, making dares. Prudent citizens retired to their own tents or rooming houses.

Sam, knowing Spanish, led a group of some twenty men to the saloon tent of Dominguez Cruz at Clark's Point. Inside, along the bar, he saw the backs of twenty Chileans. Sam marched his party in and, with drawn pistol, ordered the drinkers to disperse. Dominguez recognized Sam, the ex-sailor from Valparaiso, and served his men a round or two of drinks. They proclaimed his saloon their headquarters, then marched out. Thus, if a full-scale riot ensued, one Chilean saloonkeeper would be on the rioter's side.

The next stop of Sam's gang is impossible to determine, although the destruction of many Chilean rowboats along the shore was probably done by this jealous boatman or his ruffians. In other parts of town various gangs of roustabouts and sailors in grotesque costumes, some with blackened faces, were also making the night hideous with shouts, shots, and rumbling drums, each eager to outdo the others in acts of vandalism. Gangs of men would stop at a tent door and if the owner replied to them in English the band passed on, but if he spoke in Spanish they burst in, upsetting beds, opening trunks, destroying everything they could not carry off. Sometimes, when the loot was rich, they held an impromptu auction, selling hats, clothing, and jewelry to the highest bidder.[14] At the tents where Domingo Alegria and his family lived, all had gone to bed when the rioters burst in, upsetting furniture and driving out father, mother, and daughter. Two sons showed fight and were shot, one in the hand, the other in the abdomen. Both wounded men escaped, staggering away into the night.

In another tent the occupant saved himself by crawling through a hole he cut in the canvas wall with his knife. Several fled for protection on the nearby *Jeneral Freire*, a ship named for the popular, liberal president[15] under whom Carlos Wooster, hero of the War of 1812, had served when he joined the Chilean navy. No refugees of record boarded the Peruvian *Jeneral Gamarra* which was also in the harbor, although she made two trips later to Peru with disappointed gold seekers.[16]

During the disturbance Mr. Krafft, according to the fictional account, attacked some five or six rioters who had set fire to a tent on Dupont Street and were quarreling among themselves over a Chilean girl they had captured. Krafft, a skilled swordsman, schooled in Germany, felled four of the men with quick blows from his gold-headed Malacca cane, then disappeared in the dark, leading the terrified girl as he hummed Sir Edgar's part of the duet in the first act of *Lucia di Lammermoor*: "Io son rico, / Tu sei bella."[17] The Chilean girl probably did not understand Italian, but she stopped crying even though the disconsolate raiders fired a shot or two at the distant sound of Krafft's voice in the dark.

The extent of the depredations committed by Sam and his gang cannot be determined. Certainly he tried to recruit followers from other gangs by attracting attention with fife, drum, and shouts of encouragement through his megaphone. Before dawn, however, he returned to Dominguez' saloon, bringing loot to be stored there.[18]

The next morning many outraged citizens appealed to the alcalde, who claimed that he could do nothing without an armed constabulary, or what the Chileans called *vigilantes*, an ominous word in California history. He did, however, call a mass meeting in the plaza for three o'clock that afternoon. Some Chileans believed, erroneously, that the alcalde had resigned,[19] a natural assumption when they saw distinguished citizens assemble to take the government into their own hands. At this meeting Sam Brannan, always eager to address any audience, spoke out in his best auctioneer voice, insisting on justice for all Chileans, the good people from a neighboring republic.[20] California, Brannan boomed, depended on Chile for flour, on her skilled artisans for laying bricks, on her bakers for bread. He did not mention that Chileans under Pérez Rosales had paid him well for poor accommodations on his decrepit craft to Sacramento, but he insisted that a collection be taken to reimburse those who had been robbed. The Hounds, he thundered, must be suppressed.

The crowd followed Brannan's oratory by organizing a police force of 230 men, many of them armed with their own guns. Several Chileans enlisted. All were sworn in as they stood around the flagpole in front of the long, rickety porch of the old, adobe customhouse in the plaza.[21] Two judges were elected to serve with the alcalde. One of them was William Gwin, a professional politician from Tennessee who was destined to be a United States senator from California. In this instance he undoubtedly helped give the extemporaneous trial of the Hounds a true legal form. Attorneys for the defense and prosecution were appointed,[22] as was a grand jury of twenty-four men. The latter promptly brought in a true bill indicting Sam Roberts on four counts: (1) conspiracy to rob, assault, rape, and murder the peaceful people of this community; (2) assembling men with deadly weapons to rob and assault Domingo Alegria and his family; (3) causing bodily injury to thirty-eight persons and stealing their property; (4) assaulting Leopold Bleckschmidt with intent to kill.[23]

Somewhat different indictments were rendered against nineteen other Hounds, and seventeen of these men were arrested immediately. Since there was no jail in San Francisco, they were confined on the United States war sloop *Warren* in the bay. Three Hounds, including Sam Roberts, could not be found in town, but before arraignment two days later they had all been apprehended. Roberts was on a schooner headed for Stockton.

The trial commenced on July 18. Prompt justice surely![24] Pioneers did not believe in legal procrastination. Many witnesses were called, including Sam's woman, Felice, and the badly wounded Rinaldo Alegria, whose mother and sister helped him into court. The poor fellow died soon afterward from the bullet in his abdomen.[25]

According to the evidence, thirty-eight Chileans had been either assaulted or intimidated. Rioters had stolen $6,300 in coin, gold dust worth $1,500, and clothes, jewelry, and firearms valued at $1,400. In addition, the looters had carried off many casks of wine and brandy.

The defense attorney cross-examined all witnesses with care, and in his concluding argument begged for leniency, basing his plea on General Smith's proclamation against foreigners and a lack of identification of the looters. He proved effectively that there were no organized Hounds, although an unfinished constitution had been written to form the Regulators into an association for mutual benefit in case of illness.[26]

Several witnesses testified that the leader of the rioters wore a military uniform. Some described it to be more like a major general's than a lieutenant's uniform, and the jury decided that the resplendent man must be Sam Roberts. Consequently they adjudged him guilty on all counts in the indictment. He was sentenced to hard labor for ten years in whatever penitentiary the governor of California might select. The other prisoners who were found guilty received lesser sentences according to their crimes, but for one reason or another none of the terms were served.

The prompt decision from the jury and the severity of the sentences might have been consoling to some Chileans in San Francisco, but hundreds of their fellow countrymen had already returned to Valparaiso[27] with bitter memories of their treatment in California. By the time they reached home, dozens of ships carrying Argonauts from the eastern United States would be stopping at Valparaiso. What a chance to give those yanquis some of their own medicine when they came ashore! Trouble between the two peoples seemed sure to erupt next in South America.

PART IV
Life in Chile and Peru
During 1849

14

Ya No Voy a California

*For every sentence uttered, a million
More are dumb;
Men's lives are chains of chances, and
History their sum.*
—Bayard Taylor, *Napoleon at Gotha*

During the months preceding the San Francisco riot, the gold rush had had an amazing influence on Chile. From the beginning, unconfirmed accounts of minor confrontations reached Valparaiso. In 1848 a semiliterate workman wrote, in crude characters, to friends in Chile that a gang of Yankees had taken his claim, but two of them, he said, were now where "they will enjoy bigger placers if heaven receives gringos."[1] Such accounts were accepted as roto boasting, for the rush to California did not abate. In January, 1849, the owners of sixteen vessels advertised for passengers, and others offered their ships for charter. The usual fare was 10 ounces for cabin-class passage, 5 ounces for tween decks, and 3 ounces for peons in steerage. Two thousand gold seekers are reported to have left Chile that month.[2]

Bands of peons continued to trudge in from distant villages. Having no money, they took employment with new patrónes who boarded them on vessels in the harbor.[3] Contrary to statements that no women went to San Francisco, many families, including wives and daughters, embarked.[4] Merchants took advantage of the rush by advertising their shops as "a bit of California in Chile." Goods for sale were labeled in Spanish, "as like in California." Dealers offered "Sierra Nevada spades" and broad-brimmed mousquetaires' hats which they called "California sombreros." Dry goods soon fetched twice their normal value in Valparaiso because speculators hoped to resell in San

Francisco for prices four or five times higher.[5] Portable houses became good investments. Derricks hoisted them to the decks of California-bound ships. Agricultural supplies doubled in value, as wheat, barley, maize, beans, potatoes, and dried fruit were all in demand.

The high price paid for flour in San Francisco revolutionized the raising of wheat in Chile. Farmers plowed more ground to supply the future market.[6] The acreage in wheat more than doubled, most of the grain being raised near Concepción and on the bare hills around Santiago. Wages paid to farm workers rose from one-half and one real (6¢ and 12¢) a day to two reales.[7] Chile's eight flour mills, operated by North Americans in 1848, filled only 100 bags a day;[8] the bags were made of cloth imported from the United States. The foremost market for the flour was Peru, although shipments were also sent to Ecuador, Mexico, and Tahiti.[9] This pattern changed with the gold rush of 1849. New mills were built to supply the increased demand, and California was soon buying twice as much flour as Peru. In no time, commission firms in Valparaiso began competing for a monopoly in flour shipments. Among the leaders were Guillermo Gibbs y Cía. and A. Hemenway y Cía.[10] The house of Alsop y Cía. entered into a contract with all the millers in one southern district to deliver their wheat in Valparaiso at a fixed price.[11] Another dealer, Josué Waddington, contracted with wheat growers of the south for their entire crop, thus squeezing small mill owners to the wall.[12]

The economic dislocation worried many middle-class families, and Valparaiso's drama school principal, Rafael Minvielle, saw these unhappy individuals as a possible audience for a comedy ridiculing the gold rush. In haste he wrote a drama, *Ya No Voy a California*, and began rehearsing actors to play in it. He was one of those writers who persistently deride something or somebody. Born in Spain in 1800, the son of a French diplomat, he had been educated in France, where he ridiculed the reestablishment of a king in the land of "Liberty, Equality, Fraternity." In 1829 he emigrated to the free-wheeling city of perpetual revolutions, Buenos Aires. Here his radical writings got him into trouble with the dictator in power. A new location for his talents became imperative and he was attracted, like Pérez Rosales and other independent thinkers, to liberal Valparaiso, where he established a drama school. He achieved a reputation as a playwright and contributed opinions, couched in poetic language, to *El Mercurio*.[13]

The play he wrote to ridicule the gold rush concerned a man, a woman, her daughter, and a friend who were discussing a move to California. The leading part was to be enacted by popular Francisco Arana, and the opening performance was set for December 28, 1848. On that day a scathing editorial in *El Mercurio* should have helped the play. Under the heading MOVI-MIENTO DE POBLACIÓN, Pedro Felix Vicuña deplored the gold rush. He complained that the 2,000 emigrants to California had already taken a million pesos in cash from Chile, besides depriving the country of $6 million in services. He asked what the government was doing to stop the outflow. Valparaiso's skilled artisans, he said, left fine buildings in the city vacant and unattended. Houses that sheltered 2,000 souls stood empty while multitudes of rural strangers trudged through the streets. The only sound that relieved the silence caused by these vacancies came from the excited voices of men seeking passage to California.[14] An election was due to be held soon, and Vicuña urged readers to vote for a candidate who would restore the city's earlier ways of life. Here was the opportunity Andrés Bello had longed for!

The Valparaiso drama was staged in El Teatro de la República, a lofty, well-furnished building that seated from 1,800 to 2,000 persons.[15] On the opening night a discerning observer might have noticed that many of the ticket purchasers were California-bound emigrants who came for the fun of disrupting the play. When the lights were turned down for the raising of the first curtain, the usual constellation of sparks from smokers striking flint on steel to light their *cigarros*[16] seemed ominous. The crowd sat quietly, however, with only occasional hisses or applause from the pit when California was mentioned. But young men were busy in the gallery, and before long a huge imitation turkey, decorated with rattling tin cans, soared out across the audience. It was greeted with a peal of laughter, and the scenes that followed were interrupted by shrill whistles.[17]

This form of substantial criticism was repeated for an entirely different play four months later in New York. At the Astor Place Opera House, the gallery "b'hoys" protested a performance by throwing a chair down into the orchestra, causing "a prestissimo movement . . . not set down in the original music."[18] Later, the butchered carcass of a sheep sailed out from the gallery, much as the imitation turkey had in Valparaiso, and crashed at the feet of the leading man. The New York hoodlums might have learned these tactics from Valparaiso, but that is unlikely. Such exuberant demonstrations seem to have been fashionable both north and south of the equator.

In Valparaiso, at the end of the first act of *Ya No Voy a California*, the curtain remained down longer than usual and the audience grew impatient. Finally the theater manager came out to announce that Señor Arana had become suddenly ill and that, with the audience's permission, the performance would not continue. His statement caused renewed disorder, with shouts and shoving between men who wanted to talk and those who wanted to stop them. Some insisted on praising the gold seekers, saying they would come back rich men and, while in California, would enhance the reputation of Chile. Others, equally vociferous, censured their countrymen for interrupting a play that might stop the rush by making fun of it—not only stop the rush but save the gold seekers from terrible hardships and eventual disappointment.[19]

The comedy was performed once more, on January 4, 1849. This time Minvielle himself, the playwright and professor of dramatic art, played the leading part, but a contest between hisses and applause interrupted every act. Evidently supporters and opponents of the gold rush had come again, and they showed more interest in bombarding the actors with volleys of invectives than in listening to the theatrical dialogue. The editor of *El Progreso* in Santiago reported that the author may have created many dramatic incidents in his comedy, but anyone desiring to learn the truth about the gold rush would find the play uninteresting. The drama, he continued, although sustained, failed to hold the audience, and Professor Minvielle spoke his lines without animation.[20] An even more damning review appeared in *El Mercurio*, the paper that had supported Minvielle's project.*

A second comedy decrying the gold rush, written by playwright José Miguel Gacitúa, was *Consecuencias de un Viaje a California*. It also turned out to be a box-office mistake. Both Minvielle and Gacitúa failed to sense the spirit of adventure which motivated so many Chilean gold seekers.[21]

On February 5, 1849, the American, square-rigged *Huntress*, sixty days out of San Francisco, sailed into Valparaiso with 100,000 pesos worth of gold. On the same day the French brigantine *Perseverant* arrived, having made the trip from California in the record time of fifty-five days. She came in ballast, commanded by a captain eager to load goods, almost any kind of goods. He predicted profits of 400 percent, especially for Chilean flour.[22] The next day *El Mercurio*, under the caption ORO DE CALIFORNIA, printed extracts from the *Californian* disclosing that immense amounts of gold were being washed from the streams. One man, the paper said, washed 20,000 pesos worth in six days. Three others, in one day, washed out 36 pounds of pure gold.[23] Verifying these fantastic newspaper stories, a vessel arrived with $200,000† in gold. Reports said that every passenger and every sailor carried the precious metal. One man handed his wife a nugget weighing 18 ounces. The newspaper editor suspected that much additional gold was not declared. It could be smuggled easily and a sly man might not confess how much he had brought.

Letters that came from California were passed from hand to hand until they were worn out. All of them told about the remarkable breakdown in social classes. Men from the highest stations in Chile became laborers. The lawyer, the doctor, the deserting sailor all ranked equally, and no one carried a document showing the country of his origin.[24] Under the spell of

---

* Critics of drama since that day have adjudged *Ya No Voy a California* to be Minvielle's poorest production (José Pelaez y Tapia, *Historia de "El Mercurio"* [Santiago de Chile, 1927], pp. 82–83).

† In Spanish-American countries the dollar sign means "peso," not the United States dollar, although the value was approximately the same in 1849. Some Spanish writers put the symbol after, instead of in front of, the figures.

this news, applicants for passage to California pestered ship-masters until they refused to take any more on their over-loaded craft.[25] Many conservative Chileans saw the danger of losing the country's most vigorous citizens, and *El Mercurio* warned prospective emigrants that San Francisco with all its wealth, with gold as abundant as stones in the road, was still a city without government, a flimsy wooden city without a fire department and without doctors. The editor claimed that few intelligent people in the California city had any aspirations higher than the acquiring of wealth.[26]

The amount of gold being imported prompted *El Mercurio's* editor to urge the government to establish a bank in Valparaiso, or at least a branch of the Santiago bank which could mint gold coins.[27] The cost of shipping bars of gold in wagons across two mountain ridges was a useless extravagance, especially since the gold coins minted in Santiago would be hauled back to Valparaiso to be spent in foreign trade, a trade destined to make Chile one of the great nations of the world.[28]

In Santiago, both *El Progreso* and *La Tribuna* opposed the suggestion of establishing a mint in Valparaiso, and on Febru-ary 23 *El Mercurio* began a literary debate with *La Tribuna*,[29] the government-subsidized "paper of the people." *El Mercurio's* editor opened the discussion with a philosophical essay. He re-viewed Valparaiso's miraculous growth between 1833 and 1843, a period in which the city had became the most frequented port in the Pacific with the most cosmopolitan population. In that decade, he pointed out, Valparaiso had developed the largest merchant fleet in the Pacific, had become a center for copper exports, and had given Chile a reputation for progressive pros-perity throughout the world. All this, he said, was in danger of being revolutionized by the United States annexation of Cali-fornia. In direct competition with the norteamericanos, Chile might soon lose her superiority. Destined to be pushed into ob-scurity, it behooved her to profit as much as possible from the present California trade.[30] Already the cost of living had gone up. The price of rice had tripled, the charges for personal ser-vices had doubled, and transportation costs had become unbe-lievably high.[31] In May a sudden small-business boom added to the inflation. Shopkeepers who in the old days had barely survived on petty sales began taking in several hundred pesos a day.[32]

This boom came with the arrival of the first of the 8,000 Argonauts who left the eastern United States in January and early February.[33] Many of them had sailed on vessels barely seaworthy which stopped at Valparaiso for repairs and to restock their larders. The passengers, after months on shipboard, landed to stretch their legs and see the sights. On May 2, 1849, *El Mercurio*, noting that Valparaiso's streets were filled with fine young men glowing with the hope of riches, editorialized: "Here is a preview of the California of the future! With money in their purses the *Yanquis* buy everything, fill the theaters, lodge in the hotels. Here are a new people, reflecting the civilization of Europe, going to exploit a virgin territory."

El Comercio was sure to report the immigration differently from *El Mercurio*, and on the same day the former announced:

Valparaiso has been invaded by 500 citizens of the United States who fill the streets with the hats of Quakers or caps of oilcloth. These persons promenade along our thoroughfares with the aplomb of ancient Romans in a foreign city. At the sight of a coach such as they are used to seeing, they exclaim that it must have come by air from "Filadelphia." When forty or fifty walk along together the entire pavement is blocked. In the hotels they drink to the health of their country at all hours. They clean out the streetside peddlers of fruit, paying twice the asked price. At the theater they make a terrible noise, enter the first box they come to, and sit where they please.

Nevertheless these immigrants belong to a great nation whose power consists of the strength of its sons who travel around the world with complete indifference, and one wishes that they might return with their excellent qualifications and preoccupations to their own country. Without doubt these people have a promising future. They may be our salvation. With all their faults they have the strength of a great nation. As we have said previously, the egoism of these people is a decided virtue, and with this virtue they will go far.

To serve the tidal wave of American gold seekers, signs in English appeared throughout downtown Valparaiso. At the landing, immigrants were welcomed at the California Chop-House. Another restaurant announced in big letters that it was the Hole-in-the-Wall. Both were operated by Yankees. A dramshop proclaimed itself to be the Golden Lion. Other hotels, managed by men of various nationalities, bore such names as Star Hotel, Ship Head, Spanish Hotel, Chilean House, European Hotel, Hotel de France, and Victoria Hotel. The cost of board and lodging was reckoned in onzas, thus giving Americans their first taste of California, but the usual price amounted to only $1.50 a day.[34]

Travelers were offered souvenirs of every description, even birds of all sizes, from tiny parrots to gigantic condors with rings in their beaks. The latter were caught in the Andes, sometimes by a man who, lying under a fresh hide beside a carcass, snared the bird when it landed to eat. Condors were also trapped by killing a horse in a corral so small that when the birds came to feast they could not escape, for they needed more space to become airborne. One traveler measured the wingspread of a condor offered for sale and found it to be 11 feet, 10 inches.[35] Unlike most wild creatures, a full-grown condor, when captured, usually adjusted philosophically to its new surroundings, but still it was an inappropriate pet for a long voyage. In California, Argonauts would learn that prospectors used North American condor quills to carry gold. A single quill might store more than $100 worth of the precious dust.[36]

North American boys laughed at the sight of a cab with one horse in the shafts and another alongside pulling on a rope from the ring in a rider's saddle girth—birlocho fashion.[37] They laughed less heartily when Valparaiso's *vigilantes* arrested their comrades for riding horses at a gallop along the city streets. Four youths from Baltimore learned to their sorrow that *vigilantes* were good horsemen and also experts with ropes. These boys, seeing a livery stable, had hired horses and raced away. A *vigilante* called to them to halt. Three of the horses understood the command and stopped so suddenly that the riders slid front on their mounts' necks. The fourth rider, showing North American ego, clapped spurs to his horse. In an instant the *vigilante's* riata shot out, encircling and jerking him from the saddle.[38]

Most of the Argonauts, however, were law-abiding and hence were greeted hospitably in Valparaiso. They spent money freely.

The San Francisco riot had not yet occurred and newspaper accounts made earlier fights at the placers seem unimportant. Yet many Chileans still hoped to discourage emigration to California in spite of the failure of *Ya No Voy a California.* Another plan was tried by *El Mercurio,* which in June published a translation of Dr. J. Tyrwhitt Brooks's *Four Months among the Gold Fields,* a hoax used in English-speaking countries to discourage gold seekers. Entitled *El Nueva El Dorado,* the text was pure fiction in which the imaginary Dr. Brooks described his imaginary hardships and his lack of success in California. The book, accepted as truth by good authorities in England and in Australia, was quoted as a warning to prospective emigrants,[39] so *El Mercurio* may be excused for circulating it in Chile.[40]

On July 3, 1849, *El Mercurio* tried still another strategy, this time to discourage shippers. Heading a column TRIPULACIONES PARA NUESTROS BUQUES EN CALIFORNIA ("Crews for Our Vessels in California"), the paper warned sea captains that their crews would desert in San Francisco, leaving the vessels stranded. Speculators were told that the days of big profits had passed. Supplies from Australia had arrived in California as early as April and May. Now English, French, and German vessels must be unloading cargoes there, and only flour remained a profitable shipment. Then, on July 7, *El Mercurio,* still intent on stopping the gold rush, began to publish letters from California at the rate of almost one a day. These letters, written some two months before the riot in San Francisco, told of hardships and dangers, of conflicts with gringos over placer claims, but all the fights seemed minor and *El Mercurio* noted honestly that the reports were unconfirmed.

On the day the first letter appeared, *El Comercio,* always eager to outdo *El Mercurio,* became eloquent concerning gold in general and gold rushes in particular. The editor said the precious metal was a subject for poets and philosophers. It had caused strange vicissitudes in the lives of men, had made possible the amassing of great fortunes, and had visited many calamities upon mankind. Only the pursuers of occult ends, the seekers of mysterious treasures, or the inheritors of poor estates would be tempted to go to California. The act of looking for gold was not a legitimate occupation or a pursuit that encouraged stable habits or useful arts. Instead, it could be compared only with gambling. Even when it brought abundance and prosperity, it ruined the population for regular industry, making citizens incapable of performing work that created true wealth.[41]

Such speculative preaching fell on unhearing ears. Valparaiso businessmen were too busy dealing with the constantly increasing stream of gold seekers who stopped on their way to California. As early as May, hotelkeepers began putting up signs in English to attract patronage. Now, in July, big commission firms like Cross, Hobson y Cía. advertised their goods in English as well as in Spanish.[42] El Mercurio also announced in both languages the titles of books it had printed[43] in addition to Dr. Tyrwhitt Brooks's opus. These books were designed for North Americans coming ashore daily and for Chileans intent on perfecting their English to help them in business at home or on a trip to California.

For many Chileans the gold rush, like the Foreign Legion in France, had become a retreat for lost souls, for failures, for gentlemen ostracized after cheating at cards, and for swains disappointed in love. The tale of Joachim and his Mariquita* was typical, and Minvielle might have done better with Ya No Voy a California had he employed such a sentimental drama. According to a world traveler who visited San Francisco in 1849,[44] Joachim Vallenilla was a young and thriving merchant in Valparaiso. His wife, Mariquita, was romantic. His best friend, José, sang to Mariquita over the guitar. José and Mariquita lighted cigarettes together on the glowing coals in the silver brazier in the sala and watched the moonlight together from a vine-covered veranda. Joachim's friends, who never smoked cigarettes and had no ear for romantic music, put ideas into Joachim's businesslike head. Full of suspicions, he told Mariquita that he was going on a business trip to Santiago, to be gone

---

* The name "Mariquita" is important. Gauchos called a popular folk dance for two the Mariquita Machacha (Tito Saubidet Gauche, Vocabulario y Refranero criollo [Buenos Aires, 1943], p. 234). The Hebrew name Joachim was in common use until the nineteenth-century revisions of Spanish changed it to Joaquín.

a week. He kissed her good-bye in the afternoon; then, at midnight, leaving his shoes in the hall, he tiptoed into his wife's bedchamber. Pulling aside the curtains he saw two persons asleep.

It was not Joachim's purpose to disturb the repose of persons who were no doubt fatigued. Instead, he left his hat and dirk on the table and retired, as quietly as he had entered, to another chamber where he went to bed. In the morning, a lovely morning, Joachim arose at his usual hour and, when breakfast was laid, commanded the servant to say to his mistress that her husband waited, affectionate and hungry. Mariquita sent back word that she had a dreadful headache, having passed a wretched night. Would her "dear, kind love" excuse her?

Her dear, kind love would not. For him her presence was essential to his appetite; he could not live without her. The servant took this message and returned with another plea: "Only this once, dear Joachim. Indeed, she cannot come now; this evening, this afternoon, in an hour or so."

Joachim sent back his reply: Your "dear Joachim" is anxious now, really alarmed; he will come to his darling, his Mariquita, his Mariquita, his Mariquita, his pet of the endless diminutives; he will bring to her bedside the plantains and chocolate.

"Oh, no, no!" Mariquita will not hear of that; her Joachim shall not go to all that trouble for a foolish headache; besides she is better now and will come at once.

At this point in the story the reader is told that there is in Chile a quaint satirical rogue of a law which requires that if a man detect his wife in wantonness, he shall not take her life or maim or bruise her. He may, however, dismiss her from his bed and board, drive her out into the highway, naked if he will; only he shall first give her shoes for her feet and a loaf of bread, or its equivalent of one real.

When Mariquita came down to breakfast, pale, hoarse, rigid, biting her lips, all was as usual—plantains, chocolate, buns, flowers, and Joachim—except that at her place, beside her plate, were a pair of old slippers and a battered real.

At first she would have fainted, and then she would have fled; but just in time her eyes met the eyes of Joachim and found something there which forbade either movement. So she sat still, very still, toying with her chocolate while he, the sublime genius of ruthless retribution, talked carelessly about the mists in the vineyards, the white nightcap of Monte Diablo, and the glancing gulls seaward. Finally, at the end of what seemed to her an accursed lifetime, he arose and bowed; then she, without a look or a word from first to last, retired to her chamber.

So it went on for a month. Joaquim met his wife only at breakfast, and always there were the slippers and the real, the silence and the flippant mockery, the agony and the anguish. Once Mariquita thought of escaping, but the closed doors, with their bolts and bars, mocked her, and paid servants were deaf and merely bowed to her. Once she flung herself, abject, at Joachim's feet and would have clasped his knees, imploring him to slay her, to beat her to death with slow installments of stripes, if only he would take away the slippers and the real. But Joachim tapped the bell, forcing her to pick herself up in awkward, foolish confusion.

In another month she was happy, playing idiotically with the real and maundering baby songs over the slippers. Joachim then converted all his wordly goods into a piece of paper and sent her home with it to her father. As for José, if he did not die a natural death, he is probably living now. "¿Quién sabe?" thought Joachim, who took $100 and sailed for San Francisco, where he became the Spanish permit clerk in the Old Adobe.

15

French Aragonautes
Become Argonautes

Ya No Voy a California had been hooted off the Valparaiso stage in the midsummer months of December and January, when the roads were open for emigrant gold seekers to flock in from Santiago and other smaller towns. In May and June the cold, rainy season commenced. Poplar trees along the irrigation ditches dropped their leaves in golden showers, and after every storm, when the clouds lifted, nearby mountains displayed caps of snow. During these winter months the attitude toward the gold rush became much more critical and severe. To enact legislation regulating emigration, the people of Valparaiso had elected Andrés Bello a senator in the Chilean congress (the Cámaras).

Although the San Francisco riot had not yet occurred, debates concerning California were already bitter, and in May a ministerial crisis loomed.[1] Reports of Senator Bello's activities came to Valparaiso almost daily for printing in the newspapers. Readers learned that he continually warned his colleagues about the effect of the gold rush on Chile's economy. The new market for flour seemed excellent, but shipping it and other merchandise to California had emptied Chilean harbors of vessels. Normal commerce had been interrupted, and communication and trade with coastal towns all but destroyed. Bello, viewing the situation with alarm, said that something must be done at once; a remedy was *"urgente."*[2] With his usual literary flair he told the senators that 119 vessels had formerly traded along the Chilean coast and that now only 27 of them remained. All the others had gone to California. These were the vessels that had crowded the harbor at Mazatlán when the *California* anchored at its entrance. During their absence from Chile farm products of the small agricultural communities reached Valparaiso only at rare intervals, making the home market as uncertain as San Francisco's. If conditions became worse there might be a food shortage.

This dilemma and *Ya No Voy a California*'s failure made the opening of a new play concerning the gold rush a risky undertaking, especially since more ships and more gold seekers were going constantly to California. Then, to make the situation worse, the president of the Senate, Diego José Benavente, announced that only 3,000 passports had been issued although a much larger number of emigrants had left. He suggested that the Senate, instead of winking at evasion of the law, should pass legislation that would abolish the passport system, thus saving trouble and expense.[3] Although making emigration easier instead of harder seemed to be against the interests of Bello's Valparaiso constituents, a law was prepared for that purpose. Before it came to a vote the big, 678-ton French *Édouard* sailed into the harbor on August 2, 1849, with a theatrical troupe on board.[4] The *Édouard* had left Le Havre-de-Grâce, as Le Havre was then called, more than four months earlier, and on the voyage the impatient passengers had quarreled with Captain Curet. In Valparaiso they appealed to the French consul for redress— a common practice in gold-rush days. No doubt the vessel needed repairs because she remained in port almost two months.

The presence of a French ship with unhappy passengers may seem irrelevant to debates concerning the gold rush in the Cámaras across the mountains at Santiago. The passengers on this ship, however, were professional actors who planned to make a little money while in port, and their reception might indicate whether the popular attitude toward the gold rush had changed since mobs had closed earlier theatrical performances. A few wealthy families were making money in the California trade, but others certainly were not. Although more coal was being mined in southern Chile than ever before,[5] many of the finest residences in Valparaiso could no longer be heated during the cold winter season because few barges were available to bring the fuel north from Concepción.[6] Indeed, wealthy persons might well be reduced to the charcoal living standards of peons. As for Pisco brandy in pear-shaped crocks, no vessel was regularly importing it. Worst of all, merchants might soon lack supplies to sell to the passengers on the five or six foreign vessels that dropped anchor almost every day in Valparaiso.

This trade had become important. Each vessel paid $500 for port fees and visas,[7] yielding a good income for the port authority. In addition, if fifty passengers from each vessel—a conservative estimate—came ashore with only $10 apiece to spend, and no merchandise was available, city shopkeepers would lose $500 in sales from each of the five or six ships docking daily, or at least $2,500. Records show that visitors from the United States alone spent from $1 to $1.5 million in Valparaiso during the first twelve months of the gold rush, and many vessels carrying Argonauts from Europe added to this amount.[8] The excess of currency and a limited supply of goods had already led to a dangerous rise in prices, and as gold became more plentiful and goods more scarce inflation threatened a real economic disaster.

To prevent a possible shortage of merchandise, some members of the Cámaras suggested that foreign vessels be allowed to engage in the coastal trade and that foreign owners pay license fees no larger than those charged Chilean owners. The local navigators' representatives objected to what they deemed unfair foreign competition. Conciliators suggested that the plan be followed for only one year, but even this proposal was voted down. Finally a compromise was agreed upon: foreign traders were granted equal rights until Chilean vessels returned from California.

Some wealthy traders who had lost money shipping to California complained that United States customs fees favored importers from other countries. They demanded that a new treaty be negotiated.[9] The statesmen agreed, but another shipping problem had to be settled by compromise—one of those arrangements that seemed to be a compromise although only one side benefited. Speculators who found their cargo duplicated by half a dozen other vessels in San Francisco had lost heavily. Old established firms, operated by Chile's best families, were reported to be on the verge of bankruptcy. To favor them, the minister of finance proposed a law to exempt them from paying import duties on goods for a specific period. His bill passed with a tricky amendment that kept it from going into effect until after the exemption period had passed.[10]

In the midst of these political shenanigans in Santiago, the French actors made plans for their first performance in Valparaiso. They called themselves gold-seeking *Aragonautes*, not *Argonautes*. Both names had dangerous connotations in town. Would the actors' performance contain the objectionable features that ruined *Ya No Voy a California*? The actors explained that the name they had chosen was a tribute to their leader, Jacques Arago, a popular writer who had lost favor in France after his brother François had taken a prominent part in opposing the election of royalist Louis Napoleon to the presidency. Jacques, a world traveler, had visited Valparaiso earlier. Now fifty years old[11] and blind, he was internationally known as a novelist, a playwright, and a critic of both opera and ballet.[12] *El Mercurio* had approved the propaganda against the gold rush in *Ya No Voy a California*, criticizing only the dramatic composition. The newspaper's editor greeted the new players with enthusiasm, saying nothing about the gold rush. Instead he lauded Jacques as the author of the widely acclaimed drama, *Carcajada* ("Loud Laughter"), a Spanish translation of his *L'Éclat de Rire*.[13] Here was a French artist much greater than Rafael Minvielle who had also departed king-ridden France, seeking liberty in Latin America.

Educated Chileans always considered good drama more important than searching for California gold. French art and French music were invariably admired by the "best people," but there might still be a few radicals in town waiting for an opportunity to heckle the actors, as anti-gold rush enthusiasts had heckled *Ya No Voy a California*. Yet the editors of *El Mercurio* and *El Comercio* prophesied no trouble. Both reflected

Chileans' love of France and, to keep readers in touch with French culture, both printed French novels serially in each day's issue. *El Mercurio's* readers could peruse one of Paul Feval's novels, *El Hijo del Diablo* ("Son of the Devil"), while *El Comercio* was treating its subscribers to a translation of Eugène Sue's *Teresa Dovoyer*.

With the arrival of Jacques Arago, both papers announced with apparent delight that a great connoisseur of the arts—albeit a gold seeker—had come to Valparaiso. Here was a man personally acquainted with Balzac, Dumas, Victor Hugo, and George Sand, a man from the operatic world of Chopin, Liszt, and Schumann, who had listened to Madame Grisi's soprano interpretations of Rossini's operas and had seen, before his eyes failed, Taglioni toe-dance across the stage, light as thistledown, a form of dancing now at the peak of perfection and popularity in Europe.[14] The editor of *El Mercurio* saluted the illustrious French visitor with a special editorial, and Jacques's published reply may be translated as follows:

Yes, Señor, although blind, I am taking to California fifty energetic men, all with promising futures. They have faith in me and I in them. We go forward like soldiers advancing against the fury of the elements. As good soldiers they remove the difficulties ahead. They shorten the lengthy pilgrimage.[15]

Aided by the favorable newspaper publicity, the theatrical troupe made an alliance with Mateo O'Loghlin, manager of Valparaiso's theatrical stock company. A joint performance was prepared for Monday, August 13, and the newspapers congratulated Señor O'Loghlin for enlisting such distinguished actors. Two days before the first show both papers announced that the French players, on their way to establish a colony in California, would render songs and music from the best French operas. Neither paper suggested that the performance might be interrupted.

When the curtain rose on the opening night, Jacques Arago sat in a box between two young ladies dressed in white. Chileans appreciated good music and the theater supported an excellent orchestra. The program included a sentimental playlet Jacques had written, entitled *Un Dia en Valparaiso*, and one observer reported that many white gloves in the audience split during the enthusiastic applause. Blind Arago stood up and bowed his white head in appreciation.[16] No heckling marred the performance. Valparaiso had become reconciled to foreign gold seekers, especially if they were French.

The next day the ever poetic *El Mercurio* praised the play, calling the actors "gifted pilgrims bound for strange lands, like birds of passage that pause for a moment on some branch where they sing with exuberance before renewing their flight and leaving the land that has sheltered them for a day. . . . In all sections of Valparaiso they have found the same sympathy and appreciation."[17]

Perhaps it was more than a coincidence that the next issue of *El Mercurio* carried an advertisement for passengers to California on Captain Curet's "hermoso *Édouard*."[18] Had some of the gold-seeking actors, entranced by their reception, decided to remain in Valparaiso? Did they remember their quarrel with the captain and their appeal to the French consul for redress, or was the captain booking additional passengers and hoping to be rid of actors? Time would tell. Certainly he was offering cabin-class and tween-decks passage to California for 200 and 100 pesos, respectively. However that may be, Arago and three of the actors, Prat, Delamarre, and Féron, announced their participation in another performance on August 21, and the papers made it a point to maintain that the troupe was still on its way to California.

This *grande función extraordinaria* commenced at eight o'clock in the evening. That same day five vessels bound for California sailed into the harbor,[19] so the theater's pit and gallery were sure to be crowded with North American gold seekers as well as local townsmen. The performance comprised three acts, the first a playlet entitled *The Little Grandfather*. The second act consisted of five skits and songs ending with "La République," sung by Prat, Delamarre, and Féron. This patriotic lyric, written by Arago after he had become disillusioned by republicanism in France, received such hearty applause that the blind author appeared for a curtain call. Feeling his way with one hand on the curtain, he faced the audience and expressed in a few words his appreciation of the response, adding that he had found in Chile a second home.[20] Here was another hint that the troupe might not go on to California.

Act III repeated Arago's *Un Jour à Valparaiso*, with the Frenchmen speaking in their language while O'Loghlin spoke his part in Spanish.[21] Once more applause rocked the house, and when the last curtain came down some of the actors, washing the makeup from their faces, may also have washed away their eagerness for prospecting in California. Perhaps gold was easier to find in this hospitable city than in San Francisco. Two of the performers, Legier and Mirlin, accepted further employment, the former to sing extracts from the ever popular *Lucia di Lammermoor*.[22] Two other Frenchmen appeared in a French comedy translated into Spanish and renamed, *Tio Pablo o la Educación*.[23]

Chile's winter rains had stopped, and the actors, quaffing tintos at little tables in the side streets, could see that the surrounding mountain ridge had turned green. Wild flowers twinkled on the slopes and the air smelled as fresh as springtime on the Champs Élysées. Did the actors remember other flowers twinkling beneath the Paris chestnut trees when the air smelled fresh in May? Did they long for that wide boulevard and its ever flowing river of humanity speaking their own language? But Paris under an emperor would never again be the Paris they had loved. For these devotees of art and believers in democracy, the Comédie Française and the Quai Voltaire must henceforth be only memories. Gone from their lives forever were the animated men at streetside tables who discussed the latest play as they sipped drinks, iridescent as liquid jewels in their glasses. California might promise liberalism and gold, but gold would not buy the Paris of their dreams, and the fogs in San Francisco, come winter, were sure to be cold and disagreeable. Indeed, the temptation was strong for men of the theater to remain in Chile where they were appreciated. But would they?

The *Édouard* was not due to sail for another three weeks and, although the French actors worked continually to keep their names before the public, other distractions occasionally disturbed and amused the city. Every day one to two hundred foreigners from California-bound vessels came ashore, wandered through the streets, laughed at the North American names on bars and restaurants, hired saddle horses to ride up the ridge above Valparaiso, tarried in the market buying oranges and lemons for a few pennies, paying higher prices for the sweet potatoes imported from Peru and for *Aconcaguas*, giant strawberries named for the big mountain.

Late in August the crew of a German ship bound for California mutinied and came ashore. The captain appealed to the police who put the sailors in barred wagons, like circus animal cages, and returned them to their vessel with a warning not to land again; they could do as they pleased in San Francisco, but not in Valparaiso.[24] The *Édouard* was still unprepared to leave for California when another German vessel, the *Reform*, arrived in port. Her dissatisfied passengers appealed to their consul for the usual redress, but, pleading previous commitments, he postponed a hearing. After eight days the passengers had spent all their money living on shore so they returned to the vessel. Like it or not, they were obliged to continue their voyage to California.[25]

During these delays the French actors appeared in various plays, always emphasizing their French background and the sophisticated Paris from which they came. Yet they never let audiences forget their adventurous quest for golden fleeces in California, and invariably they were applauded. No performance was interrupted by the derision that had greeted *Ya No Voy a California*, although the newspapers continued to warn speculators about the risks of trade in the gold country. One editor observed, with poetic metaphors, that prices in San Francisco were like the ocean tides, high when goods were scarce and dismally low when several vessels arrived at the same time with similar cargoes. Merchants who believed themselves far-sighted had shipped portable houses for the fast-growing metropolis, only to find such habitations abundant. The unloading charges and sales commissions consumed any profit.[26]

After a performance on August 23, the actors probably read a letter printed in that day's newspaper[27] which made them pause and ponder while still humming the melody of *Un Día en*

Valparaiso. The letter, written in San Francisco, was dated June 11, 1849, more than a month before the riot. The newspaper editor assured his readers that the writer was a mature and energetic man who feared neither work nor fatigue and who wrote with the sincerity of one brother to another. A translation follows:

Here a man must be a natural philosopher willing to exchange intellectual for bodily pleasures. If born into another world, totally different in customs, he will not die here of hunger, but he may die of fatigue and infirmities.

There is gold in the mines and it may be had with work. Each time I think about the amount I am carrying it scares me. To come here one pays a huge price in bodily punishment for his ambition, and at the same time one exposes oneself to uselessness.

The French actors, searching through the papers for news about themselves, must have seen the letter and, being interested in California, they probably worked hard at translating it. If so, they learned that California:

. . . is a country of anomalies. He who arrives with food casts it into the sea in spite of the fact that it sells for a high price on shore. This is natural considering conditions in town and the high wages there. No religion dominates here and the only fiesta is Sunday when nobody works although there is no law against it. The governor is as small a figure as the captain of the port. A man may be threatened with hanging for stealing two dollars. Other crimes are ignored. Gambling is allowed in public and is even protected.

Life here is chaos [*Esto es un caos*]. Many are preparing to return to Valparaiso, weary and infirm. They are beginning to despair of finding gold anywhere on the American continent. As for me, I went to the mines without illusions. I came to taste adventure at any cost.

May I tell those friends who had the prudence to wait for positive reports from this country that they are lucky? [28]

Perplexing letters of this kind in newspapers[29] may have enlightened persons "born into another world, totally different in customs." Certainly the so-called *caos* in California put an idea into the head of a clever *coyote* ("sly manipulator"). Colonel Correa da Costa arrived in Valparaiso with excellent recommendations. He came with a letter of introduction to Pedro Alessandri. Don Pedro was a patron of the arts, for which Valparaiso was famous, and he eventually operated the Teatro de la Victoria where the French actors played. During the days when Valparaiso was agog over the Frenchmen, a letter to Señor Alessandri was an introduction of importance, and the colonel made the most of it. He offered to help Spanish-speaking investors who wished to send goods to California. Speculators who had failed in the past, he said, had nobody but themselves to blame. Many of them spoke no English, showed no respect for North American practices, and made fun of gringo manners. He told prospective speculators that shippers who did not understand North American courtesies of trade would find the road to success if they consulted him in his room at the Hotel de Chile. He charged only the usual commission and the cost of remitting sales profits to Chile.[30]

How many shippers engaged the colonel's services cannot now be determined, nor is it known whether any goods loaded on the *Édouard* were in his charge when she finally cleared to sail. The French actors were on board, but Jacques Arago was not with them. They had continued their performances until the day before sailing without making any references to abandoning their leader. The first intimation that they were leaving him came in the official announcement of the "Last Grand Function of the French Artists," which merely failed to include his name in the play's roster.[31] The announcement did say, without further comment, that the performance would conclude with a ballet entitled *La Jota Aragonesa* ("Aragonian Folk Dance").[32] Did the adjective refer to the province in Spain or was it a pun on Jacques Arago's surname? The female dancer in the act was a new performer, listed as Señorita Charlotte, a black-haired damsel who no doubt romanticized her eyes with belladonna and etched her lashes with mascara.

The next day the omission of Arago's name was explained in the players' grand finale, which they "performed" in the press, not on the stage. Both papers announced that Jacques Arago would not lead the "fifty energetic men" who were to follow him "like soldiers advancing against the fury of the elements." The announcement was made by Jacques himself in the form of a long personal farewell to his followers. Written in French, a

Spanish translation followed it. In part, Jacques said: "My companions go forth seeking adventure. I am old but I go on with them in spirit. They will work in water to their knees in a land of bears, of the puma, and the antelope, in the Mountains of the Rocks, but they have good hearts and red blood." The letter concluded: "Courage, then, my friends, and stay together. I say not adieu to my Aragonautes, but au revoir. Jacques Arago."[33]

The blind man had spent many hours composing this document, and on October 3, 1849, the day after it was published, the *Édouard* set sail. Along her lofty yards topmen clung where square sails were furled. A fresh breeze whipped their bell-bottom trousers. At a sharp command the heavy sheets fell and filled with wind. Down on deck a fifer played "La Marseillaise," and the French actors were off at last for California. Before sailing they had written their leader a flowery reply, signed "Les Aragonautes." Both newspapers printed it in French and Spanish on the day the *Édouard* sailed out of sight.[34]

The editor of *El Mercurio*, smelling manure under the lush language, asked pointedly why this troupe was leaving its blind leader in a strange country, without relatives or money.* Several reasons may have caused the players' breakup. Fear of violence against foreigners in California seems the most likely. The French *Chateaubriand* left San Francisco on July 8, at the time Chileans were flocking into town after being expelled from the diggings. She reached Valparaiso on September 24,[35] with reports easily understood by Frenchmen. Then, two days later, the really bad news arrived. A British coastal steamer from Callao brought a copy of *El Comercio de Lima* which contained a detailed description of the San Francisco riot, translated from *Alta California* of August 2, 1849. With the long account available in Spanish, *El Mercurio* devoted three columns to Samuel Roberts and his rioters.[36] The report probably convinced Jacques Arago and his company that California was no place for a blind poet who was no longer young, no matter how eminent his talents.[37]

---

* Jacques Arago died six years later when the vessel in which he was traveling stopped briefly in Brazil.

Arago's actors, however, men to the manner born, still saw the gold rush as a curtain call to the drama of a lifetime. Undaunted, these French Argonautes sailed away, taking with them one thing that men "born into another world, totally different in customs," can always take, even into the most primitive society, something that no mob and no misfortune could take from them: a knowledge of, and a feel for, the best music of their time.

Businessmen in Chile
Promote Washington City
in California

Gold, gold, gold, gold,
Hard to get and harder to hold!

When the French players left Valparaiso in October, 1849,[1] the debates in the Chilean congress had reached a bitterness that led directly to the second government crisis. This crisis of 1850 ended in revolution, an unusual catastrophe for the normally durable establishment in Chile. During the summer of 1849 the debates had shifted from the expediency of protecting commerce and ameliorating the lot of Chilean gold seekers in California to a question of national honor. The senators began to polarize on the policy to be followed, and the minister of marine requested an increased appropriation to build ships for the Chilean navy.[2] He complained that the sun was setting on Chile's great naval heritage. The best young men sought other careers. Seventy-three of the eighty youths being trained at the naval academy in the tradition of Lord Cochrane had already gone to California and might never return.[3]

Members of the minister's party applauded his request for more money. Certainly, they said, Chile's four sailing vessels and one steamer formed an inadequate navy,[4] and unless more war vessels were built Peru's new president, the aggressive Castilla, would rule the South Pacific. Had he not already boasted that he would build two vessels for each one constructed in Chile? Had he not already sent his warship, *Jeneral Gamarra*, to protect Peruvians in California? Chile, proud of being the outstanding naval power of Latin America, must send a comparable vessel, at least the frigate *Chile*.[5]

The minister of marine's request for money and the oral support of his backers brought the simmering debate in the Cámaras to a boil. The bad treatment of Chileans at the California diggings, even before the San Francisco riot, had been mentioned continually in the congress, but now these outrages became a decisive element in the government crisis.[6] One group, opposed to sending a warship, pointed out that Peru's *Gamarra*, although arriving before the riot, had failed to prevent it.[7] They argued that all Chile could expect, by sending such a vessel, would be the probability of war with the United States. The opposition shouted, with their best patriotic oratory, that Chile must not permit inferior Peru to outdo her in this international affair. Perhaps the *Gamarra* had failed to stop the riot in San Francisco, but she had aided the merchant marine in the harbor.[8] Sending a vessel to protect human lives would never be construed as an act of war. The Peruvian *Gamarra*, instead of causing war, had been saluted by the United States as the representative of a sovereign power. Chile deserved equal recognition.[9]

Chilean newspapers joined the politicians in this debate, eager to defend or defeat any resolution to send a warship to California. One editor said that a sampling of letters from gold seekers disclosed that some had been treated well while others were less fortunate. Certainly the average emigrant should be prepared to take his chances. Of the 4,000 or 5,000 people who had gone from Chile, only a few had appealed for protection. Did this small number of complaints justify the exorbitant expense of sending a warship?[10]

The dispute was settled temporarily by a compromise of sorts. Chile enjoyed unusually friendly relations with Great Britain. Indeed, British warships carried Chilean mail along the coast,[11] and Captain Shepard of the man-of-war, *Inconstant*, was requested to bring back from California any Chileans who desired to come. The Cámaras voted 40,000 pesos for their repatriation, and the *Inconstant* sailed on August 20, 1849.[12]

On December 24, 1849, the *Inconstant* returned, bringing a

copy of California's new constitution as well as news of the situation in San Francisco. Captain Shepard reported that he had permitted none of his sailors to land. When going ashore himself, he was rowed by midshipmen. He said that he had put sufficient men on board several stranded vessels to enable them to sail. He also reported that Great Britain was sending spare crews to California to bring back deserted British ships.[13] As for the distressed Chileans Captain Shepard was authorized to bring, he arrived too late to prevent a tragedy greater than the San Francisco riot (an event to be recounted later). In spite of his offer of free transportation home, only six homesick Chileans came with him.[14] The small number gave both factions in the congress a new premise for their arguments.

During the long debates over sending the warship to California, giving relief to speculators who had suffered in San Francisco, and aiding Valparaiso merchants who could not get supplies to sell, ship after ship arrived from California with more gold. In one period of six days, three vessels brought 3,533 ounces of dust.[15] This amounted to approximately $60,000 of currency in addition to the $2,500 that was often spent every day in Valparaiso by passengers coming ashore from northbound vessels. So large an inflow completely upset the economy of a town of 30,000.[16]

Indeed, California gold had become commonplace in Valparaiso, and merchants often attracted customers by displaying unusually shaped nuggets. *El Mercurio,* under the heading PEPITA MONSTRUO DE ORO, announced that a person recently returned from California had brought back a chunk of quartz the size and shape of a human foot, laced throughout with gold. This curiosity, on display in a store on Calle del Cabo, weighed 90 ounces and cost the owner $1,200 in San Francisco.[17] Many North Americans on their way to California saw their first gold in Valparaiso and purchased samples of it to keep as relics.[18] Gold in another form, also a novelty, soon appeared in Valparaiso. Gold eagles, minted in San Francisco, became accepted currency in town. Also in circulation were United States half eagles, which were described as being slightly smaller and thicker than the Chilean half ounce.[19]

With this influx of gold, and almost daily additions to it, the stories of persecutions in California seemed inconsequential. Gold, gold, and how to go to California for more gold, became the topic of the day. Shipowners advertised nine vessels for San Francisco during the week the French actors sailed. Then, the following week, the Ecuadorian *Ann McKim* arrived from California with passengers whose experiences might make the bravest adventurers reconsider the ocean voyage. She brought 1,533 ounces of gold, but she had put to sea with insufficient water and, before reaching Valparaiso, ten passengers were prostrated by dehydration.[20] Here was a situation that port authorities determined should not happen again. The *Ann McKim* was taken from Captain Vanpelt, and she sailed back to California in December under Chilean registry.[21]

In the first week of November the Chilean *Jeneral Freire*, to which the refugees had fled during the San Francisco riot, sailed into Valparaiso and dropped anchor. She and two vessels with her brought 200,000 pesos worth of gold.[22] Within a week more gold, valued in excess of $20,000, arrived.[23] The Chileans bringing this treasure had all become rich men and, like most men who have survived hardships and become rich, they showed little concern about their treatment in California. Life had been difficult for many of them in Chile, but, as true rotos, they could work or fight furiously or take adversity with fatalistic calm.

The boom in the last quarter of 1849 attracted new English-speaking businessmen to Valparaiso. In 1848 Spanish-language newspapers had announced big transactions like ship auctions in English and Spanish. Since July, 1849, commission firms had offered their services in both languages.[24] In August the United States customs duties were printed in English,[25] and in September the number of business advertisements in both languages increased markedly. The Board of Underwriters stated in English and Spanish that any master who deserted his vessel in California would be suspended and no insurance would be paid on his craft.[26] To prevent debtors from escaping their obligations by going to California, the names of all passengers were published before each vessel sailed.[27]

During the entire year of 1849, records showed that 303 cargo vessels sailed out of Valparaiso for California,[28] and that 53 of them were Chilean.[29] The shipping from other Chilean ports also increased. At Talcahuano, the port for Concepción on the Bio-Bio River, 70 United States vessels had called in 1848. In 1849 the number rose to 135, and in 1850, the peak year, 198 ships stopped there.[30] Don Pedro Río y Cruz, who had operated 70 vessels in the coastal trade, sent all of them with cargoes to California in 1849 and began to build more ships. Josué Waddington, who was trying to corner the southern Chile wheat crop, joined with Don Pedro and other capitalists to organize the Compañía Nacional de Valparaiso which established seven shipyards* at Constitución, a much safer harbor than Valparaiso.[31] In spite of Senator Bello's predictions, many Chileans were prospering. The 119 vessels in Chile's merchant marine increased to 159 in 1850 and to 257 by 1855.[32]

This economic explosion appears exciting on paper and it surely must have been for many men, but some who were in the thickest of it failed to realize its importance. Perhaps the incidents that historical writers preserve for posterity were unimportant to many contemporaries. In the United States the great historian, Francis Parkman, failed to see the significance of the Oregon Trail although he traveled along it during one of its best years. During the French Reign of Terror, actors performed regularly for undisturbed Paris audiences. In Valparaiso, on October 25, 1849, when Lieutenant J. M. Gilliss arrived in the harbor on his way to Santiago,[33] he noted in his journal that the harbor was full of vessels but he said practically nothing about a gold rush. He was a scientist, not a gold seeker, and instead of sailing around the Horn he had crossed the Isthmus of Panama and cruised down the coast counter to the northward emigration, stopping at both Callao and Valparaiso.

Lieutenant Gilliss planned to establish a meteorological observatory sponsored by the American Philosophical Society of Philadelphia. A close observer, he was trained to record details carefully, but he failed to note any difference between the activi-

---

* Seven seems an excessive number of shipyards. The author may have meant slipways or building ways, but the literal translation of his Spanish word *astilleros* is "shipyards," or what the British call "dockyards."

ties in the Pacific harbors and those in Philadelphia and Baltimore. He did, however, show deep interest in an odd occurrence in Santiago which has been overlooked in gold-rush narratives.

In Santiago, where the debates over the gold rush had become really malicious, Lieutenant Gilliss, after registering at a hotel on November 8, retired for the night. Suddenly he was awakened by a jolt, and his bedstead hammered repeatedly against the wall. He stepped out on the trembling floor and looked into the patio. Guests were assembling there or running into the street, and some women, he said, wore clothes that perhaps were permissible for a costume ball but certainly were not a la mode.[34] Gilliss had never felt an earthquake and he recorded this one in meticulous detail. Before the end of the month he would record thirty more quakes, temblors that terrified the natives but somehow have been omitted from gold seekers' accounts. Perhaps the vessels in Valparaiso harbor did not shake.

Lieutenant Gilliss noticed that the citizens in seaport towns differed sharply from those in Santiago, where the lower classes seemed to have more Indian blood; certainly the faces in the Guardia Nacional were copper-colored.[35] He noticed, too, that drinking water in Santiago was as scarce as it was in Valparaiso. Mules brought the water down the streets in eight- and ten-gallon kegs. A water boy usually sat on the mule's back between the kegs. He served the water through spigots, being careful to keep a balance on each side of the mule. Sometimes, as the mule jogged along between the adobe houses, one of the spigots fell off, and water gushed out. The loss of weight upset the balance, and the full keg dragged the packsaddle over, unseating the boy and amusing pedestrians.[36]

As has been said, the Chilean congress was in session during these earthquakes, and the debates were bitter. Perhaps jealousy of the prosperity for some people in Valparaiso added to the spitefulness. The vast majority of Chileans were poor and many of them ignored the gold rush entirely. Certainly the gold rush had no effect on Santiago's public market, where each morning smelly, straw-hatted peons from the country trudged in with donkeys bearing live chickens, fruit, cantaloupes, watermelons, bread, and crocks of milk.[37] In hastily constructed cloth booths, merchants offered *helados* ("ices") flavored with cinnamon, coffee, or chocolate.[38] These delicacies were made from snow or hail brought from the Andes.

At noon the country people packed their goods and trudged homeward. None of them seemed concerned about the debates on California in the congress. Downtown shops closed for the usual siesta, and when they reopened ladies of the upper classes appeared for the first time to shop. They usually returned home before the sun sank behind the western mountains and the church bells announced the *oración* ("evening prayer"). At that time every man stopped and uncovered his head for a few minutes.[39] Soon afterward, lanterns were lighted and trading continued until midnight.[40]

The fatalism so characteristic of the Chilean miners in California who clung to their claims against overwhelming odds or returned to them in the face of imminent danger was noticeable in their home country. Acceptance by the poor people of disaster and death could be seen in Chile when a man was convicted of murder. On the day of execution a hundred poor people might assemble when the convict was dragged off on a hurdle. Without remonstrance they would watch the victim die, and as his life flickered out, they all cried, "Ave! Ave!" Then the peons would spend some of their scant money to buy candles to mark the spot where a human soul had passed away.[41] Such people, as Californians had learned, can be killed, but their faith is eternal.

A very different picture of people in another Chilean city during the gold rush has been drawn by Enos Christman, a twenty-year-old apprentice printer from West Chester, Pennsylvania, who sailed into Valparaiso aboard the *Europe* on November 23, 1849. Within six months he would be editor of the *Herald* in Sonora, California, so his first impression of the Chileans he later knew so intimately is interesting. While still on the ship he noted that there were seventy to eighty vessels in the harbor, with three or four arriving or leaving every day. He estimated that half of them were from North America.[42] In fact, ninety-six vessels from Atlantic ports left Valparaiso for California in November, 1849.[43] Christmas watched boatloads of men, both passengers and crew, visit back and forth from ship to ship. Toward evening bevies of Chilean girls came out in rowboats and there was dancing and drinking on quarter-decks until midnight.[44]

In the morning Christman hired a boatman to row him to shore. The fare, he said, was 1 to 2 reales[45] (a real was worth 12½ cents), according to the customer's ability to bargain. Walking up the cobblestone streets, Christman looked at the one-story, floorless houses, roofed with what he called "hay," and thought them very primitive. A few, he admitted, had three stories, but all the windows he could see were behind iron bars. The bars seemed so different from the painted shutters on West Chester's neat brick residences. He also noticed big houses on the hillside, surrounded by beautiful rose gardens and orange and peach trees. Men in the streets wearing ponchos amused him, and he marveled at the magnificent sculpture in the cemetery[46]—the Waddington memorial, of course.

The Pennsylvanian was surprised to learn that all shops were open on Sundays, with business as usual;[47] shopkeepers wanted their share of the $2,500 spent by traveling gold seekers every day. He also noticed that all the businessmen seemed to be foreigners. None wore ponchos. Christman walked into a hotel and found the manager to be a Yankee married to a pretty sixteen-year-old Chilean.[48] Drinks at the bar cost 1 real each. The bartender served a customer by setting out the brandy bottle, a small pitcher of water, and a glass, along with a saucer of loaf sugar and a spoon for stirring the drink.[49]

On the crowded streets Christman heard quarreling, much of it in English. Discharged sailors argued over wages. Crewmen or passengers from almost every ship that arrived were at odds with the captain or with the cook. They appealed to the consul for relief[50] or told their woes to any bystander who would listen. One captain was reported to have become so angry with his passengers while at sea that he threatened "setting fire to the magazine and blowing up the whole ship, as he had as many friends in hell as any one!"[51] Some disgruntled captains sailed away without the troublesome passengers, regardless of whether or not their passage had been paid.[52]

The unpleasant antics of gold seekers which Enos Christman observed in Valparaiso compared unfavorably with the deportment of natives, and the sympathy he showed for Spanish-speaking people later, in California, may have originated in Chile. When he returned from his shore visit to the *Europe* he witnessed another example of Yankee behavior. On a nearby vessel the American flag was raised with a knot tied in it. This odd signal was immediately understood by the commander of a Chilean man-of-war in the harbor who sent a boatload of marines to the American vessel. They boarded the ships and took to shore two passengers who were fighting over one of the men's wives.[53] To Chilean authorities the norteamericanos must have seemed incorrigible!

On other ships, crews and passengers, ignoring the captain, sometimes inspected the water and supplies to be sure of sufficient quantities for the voyage. In some instances they tested the pumps and either repaired them or demanded that new ones be purchased.[54] Christman, with time on his hands, learned that there was good fishing in the bay and he caught enough fish for two meals every day. This sport appealed to some of his fellow passengers and, before sailing on to California, he and seven companions caught and salted a barrel of fine fish.[55]

Christman, like Lieutenant Gilliss, failed to notice the debates concerning California in the Cámaras which eventually became so fatal to the government. Even the Valparaiso newspapers, by the fall of 1849, seemed more concerned with the news from California than with events in their own capital. *El Mercurio*, which had never favored emigration to California, headed a two-column article with ESPÍRITU YANKEE.[56] Under this caption the editor described California's marvelous civic growth. Within a year's time, he said, the people were building cities. There was "Stokton" in the interior and on Suisun Bay, at the mouth of the San Joaquin River, a "New York of the Pacific" was being built. This city, according to its founders, was destined to be the terminus of the transcontinental railroad which would undoubtedly come down the San Joaquin Valley.[57] The editor, reminding his readers that Chile had a back country as vast and fertile as California's, urged Chileans to study Yankee methods and to develop their own natural resources with "Yankee spirit."[58]

El Comercio, true to form, published a counterarticle on the following day. The editor outperformed his rival by describing, in an equal number of columns, the large number of California's newborn cities. Lest readers question his statements, he listed the following: Fremont, Vernon, Boston, Sacramento, Sutter, Webster, Suesen (*sic*), Tuolumne, Estanislao, Stockton, New York, Benicia, Martinez, Napa, Sonoma, San Luis, San Rafael and Sausalito.[59] The young state had produced a remarkable number of towns.

The rapid settlement of California stimulated a national effort in Chile to encourage settlement in that country's vast hinterlands. The hacienda-controlled government wanted to keep labor on the estates,[60] but prospective immigrants from France and Germany[61] were offered homesteads in the dripping, fertile southern forests as well as in the lake region east of Valdivia, the country Pérez Rosales had known in his vagabond days. Although the Araucanian Indians were still dangerous, Chile was prepared to send soldiers to keep the peace and to help open more land for settlement.[62] The congress had been discussing this project all summer, and within a month of the newspaper descriptions of the California settlements, a regiment recruited in Santiago marched into Valparaiso to embark for the southern ports. True to a Latin-American custom, wives and sweethearts traipsed along behind the soldiers, vociferating their grief as the men were rowed out to the waiting transports.[63]

The change in national policy came too late for some well-to-do businessmen in Valparaiso who had already established connections in San Francisco. They were making plans to outdo the North American promoters who had founded Boston and "New York of the Pacific." In short, they had decided to build a Washington City in California. For this purpose Don Buenaventura Sánchez[64]—no doubt a brother of the owner of the famous *J.R.S.* —acquired a block of land on the east bank of the Sacramento River 9 miles north of the town of Sacramento. A brook ran through the area, promising sufficient fresh water, so important to water-hungry Chileans.[65]

Draftsmen drew a detailed map of the proposed Washington City showing a wide thoroughfare along the Sacramento River, like tree-lined O'Higgins Boulevard in Santiago. At right angles to this promenade, a main avenue would run eastward through two plazas, named Sanchez Square and Cross Square.[66] Evidently the first was to immortalize Don Buenaventura, the promoter of the city, and the second bore the name of commission merchant Alejandro Cross who, with his partners, the ubiquitous Hobsons, was interested in the enterprise. The streets of the city were named Cross, Hobson, Price, Waddington, Wheelright, and Cochrane. Two thoroughfares were named Bulnes and Taylor, the former for the president of Chile and the latter for the recently elected president of the United States. Another street was named for Brannan, who may have invested in the enterprise. Other streets bore the Anglo names of Jeffrey, Riddle, Ward, and Hooper. Two were named for prominent Chilean families, Beltrán and Alessandri. Don Pedro Alessandri's grandson would later be president of Chile.

As early as November, promoters described the project in local Chilean newspapers. A curious prospectus was published which offered investors an opportunity to make money.[67] The proposed city was described as being 160 miles nearer the gold mines than San Francisco but only twenty hours by boat from that harbor. The site was said to be at the head of river navigation, and vessels of 400 tons could unload there.[68] The city's proximity to the mines enhanced the value of the location. In addition, the temperature was agreeable and the elevation was sufficiently high to prevent the flooding that might inundate Sacramento. Also, both wood and water—two elements lacking in many Chilean cities—were ample and easily available.

Each block in Washington City was divided into twelve lots, for sale at $100 each, and the promoters assured purchasers that within a year the lots would be worth $8,000 to $10,000 apiece.[69] City lots in the inferior, flood-threatened city of Sacramento had increased as much in value during the preceding year. The prospectus also stated that a number of lots had been sold and that buildings would be constructed on them immediately. Purchasers might see a complete plan of the city in the Sánchez brothers' storehouse.*

The Sánchez brothers also offered to sell stock in Peru, where money from the guano trade was plentiful; according to reports, several Peruvian merchants invested in the scheme.[70] The real estate venture in California should have been helped by a sudden turn of bad weather. During the first week in November heavy rains began and by the end of the year Sacramento was under water, while the site of Washington City was still high and dry, but a search has failed to reveal the construction of a city there.

* Roberto Hernández Cornejo, *Los Chilenos en San Francisco* (Valparaiso, 1930), I, 177–178. The Sánchez brothers, Bernardo, Manuel, José Ramón, and Buenaventura, organized a commission firm on July 24, with offices in Valparaiso and San Francisco. *Alta California*, Nov. 22, 1849.

Chile's Pony Express
and Joaquín Murieta

Horsemen on the most remote Chilean rancho learned about California in a remarkably short time. The first ones to get the news lived along the express route across the Andes from Argentina. Four such routes were tried. Monthly mail service was established, and gold seekers from the United States and Europe who wanted to escape the hardships of sailing around the Horn could disembark at Buenos Aires, across the Andes, and reach Valparaiso ahead of their vessels.[1]

The best, although not the shortest, route crossed through Uspallata Pass and followed down the Aconcagua River to Valparaiso, bypassing Santiago. The distance was approximately 1,500 miles, considerably shorter than the nearly 2,000 miles traversed by the North American Pony Express.* The time consumed by South Americans traveling from Buenos Aires to Santiago was usually twelve days, although the trip was made once in eleven, a trifle longer than the ten and a half days allowed American pony riders. In both countries relays of horses waited at regular stations. Each Chilean rode 114 miles a day, but the Americans averaged only 75.[2] Once, in an emergency caused by Indians, an American rode 185 miles, stopping only to change horses.[3] The Chilean express began more than a generation before the North American adventure and lasted much longer.

Traveling west, gold seekers could cross the Argentine plains

* O. O. Winther (in Jay Monaghan, ed., *The Book of the American West* [New York, 1963], p. 126) says the pony express route was 1,966 miles long. The distance varied while the telegraph line was being built.

in a carriage, but everyone had to ride a horse or a mule over the Andes, stopping at government-constructed stone shelters. Travelers brought their own supplies, including charcoal for cooking food and melting snow into water.[4] Storms above timberline were frequent, with strong winds blowing sharp crystals of snow into the faces of men and animals. Horses and mules were urged forward with difficulty, but between the frightful storms that thundered along the jagged peaks, riders could sometimes see, a hundred miles to the west, the sun shining on the Pacific Ocean.

Riding down the western slope, travelers occasionally passed the half-eaten carcass of a guanaco killed by a puma and easily recognized by its camel feet. Condors feasting on the remains ran away from the riders, flapping their great wings until airborne. Below the snow line the marked trail traversed vast mountain sides cracked open by red gulches. Gigantic cacti, tall but thinner than Arizona saguaros, stood like sentinels on the dry slopes. At lower altitudes gophers, impudent as prairie dogs, sat on their hind legs to watch the riders and then scurried off chattering as though in panic.[5]

The trail eventually entered grazing country, and travelers noticed a difference between Chilean cowboys and those they had seen on the Argentine pampas. Both wore gaily colored ponchos, but their footgear and the stirrups on their saddles differed greatly. On the Argentine plains many gauchos wore heelless, colt-hide boots with iron spurs which dragged on the ground when they walked. The boot had an open toe and the stirrup was a round stick suspended on a thong which was straddled by the rider's big and little toes.[6] West of the Andes, a huaso (note the Chilean spelling of gaucho) wore heavy boots with 2-inch heels[7] and thrust his feet into wooden stirrups as big and round as wagon-wheel hubs.[*]

South American cowboys differed materially from those in California. The Chileans rode a flat saddle, often with as many

---

[*] Frederick Gerstaecker, *Narrative of a Journey round the World* (New York, 1853), p. 108. On the pampas some riders used a stirrup that had a spur shank and rowel on one side, with which a barefoot rider could spur his mount (Tito Saubidet Gauche, *Vocabulario y Refranero criollo* [Buenos Aires, 1943], p. 157).

as four thick blankets or sheep pelts strapped under or over it. Thus the rider sat on what looked like a camel's hump, and a huaso's lasso was tied to a ring on the saddle girth.* There was no horn on the saddle to which a Chilean huaso could attach his riata with what American cowboys call "dallies" or "dally wealthies," a corrupt translation of the Mexican *dar la vuelta*. Regardless of the difference between North and South American horse gear, the so-called leader of California outlaws, Joaquín Murieta, is said by Chileans to have come from Chile's very un-Californian ranch country—but more of that later!

Chilean ranchos, or cowboys' summer huts, along the express roads were built of adobe. A peaked, thatched roof covered a single dirt-floored room. There was no window and the door was seldom closed. The furniture consisted of a rude bedstead, a rickety table, two chairs, and perhaps a bench. Bins contained corn, beans, and potatoes. From the rafters, strings of onions, garlic, and red chili peppers dangled within reach of a hungry man's knife. Overhead nets held bread and cheese away from inquisitive rodents. (So wide a variety of food would not be found in a North American cow camp two generations later.) All cooking was done outside,[8] but pegs driven into the adobe walls inside held saddles, horse gear, and the inevitable guitar. A true South American cowboy was said to love only his horse, his woman, and his guitar, in that order.[9]

On the bare, cold, dry slopes of the Andes a dead animal's body might never bloat.[10] Instead, it dehydrated into natural jerky. Herdsmen had learned generations earlier that beef, cut in thin strips and laid out in the sun until black, could be baled in 100- and 200-pound bundles with rawhide covers and sold in the cities. The market extended to California after the beginning of the gold rush, and in order to meet the new demand and produce jerky rapidly, the meat was spread across a carpet of cane suckers and trampled on by barefoot boys. Four days after this treatment the jerky became sufficiently crisp for baling.[11]

Below the grazing ground travelers on the express route came

---

* Erna Fergusson, *Chile* (New York, 1943), p. 178; Gerstaecker, *op. cit.*, p. 108; Saubidet Gauche, *op. cit.*, p. 333. The South American cowboy's saddle had only one cinch.

to peach and orange orchards along the upper Aconcagua River. Perhaps 100 yards wide in this area, it was divided into many channels by dry boulders, which were covered with babbling water every spring when snow melted in the high country. Along the stream the first community of importance was San Felipe, a town with an imposing church tower, broad streets, and buildings roofed with red tiles.[12] Surrounding vineyards made the hamlet a wine and brandy center. The country from San Felipe down the Aconcagua River to the Pacific produced a large part of the alcoholic beverages shipped to California. Indeed, 5,250 gallons of wine alone were transported from Chile during the first three years of the gold rush.[13] Although shipped to California in kegs, hogsheads, and even pipes, the wine was taken from the haciendas in wineskins on the backs of mules. The wineskins were said to have been stripped from live, struggling, and crying goats suspended by their horns; the skin from a dead goat was believed to be less perfect.[14]

San Felipe's prosperity depended on copper mines operated by Englishmen.[15] Silver was also mined in the Andes, and as early as 1834 Charles Darwin saw Cornish miners at work here,[16] just as Cornishmen would be the first pit miners in California. These silver mines utilized the ancient amalgamation process that had been steadily improved in South America since the old Potosí days 300 years earlier;[17] later it was used at the rich Comstock lode in Nevada.

From San Felipe to Valparaiso a level road, deep with yellow dust, ran down the valley's flat bottom between steep, bare mountainsides 3,000 feet high. Overland travelers often passed convoys of five or six huge wagons loaded with dust-covered wine kegs, big bales of jerky, and sacks of harina tostada, the toasted flour so important to South Americans in California. Eastbound vans carried furniture, stoves, and assorted merchandise from ships unloading in Valparaiso. Each van was drawn by four to six yoke of oxen.[18] The bullwhackers, smiling under their broad black moustaches, waved to travelers.

Every 10 or 20 miles the road entered what appeared to be a city street between walls of gigantic adobe blocks, 2 and 3 feet square. These walls, usually 10 feet high and roofed with red tiles, surrounded a hacienda.[19] On one side of the street a large wooden gate led to the *hacendado*'s residence. Other gates opened into what appeared to be a store and a church. Above the wall a traveler could usually see the tops of fruit trees.

Across the street a row of doors opened into the homes of inquilinos, whose children seldom ventured out into the dangerous highway; indeed, the street usually seemed empty. Foreigners were not taunted in these villages, although one German wearing a red Argentinian poncho for the overland trip said gauchos hooted at him as a hated "kringo."[20]

Each inquilino held a plot of garden he paid for by rendering the patrón certain stipulated services. When hired for extra farm work, he received specified wages, consisting of a meager cash payment augmented by rations, which for a day's work usually amounted to one pound each of harina tostada, beans, and potatoes.[21] Most haciendas also contained a cantina[22] where the inquilinos gathered on weekends to drink and dance away the little money they had earned. The men, when drunk, often quarreled and drew their knives. On one occasion a man's abdomen was ripped from side to side until his entrails hung out. A *medica* ("female practitioner") sewed up the wound with an ordinary needle and thread. Three weeks later the man was back at work.[23] The stamina of these chilenos made them noteworthy in California.

To North American gold seekers, observing this area on their way to California, the peons seemed more degraded than slaves in the southern United States. The women, they said, seldom married, but they began having children at thirteen and continued until the age of fifty. Only the high mortality prevented a population explosion.[24] The landlords, like the rulers of primitive workers the world over, argued that their dependents would not know what to do with a higher standard of living: they would merely drink more and squander extra money on useless luxuries.[25]

The buildings on country estates seemed very crude. Roof beams, instead of being nailed down, were lashed in place with strips of hairy rawhide. Nails were expensive, and they pulled loose during earthquakes when houses shook like jelly.[26] The

tremendous gap in living standards between inquilinos and their
patrónes may have led to the common assumption that Chilean
society had only two classes, but even on a large hacienda the
storekeeper, the bookkeeper, and the various foremen consti-
tuted a modest middle class.* They lived in better quarters than
the laborers but enjoyed nothing comparable to the owner's
rambling, one-story *casa grande*, which often contained twenty
rooms opening onto several patios gay with potted flowers along
the galleries on all four sides.[27] Although separated by many
miles from Santiago or Valparaiso, these homes contained elaborate furnishings with handsome rugs on the floors and usually a
pianoforte, which ladies in every hacienda had been taught to
play. These women were also beautiful dancers. Indeed, grace
of movement was the sign of status, and a girl's social position
could be told by her walk.[28] Entertainments on the estates were
usually elaborate, with dancing until midnight when the cabal-
leros galloped away to reach their distant homes before dawn.[29]

Twenty miles from Valparaiso the road entered Quillota, a
remarkable town surrounded by vineyards. California's legendary Joaquín Murieta is said to have been born in an adobe
house here. The town, religious and extraordinarily conservative, was an odd background for the outlaw revered by Chileans.
In 1835 William Wheelwright of Valparaiso, eager to build a
railroad up the Aconcagua River to Santiago, hoped to make
Quillota a division point. As a gesture of good public relations
he published a large number of Bibles in Spanish and distributed
them in the village. To his chagrin, the outraged citizenry, re-
senting this version of the venerated Vulgate, burned the books
publicly in the plaza, just as their ancestors might have burned
a witch.

Why Joaquín is said to have come from so religious a town
remains a mystery. Perhaps his life of crime symbolized what
California might do to the finest South American personality.
Joaquín, of course, was a character in fiction, not a real man, so
he could not have been born there. "Joaquín" is a common Span-

* An occasional inquilino became an entrepreneur who hired peons to do the
work required of him on the hacienda; he might also be a capitalist owning a
few head of cattle (Arnold J. Bauer, "Chilean Rural Labor in the Nineteenth
Century," *American Historical Review*, 76 [Oct., 1971], 1064).

ish name and many Mexicans in California, driven by Anglos from the diggings, became robbers and cattle thieves. No doubt some rotos joined them. Before long, whenever there was a robbery, people said it was done by "Joaquín," as good a name for any Mexican as Diego or "Dago" was for an Italian. Soon five surnames were added to the name "Joaquín," but whether any real robbers bore these names remains unproved, since none was brought to trial. Robberies became so prevalent that the state legislature authorized the formation of a company of twenty rangers to capture the "party or gang of robbers commanded by the five Joaquins."[30] The rangers were to serve three months, and Governor John Bigler offered personally to add a reward of $1,000 for the capture or killing of "Joaquín." He stated no surname, but his offer was presumably considered good for votes.

The rangers served three months, so as to receive their full pay, and then they rode in with a man's head. The first newspaper accounts said only that it belonged to Joaquín—again no surname mentioned. To collect the governor's reward, however, the victim's full name had to be stated, and "Murieta" was selected, much to the disgust of *Alta California* which suspected the whole affair to be a farce. This head, preserved in alcohol, was exhibited in museums for some years but would undoubtedly have been cast aside had it not been for a best-selling paperback written by John Rollin Ridge, a Cherokee mixed-blood whose Indian name was Yellow Bird. Published in 1854, this pulp was entitled *The Life and Adventures of Joaquín Murieta, Celebrated California Bandit*. In the novel Joaquín was an honest, hardworking Mexican who saw Yankees hang his half brother for a trumped-up charge of horse stealing. The experience changed Joaquín overnight, and he swore a solemn oath to avenge the outrage by robbing and murdering Yankees.

Five years after publication of the paperback, the California *Police Gazette* pirated the story. A shabby trick, surely, but Ridge may have pirated part of his story from the famous *Shirley Letters*, being published serially at the time his book appeared.*

* John Rollin Ridge, *The Life and Adventures of Joaquín Murieta*, with introduction by Joseph Henry Jackson (Norman, Okla., 1955), p. xxxi. The pirating was minor. According to Dame Shirley, a vigilance committee arrested five or six Spanish-speaking men suspected, not of horse stealing, but of plotting

In the *Police Gazette* account some of the characters' names were changed. Joaquín's "Rosita" became "Carmela," and in this version the gringos not only raped but also killed her.[31]

An enterprising publisher in Spain printed a translation of the *Police Gazette* account. It caused no visible concern among the returned Chilean gold seekers. Spain, after all, was still not a country the Chileans admired, but when the story was translated and published in France it came to the notice of Roberto Hyenne, a Frenchman who claimed to have been in San Francisco with Consul Carlos de Varigny.[32] He translated the book back into Spanish and it was published in Santiago, Chile, under his name as author and with the title *El Bandido Chileño*. Hyenne moved Joaquín's birthplace from Mexico to Quillota and made him a national figure who avenged the persecutors of his fellow countrymen in California. This version was then plagiarized in Spain by "Professor" Acigar and published in Barcelona as *El Caballero Chileño*. In the meantime a reprinting of the Hyenne version appeared in Mexico with Joaquín's birthplace moved back to that country.[33]

All these cheap paperback publications in various languages by varous "authors" made Joaquín Murieta a real person in the minds of many, especially in the minds of the semiliterate who gloat over confrontations with established law and order. In Chile, Joaquín Murieta became the Robin Hood who dared defend the workingman from Yankee imperialism, and it is not surprising that the present-day leftist poet, Pablo Neruda, living only two hours' drive from Santiago in his lavish home with its shiplike drawing room on a cliff overlooking the sea,[34] should write an opera entitled *Fulgor y Muerta de Joaquín Murieta* ("The Splendor and Death of Joaquín Murieta"). This musical

---

to drive Americans from the diggings. All were found guilty. Their property was confiscated and they were driven from camp. Two of them received an additional sentence of flogging. One of these, a "gentlemanly young Spaniard," according to Dame Shirley, implored the committee to kill him. He did not want to live with the never-to-be-effaced stain of having received a punishment accorded to the vilest convict. When the committee refused to change his sentence to death, the young man swore a solemn oath to murder every American he would meet alone. Dame Shirley concluded that "he will doubtless keep his word." (Louise A. K. S. Clappe, *The Shirley Letters* [Santa Barbara, 1970], pp. 150–151.)

propaganda in five acts of brutal heroics ends with the death of Murieta, killed by a man wearing Uncle Sam's tall hat and striped trousers.

To keep his audience constantly reminded of United States villainy, Neruda composed three additional numbers to be sung before the performance and during the intermissions. The following is a translation of the first, to be sung by a male voice:

> Today they kill Negroes,
> Earlier it was Mexicans,
> Also they killed Chileans,
> Nicaraguans, Peruvians,
> Those uncontrollable gringos
> With their inhuman instincts.
>
> Who disputed their actions?
> Who challenged them face to face?
> It was a Chilean bandit!
> It was our Joaquín Murieta![35]

The second song was written for a female voice:

> Now comes Joaquín Murieta
> A defender of our people.
> Our hearts respond
> To this valiant man's rifle.
> What survives of Joaquín Murieta?
> His farm-callused hands survive;
> So do his vengeful eyes
> And his divine figure.
> What did those who killed him kill?
> If he was a bandit,
> I wish for bandits like him![36]

The third song was longer, but the following stanzas are representative:

> We proclaim for happiness!
> We protest rebelliously!
> So that all men someday
> May be contented!
>
> Whether life is good or bad,
> The Yankees will tell you:
> This is a gentle world—
> But they kill in Vietnam.[37]

The author of these lines has been acclaimed the most gifted lyric poet of the Spanish-speaking world. He holds Chile's highest literary award and has an honorary doctor of letters degree from Oxford, and in 1971 he was awarded the Nobel prize for literature. His bitterly intolerant opera was produced on the Santiago stage for eleven weeks in 1967 and for six weeks in 1968; it has also been staged in Argentina. A scene from the drama was played with little success on the various campuses of the University of California in 1968, and negotiations were made for performances in Mexico, Brazil, Italy, France, and East Germany.[38]

Needless to say, Pablo Neruda is a Communist who was elected to the Chilean Senate on that party's platform in 1944, and he used the mythical Joaquín Murieta as a present-day Saint George to kill the dragon called "investments of North American corporations." One of Neruda's supporters told me that the poet soon needed for his advancement a greater hero than Saint George. He knew Murieta to be a character in fiction, but to get votes from ignorant laborers who for centuries had lived under the influence of the Church, it was necessary to find a new Jesus who had been killed for saving men. Did any politician ever make a more damning confession? Yet to be fair to Neruda, readers should remember that he is not the first politician to live in affluence while courting ghetto votes with a recognized falsehood.

More remarkable and distressing is the article on Joaquín Murieta in the biographical dictionary of eminent Chileans compiled by that progressive and broad-minded historian, Ramón Pérez Yáñez, and published in 1953. Pérez Yáñez planned the book to interest his youthful compatriots in developing their own country. I hope that the following translation of Pérez Yáñez' account is accurate in word and fair in spirit:

Chilean workmen in California were not laggard in protecting themselves. When necessary they joined with Mexicans who were willing to be led by their friends from the south. This situation caused the tragedy of Joaquín Murieta, son of a citizen of Quillota, an honorable man who went to California with other Chilean gold seekers. Working his mine one day with other Chileans, and stimulated by the smile of his woman, Carmela [note that Carmela is the heroine of Hyenne's pirated account], he and his fellows were attacked by a big party of Americans and overpowered after a heroic resistance. Joaquín escaped, thanks to his valor, but Carmela was killed. Desperate for revenge, this honorable workman became a brigand. Three hundred Chileans and Mexicans joined his band. Many stories are told about his reckless robberies. A reward of $10,000 was offered for his head. Finally he was captured, and before he died, he put his hand on his heart and exclaimed, "My Carmela, I have avenged your death by killing those American cowards who took your life and broke mine. I was an honorable workingman, but the injustices and crimes and atrocities committed against us by these miserable usurpers forced me into bad company. I have avenged death with death and now my lips for the last time before I die pronounce your name, 'Carmela mía, adiós!' "

So ended the celebrated Chilean bandit, our honorable compatriot, a victim of injustice. If he is remembered historians should note that hundreds of non-Chileans made him what he became. Murieta was a bandit, but he was one of the great bandits of the gold country and he should be judged by his times.[39]

This odd epitaph celebrates a fictional character who was originally described as a Mexican in a cheap paperback novel. In defense of the eminent Chileans who have made this historical mistake, the same error was made by the early California historians Theodore Hittell and Hubert Howe Bancroft. Both of them accepted the fictional Joaquín as a real person,[40] but their statements were corrected years ago. Perhaps Napoleon was right: "History is a fable agreed upon." Or is it several fables disagreed upon?

18

Crusoe's Island,
the City of the Kings,
and 800 Tons of Women

A wet sheet and a flowing sea,
A wind that follows fast,
And fills the white and rustling sail,
And bends the gallant mast.
—Allan Cunningham

Gold-rush ships from Europe and the United States, after rounding Cape Horn, usually planned to stop either at Valparaiso or
at the more romantic City of the Kings.[1] Sea captains often asked
passengers to decide between the two cities. If they chose the
latter, their vessel, sailing out to sea, usually sighted the Juan
Fernández Islands. Two of the three islands were 90 miles apart,
and a vessel sometimes sailed north between them without seeing either landfall, but this was unusual. The navigators of most
vessels, tacking to the east and then to the west in the variable
winds, were almost sure to sight one of them above the horizon.
The largest and best-known of the three was called Robinson
Crusoe's island by Anglo sailors. The Chileans called it Juan
Fernández *Más a Tierra* ("More toward Land"). It stood 360
miles from the coast of Chile, was 12 miles long by 2 to 4 miles
wide, and loomed 3,000 feet out of the Pacific. Passengers were
told that a viceroy of Peru had released goats there centuries
ago to sustain shipwrecked mariners, but his good intentions
proved to be a mistake. The goats prospered, making that distant
bit of land a snug harbor for pirates. To discourage the pirates
the viceroy sent dogs to kill the goats, but this plan also failed.[2]

Goats and dogs still ran wild on the island at the time of the gold rush.[3]

In 1575, after both Lima and Valparaiso had been well established, a Spanish navigator, Juan Fernández, discovered the islands later named for him. He may never have landed, but he and at least two others attempted to found a settlement which failed. In 1616 a trading vessel belonging to a wealthy Amsterdam merchant, seeking territory outside the Dutch East India Company's monopoly, "discovered" the islands, published an account of his cruise, and the Juan Fernández Islands became known to the maritime world.[4]

Later in the seventeenth century, when the bottom fell out of the tobacco market, the Juan Fernández Islands were affected in an odd manner. Colonial planters thousands of miles away, many of them English, went bankrupt and lost their tobacco farms. Those who could afford it bought more land and more slaves and started to raise sugar. Many dispossessed tobacco farmers, having nothing left but their seagoing vessels, supported themselves by privateering for the warring nations of Europe. Soon some of them reverted to simple piracy. During these buccaneer decades at least two marooned men lived alone on the Juan Fernández Islands for several years, but the incident that made the islands famous occurred in 1709 when a British privateer, seeking French prizes, found Alexander Selkirk on Más a Tierra. He had lived alone for four years and four months after being put ashore, at his own request, by a ship later lost at sea.[5]

Selkirk's adventures were no more extraordinary than those experienced by the two men who had been marooned ahead of him, one of whom had stayed alone for a longer period, but Selkirk's story was widely published in the newspaper. In 1719 the well-known novelist, Daniel Defoe, wrote *Robinson Crusoe*, obviously a fictionalized account of Selkirk's experiences, although Defoe marooned his hero on an island in the West Indies instead of the South Pacific. Defoe's book is reputed to have had more readers than any other fiction ever written in any language. All Yankee whalemen and gold seekers knew the book well, and they recognized wind-scrubbed Más a Tierra as Crusoe's island.

In 1741 Lord Anson stopped at Juan Fernández Más a Tierra

on his famous trip around the world. He lost five of his six ships and half of his crews died of scurvy on the cruise, but he is credited with planting the peach trees that regaled gold seekers in 1849.[6] He noted that the goats, even in 1741, had been earmarked by earlier, playful buccaneers.* In 1750 Spain established a penal colony on Más a Tierra, and during the war for independence Vicente Pérez Rosales' uncle and cousin were exiled there.[7] After Chile gained independence the old jail served as a place of confinement for generals defeated in the frequent revolts.[8] But the cost of shipping supplies 360 miles west of Valparaiso proved exorbitant, and the government neglected the islands. When Lord Cochrane, commanding the Chilean navy, visited the colony in 1823 he found that the only inhabitants were four men herding cattle.

This was the era of the New England whaleships, with fortunes also being made in hides and the China trade. Yankee vessels stopped frequently at Robinson Crusoe's island for fresh water and meat. Richard Dana, on his sailing cruise immortalized by *Two Years before the Mast*, visited the island in 1834. He saw a chapel, more than a hundred huts and houses, and a few ragged soldiers wearing shoes out at the toes.[9] During the California gold rush perhaps some fifty vessels stopped at Robinson Crusoe's island.[10] An author, J. Ross Browne, on his way to San Francisco in 1849, sighted the landfall from the ship *Anteus* on May 19. His vessel, like many others, had been scheduled to stop at Valparaiso, but the passengers prevailed on their captain to go instead to Callao via the island.

Seventy miles from the well-known Juan Fernández Más a Tierra, but in plain view of the misty island, the wind stopped, and the *Anteus* lay becalmed, floating hour after silent hour on a glassy sea. Browne and nine other passengers decided to row across the still waters to the famous island; even so long a trip did not dismay men who had been cooped up for weeks on a stagnant sailing ship. One of them had brought a 22-foot sheet-iron boat which he kept on deck. During the long voyage, when

* It may have been Alexander Selkirk who caught some of the goats and earmarked them to amuse himself (Ralph Lee Woodward, Jr., *Robinson Crusoe's Island* [Chapel Hill, 1969], p. 40).

the ship stalled for lack of wind, this man had lowered his craft and amused the passengers by rowing around the vessel. Becalmed again, south of Juan Fernández, he and his friends estimated that by rowing 6 or 7 miles an hour they could reach the land before dark. They set off with a little food, a demijohn of fresh water, and a sail to be used if the wind freshened. The captain, who had visited the island, urged the adventurers to enjoy peaches from the trees planted by Lord Anson a hundred years earlier. He warned them, also, never to lose sight of the ship, never to go so far that they could not see her royals above the swell of the globe.[11]

The trip proved a harrowing experience. Browne and one ex-whaleman were the only deepwater men on board. Every time they glanced back the ship looked smaller. Her hull had sunk below the horizon, but the pale island ahead seemed to be no nearer. Then in the afternoon, to make matters worse, a storm and a choppy sea buffeted their little craft. With constant bailing they survived the night. Finally, at 4:00 A.M., when it was still dark, they saw what they believed to be a light on the island. Instead, the light came from a ship anchored half a mile from shore. She was the *Brooklyn*, out of New York with 180 gold seekers bound for California.[12]

Welcomed on board the *Brooklyn*, Browne and his friends rested, dried their wet clothes, and then, with their new friends, rowed ashore to explore the island. To them Robinson Crusoe was very real, and they prowled deep into caves they imagined he had used. They examined the ruins of the old Chilean jail and saw underground cells for extra punishment, virtual graves 5 or 6 feet long and only 4 or 5 feet high, where recalcitrant prisoners might be kept in solitary confinement. Even more interesting to Browne was the village, reduced now in 1849 to six or seven huts thatched with the straw of wild oats which grew in profusion everywhere. The total population consisted of sixteen persons, four or five of them Chilean men with wives and children. Also there was one North American deserter from a whaleship who had married a Chilean woman.[13] Five years earlier a feud on the island had ended in a murder. The Chilean government convicted the guilty parties and imprisoned them, but their sentences had expired and there was some apprehension that they might return and renew the feud.

Browne and his companions found food plentiful. They ate the peaches the captain had mentioned, also figs, quinces, and other fruit. Goats, wild cattle, seals, and pigeons provided meat. Horses, many of them wild and grown fat on native grasses, served as mounts.[14] Chickens were also plentiful. Earlier mariners, whalemen, and "dog hunters"—men seeking seals[15]—had made a practice of camping on the beach. After filling water kegs and butchering wild animals for meat, they sailed away paying for nothing.

The situation changed when the gold seekers came. These Yankees expected to be millionaires soon. One of them, with American assurance, bought a tame goat to furnish milk for the rest of the voyage to California, paid for it with a gold eagle ($10), and said, grinning broadly, "Keep the change in memory of Robinson Crusoe."[16] These North American jokers also indulged in their countrymen's favorite sport of spouting patriotic orations, and the *Brooklyn* passengers, after the usual vocal orgy, annexed the Juan Fernández Islands to the United States. Rash announcements of this kind may have influenced the Chilean government to formally attach the islands to the Department of Valparaiso in 1851.[17]

Browne and his party had camped on the beach for three days when their vessel sailed in and anchored close enough for them to row out and board her. As they passed the *Brooklyn* they saw that she was weighing anchor to stand out to sea. They also saw in the distance a small brig, beating in to take the *Brooklyn's* place, and they recognized her as a craft they had met in Rio de Janeiro. The procession of gold-rush vessels was certainly changing life on these isolated islands!

Browne's captain, eager to reach California, ordered the anchor weighed and the yards braced. With the jerk seamen know so well, the sails billowed into cumulous curves. The jibs popped sharply as they filled with wind and the *Anteus* plowed away through the cobalt waters, a white bone in her teeth, as sailors liked to say. Before noon Juan Fernández became a misty silhouette on the horizon.[18]

Some vessels carrying gold seekers stopped at other islands farther north. The *Canton*, anchoring at the Galápagos for turtles, picked up two New Bedford Yankees who had survived on wild life for nine months after deserting from a whaler,[19] but no Defoe immortalized their experiences and they, like a dozen others before and after Robinson Crusoe, have been forgotten.

The popular port of call north of Crusoe's island was Callao, gateway to the City of the Kings. Although the Peruvian people had learned about the California gold discovery on November 4, 1848, they had not yet responded to the news with the excitement demonstrated in Chile. In February, 1849, a steamer from Panama brought a copy of General Smith's proclamation against foreigners' mining for gold in California,[20] but it failed to interest many Peruvians. An attempted revolution which was crushed that month[21] may have kept some adventurers at home. Others may once more have been discouraged by letters from California which reiterated accounts of lawlessness and lack of respect for persons of the upper classes. A Peruvian, steeped in his country's tradition of viceregal discipline which was still strong in the best families, was shocked to read about "gentlemen working like beasts of burden."[22] Yet some correspondents wrote that this anomaly was accepted in California as a matter of course. In San Francisco a man was happy if he had $10 in his pocket and could get drunk. Such a society seemed unsafe for respectable persons. A man of refinement felt no virtue in walking the streets with pistols strapped to his waist. One California letter printed in a Lima newspaper said: "Gold is plenty and people keep coming, people with no concern but getting gold, people who can stand hard work and no class distinction."[23] California was obviously no place for a Peruvian gentleman, but the writer admitted that more plebeian Chileans were doing well there.

During the days when these discouraging letters were being published, a man of uncertain antecedents in Lima evidently sought a Yankee dupe among the multitude of incoming gold seekers. Claiming to be a North American, he advertised a get-rich-quick scheme in English, but knew so little of the language that it is difficult to understand exactly what he had to give for the $1,200 he wanted. The advertisement read:[24]

WANTED A PARTNER

by an experienced minor [sic], and native of the United States; who understands fusing and esaying all the useful metals.

A Sum of Twelve hundred Dollars, will be necessary, to purchase what will be required to proceed to California: so as to gain in one season's operation; sufficient for ten persons to make themselves comfortable for life.

One machine the owner reserves to himself the Patent Right as he is the sole inventor.

Enquire at this office.

The offer probably failed to find any victim ready to pay $1,200 to be "comfortable for life." At this time there seems to have been no rush to California from Peru. If emigration was being checked by General Smith's proclamation, a letter from a passenger on the warship *Jeneral Gamarra* should have had the opposite effect.* The writer said that the Peruvian consul sent by President Castilla had called on General Smith as soon as he arrived in California, asking him to apprehend deserters from Peruvian ships. The general replied frankly that he lacked the power because his soldiers had deserted, leaving only twenty-five cavalrymen in his command. Although he had twenty-five cannon, he had no one to shoot them. He expected 800 enlisted recruits but would be unable to hold them when they arrived.[25]

Although Peruvians were thus informed that General Smith could not enforce his proclamation, no gold rush developed. Yet some people continued to fear an emigration of gold seekers, and *El Comercio de Lima* tried to prevent it by the same method Australians were using to deter emigration to California. In Australia newspapers proposed local rushes to possible goldfields in the outback; Peruvian papers, as early as March, 1849, lauded the opportunities for developing gold mines in the Peruvian Andes. The first account described discoveries in 1825 which had been neglected.[26] The next article was more specific, giving details of a goldfield beyond Cuzco which had been abandoned in 1835 but would continue to yield gold when the riches of California were exhausted.[27] Ten days later, under the heading OTRA CALIFORNIA EN PERU, readers were told about an-

* The *Gamarra* arrived in Monterey on March 29, 1849 (*Alta California*, March 29, 1849).

other promising opportunity. In the Paucartambo country north of Quito, 32 million ounces of gold worth $480 million had been mined before work was temporarily suspended after a series of mishaps. Quantities of gold remained, and only men and capital were necessary for extracting it.

The accounts spurred new prospecting, and a big new field was discovered at Carabaya y Sandia, north of Lake Titicaca, some 160 miles southeast of Cuzco. There was no question about the abundance of the gold, which could be washed and also crushed from the quartz. Capital was raised for development of the field, and a French mining engineer moved in with a corps of workers.

If the redevelopment of gold mining in Peru was enhanced by the first letter from the passenger on the *Gamarra*, a later dispatch[28] from the ship's captain, José María Silva Rodríquez, must have pleased President Castilla. The captain said his timely arrival had increased the respect of all nations for Peru. In San Francisco he found a multitude of stranded ships. The crews of several Peruvian barks had deserted and he, having mustered extra men under Castilla's orders, supplied seamen to sail these vessels home. On others he kept the crews on board and forced them to leave with their ships.[29] This prompt and decisive action, the captain said, had caused the captains of vessels from all nations in the bay to applaud the *Gamarra*'s service to shipping.

Such commendable recognition of Peru caused the minister of marine, in his annual report, to state that the cost of the *Gamarra*'s cruise had been money well spent. He also said that the success of the cruise demonstrated the importance of a Peruvian navy, not only to protect the rights of individuals, especially merchants in foreign lands, but to protect Peruvian coastal cities.[30]

In addition to profits from guano and increased Peruvian shipping to California, Callao was benefiting, like Valparaiso, from gold seekers whose vessels stopped while sailing north. On a single day in October, 1849, sixty ships were anchored in the harbor, and the town boomed.[31] But, with Argonauts and quick money, came corruption. A traveler visiting Callao a few years later found a bustling town full of fine ships, elaborate saloons, and the most crooked crimps and reprobates of any port in the world. With money plentiful, a dishonest North American consul made agreements with corrupt ship captains to have their vessels condemned as unseaworthy and sold at auction. The distant owners and underwriters took the loss, while the parties who bought the vessels divided the profits with their colleagues in the fraud.[32] The proceeding was as simple as that!

Such trickery created an unfavorable North American image which was not improved by Z. W. Potter, on his way to assume the consulate in Valparaiso. He visited Lima after his steamer, running south from Panama, anchored at Callao. Registering for himself and his wife in the French Hotel, he left her there and went for a walk. On his return Potter learned that a North American named Sullivan, also on his way to Santiago, had claimed the room and ordered Mrs. Potter out of it. She left in tears, going for help to the room of General Herrera, a shipmate on the voyage from Panama. When Potter heard the details from his tearful wife he "visited" Sullivan, but got no apology and and gave him a public caning for all to see.[33] Brutal show-offs, these "more rich" norteamericanos!

On June 27, 1849, the ship *Robert Browne* sailed into Callao with 167 passengers, who were probably representative of the average North American gold seeker. As soon as the vessel anchored, Peruvian customs and health officers came on board. Later an officer from the U.S. frigate *Savannah*, which was anchored in the harbor, climbed overside. He warned all passengers going ashore to take arms,[34] but most of those who went found the Peruvians, especially the women, quite friendly. Dance halls, patronized by dozens of foreign sailors, proved noisy but safe. Masked balls were popular and exciting;[35] a fellow might even meet an upper-class damsel out on a dare![36]

The gay social whirl had its penalties. Back on their ship, sailing north, several passengers visited the doctor, complaining that the night air on shore did not agree with them[37]—a nice way of describing it! Callao's fleshpots, however, failed to attract all the young fellows on shipboard. Two Cape Ann boys, instead of going ashore, begged the captain for his yawl, and with gig and line fished all day in the harbor. Successful as Enos

Christman and his friends had been in Valparaiso, the Massachusetts boys came on board that night and showed their catch, "happy as a girl with a new bonnet."[38]

North American boys from another ship were shocked when they saw something difficult for them to understand at a dance in Callao. The room was gay with flowers. Beside the wall a beribboned cradle held a dead baby. Its mother, in party dress, danced with gaiety—obviously assumed gaiety—while her partners congratulated her for the happiness her baby must be enjoying in heaven.[39]

Many of the gold seekers whose vessels stopped at Callao visited nearby Lima. An omnibus to the City of the Kings clattered over Callao's cobblestone streets, past the mud-plastered, wattle-walled shacks, dodging burros, ragged Negroes, and cholos. Finally the bus emerged on the open desert. Half a mile from town a cross marked the place where a frigate had been washed in from the harbor by the great earthquake of 1746. Midway to Lima stood a ruined chapel which was still in use. At the entrance a priest held a cross and a cup. Next door a grogshop attendant sold drinks.[40]

Lima had a population of 60,000 in 1849. The City of the Kings had deteriorated even more than Santiago since independence.[41] A generation of democracy, so-called, had disfigured the metropolis, leaving the public buildings of former grandeur in a state of decay, but one North American who visited the city in 1849 proclaimed Lima the most interesting city in the world. At every corner his inquiring eyes beheld vistas of Lima's dramatic history—Pizarro's assassination, victims burned at the stake during the Inquisition, the viceroy's beautiful Perichole, independence, and the revolutions. The poorest woman here, he said, might be carrying a gigantic load on her back, but she wore flowers in her hair.[42] The mendicant at the cathedral door begged for alms as she patted, with motherly affection, her sleeping child's black-satin hair. Cities in the United States seemed colorless in comparison with Lima. Observers were constantly impressed by the city's viceregal past and the conservative habits of her people. Bullfights, discontinued in Santiago after independence because they were inhuman and too Spanish, still attracted crowds in Lima, where the ring accommodated 10,000 spectators.[43]

Women in Lima seemed slower than those in Santiago to discard the *saya* and *manta*,[44] that picturesque costume of an earlier day. The saya was a tight-fitting skirt that forced the wearer to take short steps and display her form. The manta, a black silk veil attached to the waist, covered the breast, the hair, and part of the face. Only one enticing eye and the white hand holding up the veil could be seen. Charles Darwin, the scientist, pronounced women wearing this costume as attractive as mermaids; he said they were more worth looking at than anything else in town.[45] Ricardo Palma, the contemporary Peruvian writer, said these girls could charm the devil to cross himself.[46] More than one North American visitor, however, registered disappointment when he saw the face behind that enticing eye.[47]

The Plaza des Armes remained the heart of Lima's activities, as it had since the days of the conquistadores. Here inquiring gold seekers might, for a dollar, view a body said to be Pizarro's in the cathedral on the plaza's south side. The eastern side was filled by the official residence of President Castilla. Sales booths and venders' awnings cluttered its walls.[48] On the plaza's other two sides Roman-arched arcades sheltered shops selling drygoods, hats, lace, crockery, pictures, and food, some raw and some simmering in pots of oil.[49] A collection of magnificent jewelry in one store awed a New York gold seeker.[50] The fountain in the center of the plaza had changed little during the revolutions. Women carrying water jugs, donkey boys filling their kegs, peddlers, and even loafers congregated here, chattering like grackles.

Every morning at 8:45 the cathedral's great bell announced the raising of the Host, and the city became suddenly quiet. Coachmen stopped their horses. Pedestrians knelt, heads uncovered. Waterboys at the plaza fountain set down their kegs. The merchant in his shop laid aside his measure. Salesmen stopped in the middle of a sentence. The monk who had extended his hand for the next move on the checkerboard suddenly became still. At the end of the bell's third stroke the activity and noise resumed.[51] The same performance was repeated every evening with the tolling of the Angelus bell.

The road from the most easterly city gate in Lima led to a country that oddly resembled places in California's mother lode. Trains of thirty or more mules came down this thoroughfare carrying ice. Relay stations along the way helped get the dripping cargo to town before it melted.[52] East of the precious snowfields the broad central valley of Peru stretched north and south. This was the Inca country which Pizarro had conquered, a broad land, high, dry, and cold, between towering mountains. On the road from Lima to this upland the first hamlet of any size was Juaja, where the surrounding hills were pocked and pitted with prospect holes[53] exactly like those the Chilean doctor saw in California on his long walk from San Francisco to Sonora. According to tradition, great treasure was hidden near Juaja during the days when Pizarro held Atahualpa prisoner at Cajamarca. The Inca ruler had tried to buy his freedom by filling a jail cell with gold to a line Pizarro drew on the wall with his sword. The cell was filled, but Pizarro wanted more gold; while it was being collected[54] he made the sudden decision to execute Atahualpa. The gold gatherers learned about the tragedy, and legends say they hid near Juaja the treasure they had collected, but it was never found.

This tale of hidden treasure is typical of many commonly circulated a generation later in California. Another story concerned an Indian who periodically brought gold to town. A young Creole, determined to find the mine, courted the Indian's daughter and induced her to drop her manta at the site of the mine as she drove the sheep past it. She did so. The young man located the vein and began digging. The girl's father joined him. Both dug together and at day's end the father offered the young man a drink of *chicha*,* which the youth soon learned had been poi-

---

* Chicha was a fermented maize beer which disappeared when corn ceased to be raised in Peru (interview with Dr. Emilio Romero, president of the Sociedad Geográfica de Lima). In order to make a superior *chicha mascada*, the corn was chewed instead of being ground between stones; it was then boiled in water and left to ferment (Johann Jacob von Tschudi, *Travels in Peru* [New York, 1847], p. 261; Philip A. Means, *Fall of the Inca Empire* [New York, 1932], p. 47).

soned. In great haste he mounted his horse, galloped to town, and said he had found the mine, but he died before he could take anyone to it.[55]

An even better Peruvian lost-mine story concerned a Franciscan monk. He was a great gambler who had been saved from bankruptcy several times by his Indian friends. Finally he persuaded them to take him to their mine. They agreed to do so if they might blindfold him. He consented, but planned to outwit them by dropping beads from his rosary to mark the trail so he could follow it the next day. This scheme worked well, but after returning home the monk heard a knock at his door. Opening it, he saw a smiling Indian holding out his hand. "Father," the Indian said, "you dropped your rosary beads on the way, and I have picked them up."[56] No lost-mine story in California quite matches this one!

In the Peruvian back country most of the mestizos owned small estates. They never did any work themselves. Instead, wrapped in their ponchos, they gossiped in groups on the village street or gambled at the local *plaza des gallos* ("cockfight ring"). They sold produce from their farms to the communities surrounding nearby mines which, like those in Chile, were usually operated by Englishmen whose Indian laborers had for generations been familiar with the best mining practices.[57] The mestizos kept remarkably well posted on California gold discoveries, and the local newspapers reprinted articles not only from Lima's *El Comercio* but also from San Francisco's *Alta California*.

In 1849 the ancient Inca town of Cajamarca had become a cluster of tile-roofed houses surrounding a Roman-steepled church. The nearby hot springs Atahualpa used for his palace baths still hissed and bubbled from the ground,[58] and the village cherished a room, probably not the correct one, as the place where Atahualpa's ransom had been collected. The Cajamarca newspaper, *La Aurora*, published an account of the discovery of gold in California as early as November 18, 1848, just twelve days after the first full account had appeared in *El Comercio de Lima*. This was fast news coverage, since the mail from Lima came only once every fortnight.[59] According to *La Aurora's* account, Governor Mason of California had calculated that the mother lode might produce 100 million pesos worth of gold each year for 500 years. Certainly Mason in his oft-copied letter to Washington gave no such figures, so gossip evidently accompanied the printed dispatches that passed from ship to ship on the long sea route which brought the news to Callao, and thence across the mountains to inland towns and villages.

In January, 1849, information about California began coming to Cajamarca directly from vessels anchored in Paita. Couriers traveled the road used by Pizarro on his famous march, and newspaper readers were told that ships from San Francisco came loaded with gold acquired in a few days, making the captains and crews wealthy. Stories of violence, mutinies on shipboard, and deaths on shore were also printed. Other accounts denied these tragedies,[60] but all verified the magnitude of the new Dorado and the contagion of what the editor called "la fiebre amarilla (alias California)."[61] Readers of La Aurora also learned that shippers of flour made immense profits.[62] One captain, having sold his whole cargo for pure gold, found himself a wealthy man without a single sailor to man his ship or sufficient flour to make a single biscuit. In desperation he shot himself.[63]

A later issue of La Aurora told a story about a United States warship which has been omitted from our histories. The correspondent did not mention the vessel's name, so a modern reader may use his own judgment concerning the story's truth. According to the report, printed in Spanish, the warship lost all her crew, except five, by desertion in California. With these five, the captain sailed to Paita where he engaged ten men. Then, having fifteen, he sailed on to Callao and enlisted a full crew,[64]—a full crew of Peruvians to man a United States ship of war!

On February 7 La Aurora reported that 7,000 men were at the California diggings, all working for themselves. This number was 3,000 more than Governor Mason's estimate, but the detail that interested Peruvians was the statement that these men worked for themselves, not under a master. Nevertheless, the peons, most of whom were Indians, never flocked to the harbors as the rotos had in Chile. Perhaps the campaign to prevent emigration by developing mines in the Andes was holding the attention of the freer spirits.

South of Cajamarca, some 500 miles down Peru's broad central valley, travelers crossed the plains where Castilla had been wounded in the cavalry charge that defeated the last Spanish army in South America. This country cherished a structure similar to the bridge of San Luis Rey in Thornton Wilder's novel. Nearby stood Ayacucho, a town of red-tiled roofs and Roman churches which looked like a bit of sixteenth-century Spain, except for the Indians and the llamas. Since Inca days the Indians had been skilled workers in gold, and at the time of the California gold rush their filigree equaled anything produced in Europe.[65] The town was in the heart of Peru's llama-raising country, and the editor of *La Alforja* ("The Llama Packsaddle Bag"), Ayacucho's newspaper, enjoyed a good joke. Having seen an article in the June 7, 1849, *Alta California* headed EIGHT HUNDRED TONS OF WOMEN FROM LOWELL, he decided to outdo the writer with a parody in *La Alforja*.

The account in *Alta California* described Mrs. Eliza W. Farnham's efforts to enlist poor, marriageable young women for California. Her success in Massachusetts, the writer said, was so good she could probably fill an 800-ton vessel with girls. The editor of *La Alforja* rewrote the story in Spanish, adding observations he considered appropriate. Under the heading OCHOCIENTOS TONELADAS DE MUJERES he told his readers that a new nation was surpassing the technology of the Englishmen, those accepted operators of Peru's mines. The skillful, progressive norteamericanos were now measuring women by the ton. A newspaper in New York, he said, reported that a bark from that harbor was carrying 800 tons of women to California via Cape Horn. On so long a trip, the editor hoped, the captain would spend some of his time giving the women lessons designed to make them more useful mothers of families in their new environment. With this theme in mind, the editor scoffed at the futile efforts of North Americans to educate the underprivileged by the monitorial system, the latest fad of liberals in the United States. The deck of a vessel, said the editor, would supply sufficient room and he hoped that the girls would learn the two things North American husbands esteemed most in their women: how to knit socks and how to prepare tea.[66]

PART V
Chileans who Remained in California and Others Who Returned Home

19

Famine, Fire, and the Anti-Chilean War

Reader, pass on—ne'er waste your time
On bad biography nor better rhyme;
For what I am, this cumb'rous clay insures,
And what I was, is no affair of yours.
—Tombstone inscription from the
Californian, August 14, 1848

The above epitaph would have been suitable for two sea captains whose negligence caused great suffering and several deaths on shipboard during the first year of the gold rush from Chile. As noted earlier, Captain Vanpelt lost command of the *Ann McKim* because he sailed from San Francisco with so little water that, when the vessel arrived in Valparaiso on October 10, 1849, ten of his passengers were prostrated from dehydration.[1] The shocking account of that voyage on an ill-equipped ship could not reach San Francisco for at least two months, and every day more illiterate peons, driven from their claims, congregated in the city. None of them knew about the *Ann McKim's* tragic cruise back to Chile, nor had they learned that the British *Inconstant* was coming to pick up homesick Chileans.

The plight of the dispossessed Chileans flocking into San Francisco caused another irresponsible shipowner to see an opportunity for making money with his *María Luisa Pérez*, a tramp schooner in the bay. These Chileans were ignorant farm workers. Driven from their claims and speaking no English, they could find no jobs in a city that, in the late summer of 1849, was filled with skilled North American and European immigrants. Almost destitute, the Chileans crowded into unsightly tents and shacks patched with tattered sails; the squalid slums were cluttered with stinking garbage, castaway clothing, and broken bottles. Haunted constantly by memories of the July riot, they eagerly accepted the offer of extra-cheap passage on the tramp schooner to Chile. She was fitted to accommodate twenty passengers, but the captain packed her with sixty to eighty of these desperate Chileans. The figures disagree.[2]

The *María* sailed early in September with the angel of death in her rigging. An average vessel could make the voyage in approximately sixty days, but she required more than eighty. To save money the captain stowed a limited quantity of cheap food on board, and this meager amount soon had to be rationed. The water supply also proved insufficient. Six of the passengers died of starvation, and the captain saw one collapse while praying for food. In spite of these conditions, he refused to stop at Valparaiso and sailed an additional 300 miles south to Talcahuano, where ten or twelve emaciated passengers had to be carried ashore.

At this port the passengers did not make a formal complaint which, according to law, had to be in writing. Since they were unable to write, the authorities sent them to Valparaiso in two small vessels. There the editor of *El Comercio*, after listening to their story, wrote a blistering editorial[3] censuring the government in Santiago which, he said, had done nothing all summer except engage in futile debates over the gold rush. Why, the editor asked, had a consul not been sent to San Francisco where he could have prevented such ill-equipped Chilean vessels from sailing? Peru had established a consulate there. Was President Castilla making his unprogressive country a more respected nation than Chile?

The Chilean government decided to act, but instead of appointing the popular Samuel Price to the position he had assumed voluntarily, a new man, Don Felipe Fierro, was sent as consul. This man, who later edited San Francisco's first Chilean newspaper, *El Eco*,[4] unearthed another tragedy. Soon after his arrival he saw, through the glass windows of a pawnshop, the Chilean colors displayed in jewels on a medal. Stepping inside, he learned from the broker that this and other valuable medals had been pawned by Don Carlos Wooster, the famous Chilean hero of Chiloé and captor of the Spanish battleship *María Isabel* in the war for independence. Don Carlos had succeeded Lord Cochrane, becoming a rear admiral, but he participated in a revolution that failed. Fleeing to San Francisco, he survived less than a year and died penniless. The once wealthy New England privateersman left only a will requesting burial under the flags of Chile and the United States, the two countries he had served and loved.[5]

The consul presented the medals to Benjamín Vicuña Mackenna, who, as editor of *El Mercurio*, visited San Francisco in 1853.[6] Don Benjamín, familiar with Valparaiso's steep shore where piers could not be constructed, was impressed by the dozens of docks protruding into San Franciso Bay. He described the city as a Venice of wood, of ships, wharves, and the sea. Big vessels that had stuck in the mud served as habitations, shops, and cafes. He found the city to be a veritable Babylon of villages—Chinese, Mexican, and Chilean. Each village had a totally different character, and on the streets he heard many languages. Men wore the clothes of all nations, the Mexican in sarape, the Chilean in poncho, the Irishman in ragged coat and crushed plush hat, the Yankee—always dominant—in red flannel shirt, heavy boots, and pantaloons held up with a belt. These gruff Americans, according to Spanish-speaking Vicuña M., talked in monosyllables, pronouncing only the middle of a word.[7] He also noted, with great interest, the Chinese in their blue blouses and pigtails, and he thanked God that the gold rush was bringing to California these inferior Orientals, so they would no longer crowd the beaches of South America.[8]

Like Pérez Rosales, who was impressed by the North Americans' coarseness, Vicuña Mackenna also noted their casual attitude toward death. When men died on shipboard, norteamericanos buried them at sea with little ceremony, he thought, and in San Francisco the surrounding hills served as rough cemeteries, although burial there cost plenty. The charge for digging a crude grave was $60, and $30 was charged for a makeshift coffin. A plank painted white, with irregular black letters stating the deceased's name, age, and date of death, cost an ounce.[9] Expensive epitaphs like REST IN PEACE were evidently scoffed at, and pranksters defaced grave markers by adding suggestions for peaceful sleep, like DRINK MILK-AND-WATER PUNCH.[10] Graves in these cemeteries, Vicuña M. said, told the grim history of Californians who died in shipwreck, died of hunger, died of grief, died of vengeance—brother against brother. Yet they had all died young, having lived only twenty or thirty years.[11]

In spite of Vicuña M.'s melancholy picture, it is noteworthy that the anti-Chilean riot failed to drive his more vigorous fellow countrymen from San Francisco. Many of them had established permanent business houses before the great fire of December 24, 1849, consumed the heart of the city. The conflagration started at about 6:00 A.M., probably in Dennison's Exchange[12] or in a nearby brothel where the flames could crackle quickly over the freshly painted nude figures, the cotton ceilings, and the tar-paper roofs. In no time the fire spread in every direction, roaring through the frail wooden buildings. Chilean cities never burned like this, even after an earthquake, but Chileans were reminded of the fires that sometimes swept across their grain fields at harvest time.[13] The Waddington offices were destroyed, as were the counting rooms of both Luis Guzmán and the Soruco brothers,[14] upper-class businessmen who had come during the first year of the rush.

A week after the conflagration a Chilean wrote to friends in South America: "I passed the place of the fire this afternoon. A large number of the houses are now rebuilt and others are being constructed."[15] He said that men had been paid $25 an hour for saving property. One owner, even while his cafe was burning, contracted for its reconstruction. The agreement promised the builder a magnificent bonus if he finished the job in fifteen days, but if he failed to meet that deadline he would have to pay the owner $500 every day until the work was completed. Other property owners, according to the writer of the letter, negotiated similar agreements, and in no time 200 carpenters were at work, each receiving $15 to $20 a day.[16]

Several Chileans of means had established themselves in other California hamlets. Washington City showed no sign of growth, but José Manuel Ramírez y Rosales* was one of the early purchasers of the original trading post in Marysville who laid out a future city.[17] Also early in 1849, the Luco brothers, Leandro and Manuel, became active businessmen in Sacramento. They had sailed their seagoing *Natalia* all the way to the site at the time Pérez Rosales outfitted there. In addition to a cargo of merchandise, they brought a goodly number of peons whose labor they offered for hire.

During the hot summer of 1849, with stagnant pools left by the receding rivers, many of the Chileans in Sacramento became seriously ill with malaria and other fevers. Some died. The Luco brothers converted the *Natalia* into an infirmary,[18] thus giving future Chilean historians a reason for crediting them with the establishment of Sacramento's first charity hospital.[19]

The *Natalia* became a haven for dispossessed Chileans during the local riots of June and July, and the Luco brothers, with their family tradition of foreign trade, made a business of supplying Anglo capitalists with Chilean laborers. The Lucos also employed their peons to pan gold for them on the Yuba River, which in 1849 became the latest bonanza. Gold seekers came to it from everywhere. One Englishman, with a Chilean partner and a gang of peons, staked mining claims for his entire party. General Thomas Jefferson Green, ex-filibusterer from Texas, moved in with a dozen Texans and fifteen Negro slaves. He staked a mining claim for each man.[20] The practice of claiming large tracts of gold country in the names of employees or slaves seemed to be the order of the day.

A tall, well-built man, with graying hair and the rugged features common on the frontier, watched with interest this method of acquiring claims. Wilson Shannon had served as congressman from Ohio, as governor of that state, and as United States minister to Mexico. In 1854 President Pierce would appoint him governor of Kansas Territory.[21] In Ohio the former governor

---

* Hubert Howe Bancroft, *History of California* (San Francisco, 1884–1890), VI, 463. Don José later became a Chilean senator. Benjamín Vicuña Mackenna (*"Terra Ignota,"* o sea *Viaje del país de la crisis al mundo de las maravillas* [Valparaiso, 1930], p. 18). Felipe Ramírez was a brother-in-law of Vicente Pérez Rosales. See his *California Adventure* (San Francisco, 1947), p. 89.

organized a party of twenty-five gold seekers, and to save money sent them by boat around the Horn while he and his brother-in-law crossed the Isthmus of Panama. Arriving three months ahead of his party, Shannon saw bands of Chileans—forty in one party—panning for gold along the Yuba.[22] Lest the supply of gold be exhausted, he decided not to wait for his party but to hire the Chileans available in Sacramento at once.

The severe illness of one of the Luco brothers halted Shannon's negotiations for laborers.[23] Perhaps the circumstance was fortunate, because independent American miners were losing patience with capitalists who took up large blocks of claims in the names of their workers. As a result, many operators were driven from the stream,[24] and the Luco brothers' Chileans were particularly vulnerable. Yankee miners had not forgotten General Smith's unfortunate proclamation against foreigners. A raid on the Yuba in December ended with the hanging of one Chilean, while others were flogged or had their ears cropped.[25]

By this time Sacramento had become completely Anglicized. Some 30,000 Americans had arrived overland in wagon trains,[26] a number six times larger than the total of those who had come from Peru and Chile.[27] The city had grown amazingly since Pérez Rosales saw it in July. S. B. Brannan & Co. now operated a handsome, wide-eaved store, whose rafters served well for hanging harness, horse collars, feed bags, hobbles, lanterns, and log chains. The half darkness inside the store made it more difficult for customers to read the scales when a clerk weighed their gold dust.

Another impressive building, the City Hotel, stood three stories high with a balcony the full length of each floor, and there was the Eagle Theater, with its false front.[28] The plan of naming streets A, B, and C in one direction and numbering them 1, 2, and 3 in the other impressed Chileans as a Yankee method by which a house could be located "with rifle accuracy."* Sacramento had indeed become a city. Many Chileans remained but

---

* "Infalible como la puntería de un rifle," according to Benjamín Vicuña Mackenna (*Pájinas de mi Diario* [Santiago de Chile, 1856], p. 9). Here is a good example showing why a text in Spanish is longer than one in English.

their day had passed, and the so-called Chilean war would be fought farther south.

As early as July, 1849, gold seekers on the Middle Fork of the Stanislaus River had expelled Spanish-speaking miners. According to contemporary accounts, this illegal action was performed by English, French, Dutch, Italian, and Portuguese miners, combined with North Americans. The prejudice against Mexicans and South Americans specifically, instead of against all foreigners, evidently arose from the fact that they had come to the country first, understood mining better, and held the best claims. The editor of the *Placer Times* in Stockton sympathized with the Spanish-speaking miners and disapproved of expelling them. Many of his readers concurred. As the conflict developed, this sympathy encouraged the Chileans[29] and precipitated the "war."

Three versions of the confrontation have been published: the piecemeal reports in the contemporary press; the story told by Colonel J. J. Ayers, a prisoner of the Chileans, and published forty-seven years after his experience; and the history written by Enrique Bunster in 1954. The three accounts differ widely from one another. Bunster's *Chilenos en California*[30] described battle carnage that turned the Calaveras River red. Colonel Ayers, in "The Chilean War in Calaveras County,"[31] showed more restraint but in the end, as will be seen, he gave himself a heroic role not borne out by contemporary newspapers. The following narrative is reconstructed from these three accounts.

The war commenced about 50 miles from Stockton. When the winter rains started in December, 1849, some Americans moved into the country where Chileans had worked dry diggings during the summer. The Chileans returned and began to work on their old claims. The Americans objected, claiming all the land. Instead of appealing to the established government, they held a mass meeting, drew up a mining code of their own which regulated the size of claims, and prohibited Chileans from filing on claims for their peons. A similar restriction had been imposed on General Green and his slaves on the Yuba. The Calaveras miners, at their meeting, established a local government of their own, electing a Virginian named Collier as alcalde, presumably because he came from a slave state and therefore knew how to deal with bondmen of color, a definition that hardly applied to Chilean rotos. The miners also elected a military captain to enforce the alcalde's decisions.[32] These acts ignored the established state government, the judge in Stockton, the county sheriff, and the legally qualified alcalde, John Scallan, who operated a shop on the Calaveras and was also interested in several stores throughout the southern diggings.

Shortly after the miners wrote and adopted their code some of them were driven from a gulch by Chileans who claimed prior mining rights there. The dispossessed Americans appealed to their pseudo alcalde, Judge Collier, who called his constituents to another mass meeting. They adopted a resolution ordering all miners who were not citizens of the United States to leave the country within fifteen days.

Many of the Chileans left, but some, true to the fatalism of rotos in South America, stayed stubbornly on their claims. At the end of the prescribed fifteen days, those who had remained were brought before Collier, who fined each of them an ounce in gold and ordered them to leave by December 25. Apparently all were packing to go, but then a leading Chilean named Dr. Concha appealed for help to Judge Reynolds in Stockton. Concha returned with a warrant for the arrest of the North American miners who, though claiming to impose fines, were legally guilty of robbery. The sheriff also gave the doctor authority to organize a posse and make the necessary arrests. Dr. Concha enlisted some sixty Chileans* who, armed with revolvers, cutlasses, clubs, and butcher knives,[33] went to an encampment known as the Iowa Cabins after dark on December 26. Surprising the Americans in their beds, the Chileans arrested the leading miners, bound their arms behind their backs, and marched them away. Similar arrests were made in other camps. At one place the posse saw a light and burst in on five or six men playing cards. A fight ensued. Two Americans and one Chilean were killed, and four others were wounded.

* James J. Ayers (*Gold and Sunshine* [Boston, 1922], p. 50) says sixty Chileans formed the posse. The Stockton *Placer Times*, Jan. 14, 1850, says eighty. Both figures are conjectural.

Colonel Ayers, in his written account of the war, says he heard the firing and considered it a massacre, not a fight. He learned later that the posse shot two men, killing one and severely wounding the other in the right arm and shoulder. The Chilean posse, he said, had mistaken the man they killed for Collier, whom they blamed for giving the order to expel them. They wrapped the wounded man in a blanket and left him. When found, he was dead. Colonel Ayers said the Chileans had probably slipped back and murdered him, lest he crawl away and warn other camps to pursue the posse and liberate the arrested men.[34]

According to Ayers, the Chileans now held thirteen prisoners. Bunster and the newspapers say there were sixteen.[35] With these men in custody, some of them coatless in the winter weather, the Chileans marched 8 miles to the tent store of John Scallan, the legitimate alcalde. Evidently loath to take sides among his customers, Scallan refused to countenance the warrants from the judge in Stockton. Instead, on some excuse, he dodged his duty and disappeared. The perplexed Chileans spent an hour looking for him and then decided to take the prisoners to their own camp, some fifteen miles away, for the night.

Early the next morning the Chileans, some on horseback, started with their prisoners for Stockton to deliver them to the sheriff. At seven or eight o'clock the party stopped at what was called "the six-mile tent," where the Chileans, according to one newspaper, ate breakfast while their prisoners drank only cold coffee.[36] They then marched 12 miles to Frank Lemon's tent restaurant, at the lower crossing of the Calaveras, where each man ate a biscuit and some cheese, with coffee. Here the prisoners described their predicament to a local ranchman who vowed to free them, saying he would arouse the entire community and overpower the Chileans.

Marching on toward Stockton, the posse and the prisoners met a man with a gun on his saddle. As he passed them, he said, "Take care of yourselves, boys."[37] Although none of the Chileans spoke English, this remark and the belligerent appearance of the rider made them decide to leave the Stockton road and tramp into the tall wild oats and creosote bushes south of the highway. The winter rains had started, obliterating their tracks. They walked slowly through intermittent showers, over hill and dale, through thickets, mud, and water. Once or twice they crossed rocky ridges where they looked back over the underbrush toward the Stockton road and saw armed men galloping along it, evidently hunting them. With no hope of escape to their rear, the Chileans pushed on toward the Mokelumne River. As the storm increased, they took shelter under the spreading branches of live oak trees. The march had been harder on many of the Chileans than on their prisoners, and only eleven of the posse remained.

At this point Colonel Ayers's narrative differs markedly from newspaper accounts. All agree that Ayers was the only prisoner who spoke Spanish, but only Ayers says that he overheard the leaders' conversation and learned that they had given up their plan to go to Stockton because they were afraid they would be discovered and stopped. A leader named Tirante wanted to kill the prisoners and then scatter, every man for himself. Another man, named Maturano, vigorously opposed this idea. The question was voted upon and the captives' lives were saved.[38]

That night, according to Ayers, the Chileans camped around a big fire which gave them some relief. Finally the storm moderated and the guard fell asleep. The prisoners saw their chance, grabbed the drowsing men's guns, and took command of the entire camp. The peons acquiesced readily enough. Indeed, Tirante was the only man who showed fight, so they bound him with a rope and kept him under guard. In the darkness the triumphant Americans did not know where they were or which way to go, but they did remember that they had marched south from the Stockton road. In the morning the sun rose in a clear sky, and the Americans, with their prisoners, started north through the dripping undergrowth. Before long they caught sight of a large tent across a gulch in front of them which they recognized as O'Neill's Hotel on the Stockton road. A man at the hotel spied them coming, and by the time they crossed the ravine a large party of armed miners stood in formation to greet them.[39]

The Chilean prisoners were turned over to this party and all devoured a much-needed breakfast. Colonel Ayers, ever thankful to Maturano for saving all their lives, invented an excuse for walking past the guard with him; when they reached the open country where the wild oats stood dense and tall, he told the Chilean to stoop and run. Maturano thanked him and disappeared. Colonel Ayers watched the swaying oat tops until he was sure that his friend had escaped.

The remaining prisoners, according to Ayers's account, were marched back to the Calaveras camp where a lynch court sentenced Tirante and two others to death, some four or five to flogging, and two to having their ears cut off. This statement is not confirmed by contemporary records. Colonel Ayers may have read about hanging and ear clipping on the Yuba and, after forty-seven years, may have thought these punishments were meted out in his camp. Ayers also says[40] that men in Stockton who sympathized with the miners made the lives of Judge Reynolds and the sheriff miserable because they had issued the arrest warrants and authorized the posse. Both officials fled in disgrace.

Like many personal narratives, the heroic details written by Ayers disagree with stories in the press. The newspapers omit the grim threat to murder the prisoners which Ayers says he heard. They also say nothing about his heroic disarming of the guard. Instead, they state that the Chileans agreed, through the Spanish-speaking Ayers, to return to the Stockton road if the prisoners would go with them to Stockton and intercede with any armed miners they might meet on the way.[41] The prisoners did agree, and the party came out at a tent on the road about 10 miles from Stockton. The tent happened to be full of Americans who immediately tied up the Chileans and started for Stockton with the entire party (thus partly honoring the agreement). On the way they were overtaken by men from Calaveras who marched the Chileans back to their encampment, while the erstwhile American prisoners went on voluntarily to Stockton to give themselves up according to the warrants for their arrest.

In Stockton the authorities examined the warrants and claimed that they found no proof that the persons surrendering themselves were the men who had ordered the Chileans off the public domain after extracting money from them. Because of this uncertainty, the defendants were released. The newspaper that reported this decision added that, according to rumor, the eleven Chileans taken back to Calaveras were hanged. Any of their countrymen, the paper added, who remained in the neighborhood would fare badly.[42]

This rumor, which Ayers enlarged upon, seems to have been groundless. As for the escape of Judge Reynolds and the sheriff from the mob violence in Stockton, described by Ayers, the *Alta California* says merely[43] that four delegates from Calaveras came to town to present the miners' case. They called a public meeting, denied that any of the Chileans had been hanged, and offered resolutions blaming the Chileans for making the arrests by force at night. How many North Americans were present to vote for these resolutions the paper does not state, and there is no mention of the flight of judge or sheriff.

Thus the "people," in a rather feeble way, won out against the law, but Chileans never forgot the bad treatment they received in the San Francisco riot, the expulsion from their claims in this little war, and, later, the Baltimore affair of 1891. Their everlasting grudge, embodied in the name of Joaquín Murieta, helped elect a Chilean senator in 1964, and in 1970 the old rancor, now called imperialism, served to elect an anti-North American president.*

* In 1850 an attempt was made to expel Latin Americans from the placers by a monthly tax levied on foreign miners by the state. The revolt against the tax was led by Frenchmen, not Chileans. Since many merchants liked the free-spending Latins, the law was repealed in 1851. By that time many Chileans had gone home, but the census of 1852 showed more than half of the population at the southern mines to be foreign. (Leonard Pitt, *The Decline of the Californios* [Berkeley and Los Angeles, 1966], p. 66; Rodman Wilson Paul, *California Gold* [Cambridge, Mass., 1947], p. 108; Frederick Gerstaecker, *Narrative of a Journey round the World* [New York, 1853], p. 209.)

20

Epilogue

Shipmates all, my cruise is up,
My body's moored at rest.
My soul is—where?—aloft of course,
Rejoicing with the blest.
    —Epitaph in Protestant cemetery,
    Valparaiso

If the California gold rush began when Sam Brannan shouted, "Gold! Gold! Gold from the American River," it may be said, with equal uncertainty, that the rush ended in Chile when rotos coming back from California participated in a revolution opposing the nomination of a conservative president in 1851. In the same year, Castilla's first term as president of Peru expired. He designated a puppet whose administration was notable for corruption, but no revolution upset the government and Castilla continued to dominate it until 1862.[1] He was killed five years later at the age of seventy. Like Pizarro, he died fighting his enemies. Oddly enough, the California gold rush did cause a revolution in Australia which, like the one in Chile, failed militarily.

In California the Australian gold seekers learned how to find and mine gold before returning to their own country. They soon outproduced the United States by millions of dollars every year, and in a decade the population of Australia trebled.[2] The effect of the gold rush on South America was quite different. Chileans and Peruvians who returned from California had been teachers, not learners. For 200 years their countries had led the world in producing gold. The wealth from Peruvian mines had made Spain the richest nation in Europe, with colonies around the world and fleets on every sea. But after 1800 the amount of Peruvian gold decreased noticeably, and from 1851 to 1855, the peak years,[3] the United States produced as much gold as South America had produced in the preceding half century.

During the first year of the California rush 5,000 South Americans emigrated. A total of some 50,000 are said to have arrived in California between 1848 and 1852.[4] Most of them were Chileans. No real rush developed from Peru. The attitude of its population differed markedly from that of Chileans, and the effort to retard emigration by redeveloping mines at home may have discouraged the more adventurous spirits in Peru. The attempt to exploit the vast gold deposits at Carbaya y Sandia had failed completely by 1850. A Frenchman with capital employed a corps of workers, but the exorbitant wages for men willing to work at that breathtakingly high altitude, the lack of roads for bringing in machinery, and the danger from neighboring Indians discouraged the operators.[5] Indeed, that goldfield was farther away from Lima, in terms of time, than California was. It also proved much more expensive to work. Although the project, while it lasted, may have diverted some Peruvians from going to California, the few who went to North America attracted more attention than their number warranted. The handful who sailed on the S.S. *California* caused General Persifor Smith to issue the circular letter that caused so much trouble for all Latin Americans in the goldfields. The general's successor, Brigadier General Bennet Riley, tried to repair the damage by saying that every person, regardless of his nationality, was a "guest" on the public domain,[6] but American miners clung to Smith's doctrine and in their proclamations against foreigners they always included Peruvians along with Chileans.

We have noted that some Chileans returned home with quickly made fortunes, but many stayed in the United States permanently, establishing themselves as North American businessmen. Others left the country with nothing but experience coupled with a North American disrespect for authority—rotos ready for revolution. The revolution in Chile, however, was not started by rotos, and the great day for Pérez Rosales came when the establishment crushed the rebels. The trouble was started by Francisco Bilbao, a twenty-one-year-old law student in Santiago. He had studied under Andrés Bello[7] and had published an article extolling socialism some three years before Karl Marx's *Manifesto* appeared. For this effrontery Bilbao was expelled from college. He went to France, the country admired by educated Chileans, and learned about street barricades in Paris during the revolution of 1848.

Returning to Chile in 1849, Bilbao heard the bitter debates in the Cámaras concerning the economic upset caused by the California gold rush. All around him people were impoverished by inflation while others became inordinately wealthy. This economic imbalance gave Francisco Bilbao an unusual opportunity. He organized socialistic equality (*Igualdad*) clubs to overthrow Chile's so-called autocratic republic which, under the constitution of 1833, had been ruled by men of position and wealth. Club members called these rulers *pelucanismo* ("wigged ones" or "tiewigs"), a Spanish translation of the slang term for "Tory" used in the American Revolution. Some deputies in the Cámaras who opposed the ruling majority joined Bilbao's organization.

Elections for the presidency were due in the fall of 1851, and whoever received the Cámaras nomination invariably won. President Manuel Bulnes wanted his "tiewig party" in the Cámaras to nominate Manuel Montt, who would continue his program of colonization in the unsettled southern forests and also in the Strait of Magellan area. Bulnes's opponents determined to nominate General José de la Cruz, who would decentralize the government and give more democratic self-determination to outlying communities.

There is no record that any roto from California took part in the first confrontation between the two parties, which occurred in the autumn of 1850 at San Felipe, on the pony express road between Buenos Aires and Valparaiso. In the town famous for its vineyards and imposing church, protesters took advantage of the wide main street for demonstrations. Members of La Sociedad de la Igualdad harangued any crowd they could muster, preaching redistribution of wealth, brotherhood, and equal rights for all. A banner inscribed with a phrase offensive to some was displayed at the club's window. Reports disagree on its exact wording. The conflicting mottoes may be translated as "War against Tyranny" or as the more fatal words used by Pizarro's assassins, "Death to Tyrants."⁸ A policeman tore down the banner and delivered it to the town *intendente*. Two club members who went to the city hall to retrieve the banner were put in jail.

Residents in the small town of San Felipe soon learned that their fellow citizens were being held in jail without a trial. A mob assembled, and club members urged the people to parade up and down the broad street between the red-roofed adobe houses. The local constabulary was ordered to disperse the mob and shoot to kill if necessary. Many of the police had brothers, cousins, and friends in the crowd and they refused to fire. The mob, realizing its power, seized the jail and released all prisoners, including embittered criminals who were eager for revenge against society. The situation became so dangerous that the authorities sent an express rider at full gallop to get help from Santiago, 60 miles away, where the first California gold-seeking rotos would enter the episode.

In San Felipe prominent citizens, who cared little for politics and supported neither Montt nor Cruz, organized a committee to restore order. They were confronted with the crisis common to all administrators dealing with a mob. They knew that the Chilean army could restore peace, but soldiers would probably kill some normally peaceful protesters. The committee realized, also, that the word "army" was anathema to rioters who might redouble their depredations before the soldiers arrived. Faced by this predicament, the committee consulted the Igualistas, and agreed to return the banner and bring no charges against the rioters if they dispersed. This concession restored peace. Nobody was hurt, but the Igualistas had become aware of their power.

The next disturbance occurred in Santiago, the nation's capital. When the express rider from San Felipe galloped into town at dawn on November 6, 1850, the federal Council of State dispatched troops to crush the revolution there. Police in Santiago, fearing that the insurrection might be general, watched the windows of the local Igualdad club rooms. Everything in town seemed quiet except for little groups of rotos who clustered suspiciously at street corners. Before long a disturbing rumor reported, falsely, that the revolution in San Felipe had succeeded. Equally erroneous accounts said that a victorious rebel army was marching across the cactus-studded tableland north of Santiago to arouse all liberty-loving people. Chileans knew their French history and remembered what happened when the revolutionary volunteers from Marseilles marched to Paris in 1792, singing what would become the hymn of the French Revolution.

The frightened authorities in Santiago declared martial law. Both liberal newspapers, *El Progreso* and *La Barra*, were ordered to stop publication, and the police began secretly to apprehend all known radical speakers. Some forty men, including a few members of the Cámaras, were listed for arrest. Many citizens fled the town or hid in the homes of friends. One escaped from his residence by running across the rough tile roof.[9]

The night following the issuance of these tyrannical orders was ominous because the United States minister, some days earlier, had selected this evening for a dance at the legation and radicals in the Cámaras usually attended his functions. Yankees, since colonial days, had had a reputation for lawlessness. Chileans remembered that in 1811, when Spain still ruled their country, President Madison had sent Joel Poinsett to Chile to foment a revolution and to free American prisoners, many of them Nantucket whalers, who had been captured trespassing in Spanish waters. For two years Poinsett rode with the insurrectos.[10] He helped release the prisoners, but the revolution for independence did not succeed. Since that time the United States, in Chilean eyes, had continued to represent lawlessness. Seth Barton, the impudent chargé d'affaires, had perpetuated the image, and the treatment of Chileans in California confirmed it. A ball at the American legation always attracted radicals, and the police would haunt the streets leading there. This prospect so terrified any man with liberal opinions that only a quarter of the invited guests attended.[11]

The threatened revolution failed to materialize, and most of the arrested radicals were released. The Igualistas reorganized underground and struck again in April, 1851. They still had almost five months to prevent Manuel Montt from becoming president. Public demonstrations were now forbidden by law but the

Igualistas convinced Colonel Pedro Urriola that "the people" detested tiewigs and would support him eagerly in a coup d'etat to nominate General Cruz for the presidency. Colonel Urriola was a veteran revolutionist[12] with the ominous Basque "rr" in his name. He was easily assured by scheming insurgents that a revolt on Easter Sunday would make him leader of a resurrection "as important to Chile as was that of the Savior."[13]

Flattered by this prospect and pleased by an advance payment of $15,000, the colonel appeared with a few battalions of his regiment in the plaza at 3:00 A.M. on that holy day. He announced to the early morning loafers—the poor waifs who slept in alleys—and to the donkey boys who had come to fill their water kegs that he was taking over the government in order to install a president who represented the people. These vagabonds had heard politicians talk that way all their lives. They showed little interest in politics and seemed slow to agree that Chile would be saved by the election of General Cruz.[14] Their lives had never changed much under any president. Undismayed, Colonel Urriola sent a courier to President Bulnes demanding his surrender, while Igualistas in the plaza implored every man who believed in liberty, equality, and fraternity to join the colonel's army of liberation.

President Bulnes, aroused in his palace, did not know the magnitude of the revolt, but he hesitated to arrest and imprison the courier who came for his surrender. Such an act had precipitated the riot in San Felipe. His bodyguard knew nothing about the revolution and questioned whether many regiments had joined Colonel Urriola. The city being quiet, President Bulnes dared ride through the streets, imploring the people to support his government.

In the plaza, however, Colonel Urriola had mustered 600 men, including soldiers, the Igualistas, and a few street loafers. He sent word to his fellow officers to bring their regiments, but he received only evasive replies. Were they all nonidealistic materialists waiting to support the winning side? He waited three uncertain hours, then decided to act. Surely the other regiments would join him if he led the people to victory. He ordered his little band of rebels to march to Mount Santa Lucía where artillery and ammunition were stored in the government armory. The small guard on duty there would be no match for his 600 followers. He would take the armory and everybody would join his crusade for equality, fraternity, and civil rights. His second in command, Colonel Justo Arteaga, an elderly liberal, opposed Urriola's rash order. He believed in equality and popular rule, but disliked bloodshed. He accompanied the march with apprehension.

The march proved a success. Street loafers joined the parade, shouting victorious *viva's*, but the guard at the armory slammed shut the portals and defied the enemy. At last the crisis had arrived. Urriola ordered the erection of a street barricade, like those in Paris. While it was being built street vendors came along and the insurrectos bought bread, milk, and fruit, paying with gold dust; thus they revealed themselves to be rotos from California.[15] Lieutenant Gilliss, whose American Philosophical Society observatory stood near the armory, feared that it would be destroyed.* California rotos had no love for norteamericanos. The rebels, however, were intent only on capturing the government artillery and ammunition. After breakfast some of those behind the barricade began firing at the armory. Others slipped around to attack it from streets in the rear. Several squads of daring men tried again and again to batter their way into the building.

During this bombardment other regiments began to appear, but they did not support the revolt. Instead, they came to uphold the government. A musket ball hit Colonel Urriola and he fell from his saddle saying, "Me han engañado" ("They have deceived me").[16] His second-in-command, Colonel Arteaga, who had followed reluctantly, mounted a servant's horse and, riding behind the menial, escaped to the home of a North American envoy. The fighting rotos failed to notice the loss of their commanders. With typical impetuosity they finally captured the armory, then stood dumbfounded. They had won the battle but, lacking a leader, they had lost the war. More than a hundred of their comrades lay dead around the building.[17]

* Since Gilliss himself was in Valparaiso at this time, he was in no personal danger. He learned about the insurrection from dispatches.

This engagement ended the revolution in Santiago. Manuel Montt was duly nominated and elected president, but followers of General Cruz and some regiments north and south of the city defied the government. At last the revolution had become nationwide, but it was soon crushed 125 miles south of Santiago on the Loncomilla River which drained a grazing country with enough cattle and sheep to support two armies. Federal and insurrecto forces met there on December 8, 1851, in a battle that cost more lives than any other in Chilean history. Of the 7,000 engaged, 2,000 were killed and 1,500 wounded. The Montt government won, and later in the same month the rebels in northern Chile also surrendered. The pelucanismo ("wigged ones") remained in power,[18] and Pérez Rosales, who returned to Chile at this time, began his remarkable career.

It is easy to put together with reasonable accuracy the pieces of Vicente's past which contributed to his immediate prominence. In addition to his various pioneer experiences in North and South America, he had been a disciple of the Argentine writer, Sarmiento, who was always a devoted supporter of Manuel Montt. When Montt graduated from law school and became a candidate for a seat in the Cámaras, Sarmiento had campaigned for him. After winning the election, Montt soon became minister of education and he repaid Sarmiento with government appointments in Chile. Both men were interested in education and colonization,[19] but Sarmiento's most compelling vocation continued to be his own vigorous writing, the writing that had fascinated Pérez Rosales.

Sarmiento's great book, *Civilization and Barbarism*, written in Chile shortly before the gold rush, made him internationally famous. In its pages he advanced a theory of the frontier exactly the reverse of the one voiced fifty years later in North America by Frederick Jackson Turner. The frontier that Sarmiento knew so well was no cradle for democracy. Instead, he found it the seat of tyranny. Progress and democracy, he said, must be born in the cities. The free land of the pampas could only "prepare the way for despotism."[20] The villain in Sarmiento's famous book was the dictator of Argentina, who became so enraged he charged the writer with treason and tried to extradite him for trial. Instead of surrendering, Sarmiento took refuge in his old haunts in the Andes where he continued to write, helped organize a revolution, and eventually became president of Argentina. But that part of his life is beyond our story.

When Pérez Rosales returned to Chile from California,* Sarmiento had fled. Bulnes and Montt needed a qualified person to direct the colonization that had interested the great writer. What better man could they find than Sarmiento's disciple, who knew the Chilean Andes and would also be able to deal with Indians? The Araucanians south of Concepción were blocking colonization. They had resisted Europeans successfully since the days of the conquistadores.

These Indians were not naked savages. They were agriculturists who clung to their native dress and customs. They lived in log houses, sometimes 60 feet long. They raised wheat, maize, peas, potatoes, and cabbages, wove handsome ponchos, and bred horses, cattle, and sheep,[21] but they resolutely resisted the Chilean army. In desperation the government offered them all the country from Concepción south to Valdivia—an oasis 100 miles square—if they would not harass settlers in the pine forests farther south which were now open to homesteaders, who would pay no taxes for twelve years.[22]

Settlements were started on this frontier during Pérez Rosales' youthful days of adventure, but they had never been successful. The Indians made life too dangerous. Now Vicente, accompanied by the German who had been commissioned by the government to aid colonization, sailed up the Valdivia River, a tree-bordered stream as broad and tranquil as California's Sacramento River which Pérez R. had navigated so successfully. They explored the lake region at the foot of the Andes. In 1858 Vicente went to Hamburg where, as *agente de colonización*, he established an office and served as consul. He directed the emigration of Germans who later formed the Chilean province of

---

* Pérez R. says he left California toward the end of 1850. Manuel Montt became president of Chile in October, 1851. According to Ramón Pérez Yañez (*Forjadores de Chile* [Santiago de Chile, 1953], p. 211), Pérez R. left Valparaiso and arrived in Carral on February 12, 1850. There is some error here, because Pérez Y.'s statement means that Pérez R. would have left California in November, 1849, before the fire he describes so vividly.

Llanquihue, named for a lake where many settled. In 1876 homesteaders in the province elected him senator to represent them in the Cámaras. He died in 1886.[23]

Chile and Peru, unlike Australia, did not experience a sudden social and political change immediately after the California gold rush. Both Latin-American countries conformed to a culture centuries old, a culture that many North Americans considered archaic. Yet both these Latin countries emancipated their slaves before the United States did. In Peru, President Castilla's reign became a turning point in his country's history. He built the first railroad in South America and abolished primogeniture, thus permitting the breakup of large estates. He also established mail service and instituted federal supervision of trade unions. Under his administration residents of Lima lived without fear of violence for the first time since Peru's independence. Some analytical historians maintain that Peru's age of modern maturity began with Castilla. Others disagree, saying that Peru's prosperity ended when the supply of guano failed,[24] while in California, by the time the gold was depleted, new industries and prosperous agriculture had been established.

In Chile, efforts to break up the big estates by abolishing entail and primogeniture had started before the gold rush. Some enactments during the rush caused bitter debates, but the problem was finally settled in 1857.[25] The sudden inflation caused by gold-rush vessels stopping at Valparaiso enabled a progressive city council to construct reservoirs beyond the encircling ridge[26] and provide iron pipes instead of donkey boys to bring water into the city.[27] With available water, in 1851, the indomitable Guillermo Wheelwright established the first fire-fighting company in Chile.[28]

The great demand for Chilean flour caused by the gold rush was short lived. Californians preferred Tasmanian flour shipped in barrels made from wood of that country to the Chilean flour transported in gigantic imported sacks. By 1854 Peru had replaced California as the leading market for Chilean flour.[29]

The builders of Chilean ships fared better. Their vessels were launched in time to take part not only in the California gold rush but also in the Australian rush which followed the discoveries there in 1851. The end of the Opium War against China, as well as the negotiation of treaties opening Japanese ports after Commodore Perry's visit in 1854, increased the exciting Pacific trade. Thus the California gold rush started a period of long economic prosperity for Chile. Ramón Pérez Yañez, Chilean historian, wrote as recently as 1953 that the California gold rush brought to Chile the riches that built palaces in Santiago, imported fine furniture and works of art, advanced culture, and attracted distinguished technicians. Little Chile, he said, the onetime vassal of the gigantic viceroyalty of Peru, had not been smothered by the "coloso norteamericano." Instead, Chile competed with the United States like a child, free from resentment, competing with a giant.[30]

Notes

(All abbreviated titles are given in full in the Sources.)

CHAPTER 1

1 Hubert Howe Bancroft, *History of California* (San Francisco, 1884–1890), VI, 56.
2 Charles Victor Crosnier de Varigny, *Los Orijenes de San Francisco* (Valparaiso, 1887), p. 18, and *L'Océan Pacifique* (Paris, 1888), p. 262.
3 George P. Hammond, ed., *The Larkin Papers* (Berkeley and Los Angeles, 1951–1964), VII, 286, 290.
4 Olaf P. Jenkins, ed., *The Mother Lode Country* (San Francisco, 1948), p. 13.
5 Jay Monaghan, ed., *The Private Journal of Louis McLane* (Los Angeles, 1971), p. 101.
6 Earl Parker Hanson, ed., *South from the Spanish Main* (New York, 1967), p. 145.
7 Roberto Hernández Cornejo, *Los Chilenos en San Francisco* (Valparaiso, 1930), I, 19; [Miguel Venegas,] *Noticia de la California* (Madrid, 1757), I, 58.
8 José Francisco Velasco, *Sonora: Its Extent, Population* (San Francisco, 1861), p. 125.
9 Hernández C., *op. cit.*, I, 102; Otis E. Young, Jr., *How They Dug the Gold* (Tucson, 1967), p. 51; George Findlay Willison, *Here They Dug the Gold* (New York, 1931), p. 234.
10 Erna Fergusson, *Chile* (New York, 1943), p. 124; Hernández C., *op. cit.*, I, 41.
11 *California Star*, May 6, 1848; *Californian*, May 10, 1848.
12 Hammond, *op. cit.*, VII, 290–291.
13 Frank Soulé, John H. Gihon, and James Nisbet, *The Annals of San Francisco* (New York, 1855), p. 174.
14 Hammond, *op. cit.*, VII, 267.
15 Ralph P. Bieber, "California Gold Mania," *Mississippi Valley Historical Review*, XXXV (June, 1948), 9–10; Hammond, *op. cit.*, VII, 286.
16 Bieber, *op. cit.*, p. 10.
17 Hernández C., *op. cit.*, I, 23.
18 Soulé et al., *op. cit.*, p. 149.
19 Chester S. Lyman, *Around the Horn* (New Haven, 1924), p. 21.
20 James Melville Gilliss, *Chile: Its Geography, Climate* (Washington, 1855), p. 227.
21 Enos Christman, *One Man's Gold*, comp. and ed. Florence Morrow Christman (New York, 1930), p. 51.
22 Victor M. Berthold, *The Pioneer Steamer* (Boston, 1932), p. 32.
23 *El Comercio de Valparaiso*, Aug. 19, 1848.
24 Monaghan, *op. cit.*, pp. 36–37.
25 Charles Wilkes, *Narrative of . . . Exploring Expedition* (Philadelphia, 1845), I, 165.

[26] William Perkins, *Three Years in California* (Berkeley and Los Angeles, 1964), p. 49; Ramón Pérez Yañez, *Forjadores de Chile* (Santiago de Chile, 1953), p. 465.

[27] Robert B. Forbes, *Personal Reminiscences* (Boston, 1876), p. 104.

[28] Arthur C. Wardle, *Steam Conquers the Pacific* (London, 1940), p. 16.

[29] Alexander George Findlay, *A Directory for the Navigation of the South Pacific Ocean* (London, 1863), p. 117.

[30] Thomas Robinson Warren, *Dust and Foam* (New York, 1859), p. 383.

[31] Gilliss, *op. cit.*, p. 48.

[32] Hubert Herring, *Good Neighbors* (New Haven, 1941), p. 231.

[33] Frederick Gerstaecker, *Narrative of a Journey round the World* (New York, 1853), p. 117.

[34] William Hickling Prescott, *The History of the Conquest of Peru* (New York, 1847), I, 186.

[35] George McCutcheon McBride, *Chile: Land and Society* (New York, 1936), p. 120.

[36] Basil Hall, *Extracts from a Journal* (London, 1840), Pt. I, p. 19; App. p. 66.

[37] Benjamín Vicuña Mackenna, *Pájinas de mi Diario* (Santiago de Chile, 1856), p. 1.

[38] *Ibid.*

[39] *Navigation Chart*, United States Air Force, April 19, 1965.

[40] Hall, *op. cit.*, Pt. I, p. 2; Gilliss, *op. cit.*, p. 241.

[41] Findlay, *op. cit.*, p. 119.

[42] Wardle, *op. cit.*, p. 14; Findlay, *op. cit.*, p. 118.

[43] Doyce B. Nunis, Jr., ed., *The California Diary of Faxon Dean Atherton* (San Francisco, 1964), p. 154.

[44] William Tecumseh Sherman, *Memoirs* (Bloomington, Ind., 1957), I, 16.

[45] Gilliss, *op. cit.*, p. 224.

[46] Wilkes, *op. cit.*, I, 200; Findlay, *op. cit.*, p. 116.

[47] Laura Fish Judd, *Honolulu*, ed. Dale L. Morgan (Chicago, 1966), p. 233.

[48] Hammond, *op. cit.*, VII, 303.

[49] Leonard Pitt, *The Decline of the Californios* (Berkeley and Los Angeles, 1966), p. 53; Velasco, *op cit.*, pp. 287 ff.; Doris Marion Wright, "The Making of Cosmopolitan California," *California Historical Society Quarterly*, XIX (Dec., 1940), 325.

[50] Rodman Wilson Paul, *The California Gold Discovery Sources* (Georgetown, Calif., 1966), p. 97.

[51] *Ibid.*, p. 70; Milo Milton Quaife, ed., *Pictures of Gold Rush California* (Chicago, 1949), p. xviii.

[52] Ferol Egan, *The El Dorado Trail* (New York, 1970), p. 23.

[53] Judd, *op. cit.*, p. 253.

CHAPTER 2

[1] Sergio Sepúlveda G., *El Trigo Chileno en el Mercado Mundial* (Santiago de Chile, 1959), p. 42.

[2] *El Comercio de Valparaiso*, Nov. 29, 1848; Arthur H. Clark, *The Clipper Ship Era* (New York, 1912), pp. 60–61.

[3] *El Comercio de Valparaiso*, Aug. 29, 1848, and earlier issues.

[4] Ramón Pérez Yañez, *Forjadores de Chile* (Santiago de Chile, 1953), p. 247.

[5] Thomas Robinson Warren, *Dust and Foam* (New York, 1859), p. 389;

Charles Wilkes, *Narrative of . . . Exploring Expedition* (Philadelphia, 1845), I, 201.

[6] Felix Paul Wierzbicki, *California As It Is* (San Francisco, 1933), p. 7.

[7] Alexander George Findlay, *A Directory for the Navigation of the South Pacific Ocean* (London, 1863), p. 116.

[8] James Melville Gilliss, *Chile: Its Geography, Climate* (Washington, 1855), pp. 28, 225, 230.

[9] Findlay, *op. cit.*, p. 116.

[10] Chester S. Lyman, *Around the Horn* (New Haven, 1924), p. 21.

[11] Arthur C. Wardle, *Steam Conquers the Pacific* (London, 1940), p. 59.

[12] Johann Jacob von Tschudi, *Travels in Peru* (New York, 1847), p. 17.

[13] Findlay, *op. cit.*, p. 116.

[14] Gilliss, *op. cit.*, p. 221.

[15] Wilkes, *op. cit.*, I, 169.

[16] Jay Monaghan, ed., *The Private Journal of Louis McLane* (Los Angeles, 1971), p. 116.

[17] Frederick Gerstaecker, *Narrative of a Journey round the World* (New York, 1853), p. 115.

[18] Oscar Lewis, *Sea Routes to the Gold Fields* (New York, 1949), p. 147; Wilkes, *op. cit.*, I, 165.

[19] Gilliss, *op. cit.*, p. 225.

[20] *Ibid.*, p. 465.

[21] Frederick Marryat, *Frank Mildmay or, The Naval officer* (London, 1863), pp. 14, 19.

[22] Manuel Ignacio Vegas García, *Historia de la Marina de Guerra del Perú* (Lima, 1929), p. 6.

[23] Wardle, *op. cit.*, p. 15.

[24] Edward Baxter Billingsley, *In Defense of Neutral Rights* (Chapel Hill, 1967), p. 59.

[25] *Alta California*, Aug. 2, 1848.

[26] Tschudi, *op. cit.*, p. 21.

[27] *Ibid.*, p. 86.

[28] Jay Monaghan, "Did Expansion of the Traditional West Stop at the Pacific?" in *The Westward Movement and Historical Involvement* (San Jose, Calif., 1965), p. 6.

[29] Wilkes, *op. cit.*, I, 201.

[30] *Ibid.*, p. 169.

[31] Lyman, *op. cit.*, p. 22.

[32] Gerstaecker, *op. cit.*, pp. 116, 118; Lyman, *op cit.*, p. 32.

[33] Basil Hall, *Extracts from a Journal* (London, 1840), Pt. I, pp. 6, 10.

[34] Gilliss, *op. cit.*, p. 218.

[35] Wilkes, *op. cit.*, I, 169.

[36] Gerstaecker, *op. cit.*, p. 116.

[37] Lewis, *op. cit.* p. 148; Wilkes, *op. cit.*, I, 167.

[38] Hubert Howe Bancroft, *History of California* (San Francisco, 1884–1890), VI, 125; George P. Hammond, ed., *The Larkin Papers* (Berkeley and Los Angeles, 1951–1964), VII, 355.

[39] *El Comercio de Valparaiso*, Sept. 13, 1848.

[40] Sepúlveda G., *op. cit.*, p. 42.

[41] Lyman, *op. cit.*, p. 24; Gerstaecker, *op. cit.*, p. 131.

[42] Wilkes, *op. cit.*, I, 168.

[43] Gerstaecker, *op. cit.*, p. 116.

[44] Hall, *op. cit.*, Pt. I, p. 4.

[45] *Ibid.*, p. 5; Wilkes, *op. cit.*, I, 169.

[46] Pérez Yañez, *op. cit.*, p. 249.

[47] Roberto Hernández Cornejo, *Los Chilenos en San Francisco* (Valparaiso, 1930), I, 18.

[48] Gerstaecker, *op. cit.*, p. 118.

[49] *Ibid.*, p. 130.

[50] New Brunswick *Home News*, March 22, 1902, clipping file in Special Collections, Rutgers University.

[51] Sepúlveda G., *op. cit.*, p. 42.

[52] Hammond, *op. cit.*, VII, 353.

[53] Pedro Pablo Figueroa, *Diccionario Biográfico de Chile* (Santiago de Chile, 1897–1901), III, 493–494; Wardle, *op. cit.*, p. 17.

[54] Pérez Yañez, *op. cit.*, p. 243.

[55] Hammond, *op. cit.*, VII, 353.

[56] Sepúlveda G., *op. cit.*, p. 42.

[57] Hammond, *op. cit.*, VII, 353.

[58] Hernández C., *op. cit.*, I, 20.

[59] Hammond, *op. cit.*, VII, 353.

[60] *Ibid.*

[61] Doyce B. Nunis, Jr., ed., *The California Diary of Faxon Dean Atherton* (San Francisco, 1964), p. xvi.

[62] *Ibid.*, p. xvii.

[63] Hammond, *op. cit.*, V, 308; Nunis, *op. cit.*, p. xxvii.

[64] Nunis, *op. cit.*, p. xxviii.

[65] Hammond, *op. cit.*, VII, 353.

[66] Susanna Bryant Dakin, *A Scotch Paisano: Hugo Reid's Life in California* (Berkeley, 1939), p. 204.

[67] Bancroft, *op. cit.*, VI, 125; Reuben L. Underhill, *From Cow Hides to Golden Fleece* (Palo Alto, 1939), p. 169.

[68] William Perkins, *Three Years in California* (Berkeley and Los Angeles, 1964), p. 80.

[69] Florence Marryat, "Memoir of Captain Marryat," in *Works of Captain Marryat* (New York, n.d.), I, 11.

[70] *El Comercio de Valparaiso*, Sept. 13, 1848.

[71] Hernández C., *op. cit.*, I, 20.

[72] *El Comercio de Valparaiso*, Sept. 23, 1848; Hernández C., *op. cit.*, I, 23.

[73] *El Comercio de Valparaiso*, Sept. 23, 1848; Hammond, *op. cit.*, VII, 353.

[74] *El Comercio de Valparaiso*, Nov. 13, 1848; *Alta California*, Jan. 11, 1849.

[75] *El Comercio de Valparaiso*, Oct. 5, 1848.

[76] *Ibid.*, Oct. 12, 28, 1848; Enrique Bunster, *Chilenos en California* (Santiago de Chile, 1965), p. 85; Hernández C., *op. cit.*, I, 28.

[77] *Alta California*, Jan. 4, 1849.

[78] *El Comercio de Valparaiso*, Nov. 9, 1848.

[79] *Ibid.*, Oct. 23, 1848; Hernández C., *op. cit.*, I, 27.

[80] Bunster, *op. cit.*, p. 76.

[81] *El Comercio de Valparaiso*, Oct. 22, 25, 30, 31, 1848.

[82] *Ibid.*, Nov. 3, 1848; Hernández C., op. cit., I, 28.

CHAPTER 3

[1] Roberto Hernández Cornejo, *Los Chilenos en San Francisco* (Valparaiso, 1930), I, 41.

[2] George McCutcheon McBride, *Chile: Land and Society* (New York, 1936), p. 12.

[3] Hernández C., *op. cit.*, I, 49–50.

4 James Melville Gilliss, *Chile: Its Geography, Climate* (Washington, 1855), p. 229.

5 Howard Mumford Jones, *America and French Culture, 1750–1848* (Chapel Hill, 1927), pp. 530–531, 567.

6 *El Comercio de Valparaiso*, Sept. 25, 1848.

7 Gilliss, *op. cit.*, p. 392.

8 *Ibid.*, p. 171.

9 *El Comercio de Valparaiso*, Aug. 19, 1848.

10 Laura Fish Judd, *Honolulu*, ed. Dale L. Morgan (Chicago, 1966), p. 249.

11 Diego Barros Arana, *Compendio de Historia Moderna* (Santiago de Chile, 1881), p. 288.

12 Pedro Pablo Figueroa, *Diccionario Biográfico de Chile* (Santiago de Chile, 1897), III, 266–267; Pedro Pablo Figueroa, *Diccionario Biográfico de Estranjeros en Chile* (Santiago de Chile, 1900), p. 211; Manuel Ignacio Vegas García, *Historia de la Marina de Guerra del Perú* (Lima, 1929), p. 68.

13 Jorge Luis Borges, *A Personal Anthology*, ed. Anthony Kerrigan (New York, 1967), p. 23.

14 Hernández C., *op. cit.*, I, 25–27.

15 Guillermo Feliú Cruz, *Vicente Pérez Rosales: Diccionario* (Santiago de Chile, 1946), p. 10; Figueroa, *Diccionario Biográfico de Chile*, II, 458–460; Pedro Pablo Figueroa, *Diccionario Biográfico Chileno, 1550–1887* (Santiago de Chile, 1887), pp. 291–292; Ramón Pérez Yañez, *Forjadores de Chile* (Santiago de Chile, 1953), p. 210.

16 Feliú Cruz, *op. cit.*, p. 52.

17 Gilliss, *op. cit.*, p. 15.

18 McBride, *op. cit.*, p. 289.

19 Feliú Cruz, *op. cit.*, p. 30.

20 Hubert Herring, *Good Neighbors* (New Haven, 1941), p. 231.

21 Hernández C., *op. cit.*, I, 25.

22 Feliú Cruz, *op. cit.*, p. 51.

23 Figueroa, *Diccionario Biográfico de Chile*, III, 458.

24 Claude G. Bowers, *Chile through Embassy Windows, 1939–1953* (New York, 1958), p. 223; J. Fred Rippy, *Joel R. Poinsett* (Durham, N.C., 1935), pp. 40–44.

25 Paúl Silva Castro, *Prensa y Periodismo en Chile, 1812–1956* (Santiago de Chile, 1958), pp. 127, 129.

26 Erna Fergusson, *Chile* (New York, 1943), p. 292.

27 Figueroa, *Diccionario Biográfico de Estranjeros*, p. 219.

28 J. Fred Rippy, *British Investments in Latin America, 1822–1949* (Hamden, Conn., 1959), p. 27.

29 Robert N. Burr, *By Reason or Force* (Berkeley and Los Angeles, 1967), pp. 78–79.

30 José Pelaez y Tapia, *Historia de "El Mercurio"* (Santiago de Chile, 1927), pp. 160, 170.

31 Figueroa, *Diccionario Biográfico de Estranjeros*, pp. 41–42.

32 *Ibid.*, p. 41; Feliú Cruz, *op. cit.*, p. 16; Pérez Yañez, *op. cit.*, pp. 167–171.

33 Pelaez y Tapia, *op. cit.*, p. 87.

34 Domingo Faustino Sarmiento, *Sarmiento's Travels in the United States in 1847*, trans. Michael Aaron Rockland (Princeton, 1970), pp. 7–8.

35 Vicente Pérez Rosales, *California Adventure*, trans. Edwin S. Morby and Arturo Torres-Rioseco (San Francisco, 1947), p. ix.

36 Pérez Yañez, *op. cit.*, pp. 174, 310.

37 Pelaez y Tapia, *op. cit.*, p. 83; Sarmiento, *op. cit.*, pp. 8, 21, 39.

38 Sergio Sepúlveda G., *El Trigo Chileno en el Mercado Mundial* (Santiago de Chile, 1959), p. 42.

[39] *El Comercio de Valparaiso*, Nov. 3, 1848.
[40] Hernández C., *op. cit.*, I, 28, 81.
[41] *Ibid.*, pp. 28–29.
[42] *Ibid.*, p. 32.
[43] *Ibid.*, p. 35.
[44] William Ray Manning, *Diplomatic Correspondence of the United States: Inter-American Affairs, 1831–1860*, V (Washington, 1935), 183; *California and New Mexico*, 33d Cong., 1st sess., H.R. Exec. Doc. 17 (Washington, 1850), p. 36.
[45] McBride, *op. cit.*, p. 62.
[46] Model of city in National Historical Museum, Santiago, Chile.
[47] Gilliss, *op. cit.*, p. 196.
[48] *Ibid.*, pp. 179, 192.
[49] *Ibid.*, p. 179.
[50] *Ibid.*, p. 145.
[51] *Ibid.*, p. 143.
[52] *Ibid.*, p. 219.
[53] *Ibid.*, p. 142; Basil Hall, *Extracts from a Journal* (London, 1840), Pt. I, p. 8.
[54] Hernández C., *op. cit.*, I, 33.
[55] *Ibid.*, p. 34.
[56] Gilliss, *op. cit.*, p. 155.
[57] Hernández C., *op. cit.*, I, 34–35.
[58] *Public Statutes at Large* (Boston, 1846), VIII, 436.
[59] James J. Ayers, *Gold and Sunshine* (Boston, 1922), p. 62.
[60] Gilliss, *op. cit.*, p. 156.

CHAPTER 4

[1] Pedro Pablo Figueroa, *Diccionario Biográfico de Estranjeros en Chile* (Santiago de Chile, 1900), p. 238; Roberto Hernández Cornejo, *Los Chilenos en San Francisco* (Valparaiso, 1930), I, 159.
[2] Felipe Wiegand, speech at time of visit to Cincinnati, "Consular Reports between United States and Chile, 1910–1929," Dispatch 413, enclosure no. 4, National Archives, microfilm roll 489.
[3] Ramón Pérez Yañez, *Forjadores de Chile* (Santiago de Chile, 1953), p. 102.
[4] Benjamín Vicuña Mackenna, "Don Carlos Wooster," *La Justicia* (Talcahuano), XXVI, no. 2.558.
[5] *El Comercio de Valparaiso*, Nov. 7, 1848.
[6] *Ibid.*, Nov. 13, 1848.
[7] *Ibid.*; Sergio Sepúlveda G., *El Trigo Chileno en el Mercado Mundial* (Santiago de Chile, 1959), p. 42.
[8] *El Comercio de Valparaiso*, Nov. 13, 1848; Hernández C., *op. cit.*, I, 36.
[9] *El Comercio de Valparaiso*, Nov. 14, 1848; Hernández C., *op. cit.*, I, 37.
[10] *El Comercio de Valparaiso*, Nov. 16, 1848 (translation mine).
[11] Hernández C., *op. cit.*, I, 41.
[12] Pérez Y., *op. cit.*, p. 455.
[13] *El Mercurio*, Nov. 16, 1848; Hernández C., *op. cit.*, I, 39.
[14] Hernández C., *op. cit.*, I, 39.
[15] *Ibid.*, p. 38.
[16] *Ibid.*, p. 46.
[17] *Ibid.*
[18] *Ibid.*, pp. 46–47.

[19] James Melville Gilliss, *Chile: Its Geography, Climate* (Washington, 1855), panoramic map; Charles Wilkes, *Narrative of . . . Exploring Expedition* (Philadelphia, 1845), I, 180.

[20] Gilliss, *op. cit.*, p. 143.

[21] *Ibid.*, pp. 157–158.

[22] Model of city in National Historical Museum, Santiago, Chile.

[23] Jay Monaghan, *Australians and the Gold Rush* (Berkeley and Los Angeles, 1966), p. 119.

[24] Figueroa, *op. cit.*, pp. 41–42; Pérez Y., *op. cit.*, p. 169.

[25] Domingo Faustino Sarmiento, *Sarmiento's Travels in the United States in 1847*, trans. Michael Aaron Rockland (Princeton, 1970), p. 10.

[26] Gilliss, *op. cit.*, p. 194.

[27] *Ibid.*, p. 463.

[28] Erna Fergusson, *Chile* (New York, 1943), p. 280.

[29] Basil Hall, *Extracts from a Journal* (London, 1840), Pt. I, p. 6.

[30] Gilliss, *op. cit.*, p. 352.

[31] *Ibid.*; Wilkes, *op. cit.*, I, 177.

[32] Hall, *op. cit.*, Pt. I, p. 6; Hernández C., *op. cit.*, I, 68; Wilkes, *op. cit.*, I, 182.

[33] Wilkes, *op. cit.*, I, 180.

[34] Gilliss, *op. cit.*, p. 175.

[35] *Ibid.*, pp. 344, 465; Ricardo Donoso, *Las Ideas Políticas en Chile* (Santiago de Chile, 1967), p. 110.

[36] Gilliss, *op. cit.*, pp. 352, 451; Hernández C., *op. cit.*, I, 68.

[37] Gilliss, *op. cit.*, p. 451; Hernández C., *op. cit.*, I, 68; Wilkes, *op. cit.*, I, 178.

[38] Gilliss, *op. cit.*, pp. 452, 463.

[39] Fergusson, *op. cit.*, p. 253; Hernández C., *op. cit.*, I, 58.

[40] Gilliss, *op. cit.*, p. 451.

[41] *El Comercio de Valparaiso*, Nov. 16, 1848.

[42] José Pelaez y Tapia, *Historia de "El Mercurio"* (Santiago de Chile, 1927), p. 227.

[43] Pedro Pablo Figueroa, *Diccionario Biográfico Chileno, 1550–1887* (Santiago de Chile, 1887), pp. 242–245; Pérez Y., *op. cit.*, p. 180.

[44] Pelaez y Tapia, *op. cit.*, p. 83.

[45] *Ibid.*, p. 224.

[46] Figueroa, *Diccionario Biográfico de Chile* (Santiago de Chile, 1897–1901), II, 167–169.

[47] Pérez Y., *op. cit.*, p. 183.

[48] Hernández C., *op. cit.*, I, 57–58.

CHAPTER 5

[1] Pedro Pablo Figueroa, *Diccionario Biográfico de Chile* (Santiago de Chile, 1897–1901), II, 458.

[2] *El Comercio de Valparaiso*, Nov. 10, 1848.

[3] *Ibid.*

[4] *Ibid.*, Nov. 16, 1848.

[5] *Ibid.*, Dec. 29, 1848.

[6] *Ibid.*, Nov. 16, 1848.

[7] *Ibid.*, Nov. 22, 1848.

[8] *Ibid.*, Nov. 20, 1848.

[9] Vicente Pérez Rosales, *California Adventure*, trans. Edwin S. Morby and Arturo Torres-Rioseco (San Francisco, 1947), pp. 4, 9.

[10] *Ibid.*, p. 4.

[11] *El Comercio de Valparaiso*, Nov. 20, 1848; Enrique Bunster, *Chilenos en California* (Santiago de Chile, 1965), p. 76.

[12] Roberto Hernández Cornejo, *Los Chilenos en San Francisco* (Valparaiso, 1930), I, 37.

[13] *Ibid.*

[14] *Ibid.*

[15] *Ibid.*; *El Comercio de Valparaiso*, Nov. 27, 1848.

[16] *Alta California*, Jan. 18, 1849.

[17] Hernández C., *op. cit.*, I, 37.

[18] *El Comercio de Valparaiso*, Dec. 8, 1848.

[19] *Alta California*, Jan. 25, 1849.

[20] *Ibid.*, Feb. 8, 1849.

[21] *El Comercio de Valparaiso*, Dec. 5, 1848.

[22] *Ibid.*

[23] *Ibid.*, Dec. 8, 1848; *Alta California*, Feb. 8, 1849.

[24] *El Comercio de Valparaiso*, Dec. 11, 1848.

[25] *Alta California*, Feb. 22, 1849.

[26] Bunster, *op. cit.*, p. 76.

[27] Hubert Howe Bancroft, *History of California* (San Francisco, 1884–1890), VI, 125.

[28] William Tecumseh Sherman, *Memoirs* (Bloomington, Ind., 1957), I, 15.

[29] Hernández C., *op. cit.*, I, 58.

[30] *El Comercio de Valparaiso*, Dec. 20, 1848.

[31] *Ibid.*, Dec. 11, 1848.

[32] Sergio Sepúlveda G., *El Trigo Chileno en el Mercado Mundial* (Santiago de Chile, 1959), p. 42.

[33] *Alta California*, Feb. 8, 1849.

[34] Hernández C., *op. cit.*, I, 55.

[35] *Ibid.*, p. 57.

[36] *Ibid.*, p. 56.

[37] *Ibid.*, p. 55.

[38] *El Comercio de Valparaiso*, Dec. 20, 1848; Victor M. Berthold, *The Pioneer Steamer* (Boston, 1932), p. 32.

[39] Berthold, *op. cit.*, frontispiece.

[40] *Ibid.*, p. 12.

[41] Enos Christman, *One Man's Gold*, comp. and ed. Florence Morrow Christman (New York, 1930), p. 51.

[42] Oscar Lewis, *Sea Routes to the Gold Fields* (New York, 1949), p. 225.

[43] John Edwin Pomfret, ed., *California Gold Rush Voyages* (San Marino, Calif., 1954), p. 177.

[44] *Ibid.*, p. 216; Berthold, *op. cit.*, p. 32.

[45] *El Comercio de Valparaiso*, Dec. 21, 23, 1848.

[46] *Ibid.*, Dec. 23, 1848.

[47] Basil Hall, *Extracts from a Journal* (London, 1840), Pt. I, p. 19.

[48] Pomfret, *op. cit.*, p. 21.

[49] James Melville Gilliss, *Chile: Its Geography, Climate* (Washington, 1855), p. 442.

CHAPTER 6

[1] *El Comercio de Valparaiso*, Dec. 23, 1848.

[2] Benjamín Vicuña Mackenna, *Pájinas de mi Diario* (Santiago de Chile, 1856), p. 2.

3 *El Comercio de Valparaiso*, Dec. 29, 1848; Vicente Pérez Rosales, *California Adventure*, trans. Edwin S. Morby and Arturo Torres-Rioseco (San Francisco, 1947), p. 6.
4 Enrique Bunster, *Chilenos en California* (Santiago de Chile, 1965), pp. 77, 86.
5 Roberto Hernández Cornejo, *Los Chilenos en San Francisco* (Valparaiso, 1930), I, 57.
6 Pérez R., *op. cit.*, p. 7.
7 Edward Baxter Billingsley, *In Defense of Neutral Rights* (Chapel Hill, 1967), p. 83.
8 Pérez R., *op. cit.*, p. 7.
9 *Ibid.*, p. 8.
10 *Ibid.*
11 *Ibid.*
12 Robert B. Forbes, *Personal Reminiscences* (Boston, 1876), p. 84.
13 Pérez R., *op. cit.*, p. 11.
14 *Ibid.*
15 *Ibid.*
16 *Ibid.*, p. 12.
17 *Alta California*, Feb. 22, 1849.
18 Pérez R., *op. cit.*, p. 15.
19 Hernández C., *op. cit.*, I, 87; Pérez R., *op. cit.*, p. 15.
20 Pérez R., *op. cit.*, p. 17; Hernández C., *op. cit.*, I, 87.
21 Pérez R., *op. cit.*, p. 16.
22 *Alta California*, Jan. 1, 1849.
23 Pérez R., *op. cit.*, p. 17.
24 *Ibid.*, p. 18.
25 *Ibid.*, p. 19.
26 *Ibid.*, p. 20.
27 *Alta California*, Feb. 1, 1849.
28 Pérez R., *op. cit.*, p. 20.
29 *Ibid.*, p. 21.
30 *Ibid.*
31 *Ibid.*, p. 22.
32 *Alta California*, Feb. 22, 1849.
33 Pérez R., *op. cit.*, p. 24.
34 *Alta California*, March 22, 1849.
35 *Ibid.*, April 5, 1849.
36 *Ibid.*, March 29, 1849.
37 *Ibid.*, Feb. 22, March 1, 1849.
38 *Ibid.*, Feb. 22, 1849.
39 *Ibid.*, Jan. 4, 1849; *California Star and Californian*, Nov. 18, 1848.
40 *Alta California*, Jan. 18, 1849.
41 *Ibid.*, Dec. 24, 1848; Jan. 4, 1849.
42 *Ibid.*, March 1, 1849.
43 *Ibid.*, March 2, 1849.

CHAPTER 7

1 James Melville Gilliss, *Chile: Its Geography, Climate* (Washington, 1855), pp. 218, 229; Charles Wilkes, *Narrative of . . . Exploring Expedition* (Philadelphia, 1845), I, 243.
2 Johann Jacob von Tschudi, *Travels in Peru* (New York, 1847), p. 75.

[3] *Ibid.*, p. 76.

[4] Burr Cartwright Brundage, *Empire of the Inca* (Norman, Okla., 1963), p. 309.

[5] Philip A. Means, *Fall of the Inca Empire and the Spanish Rule* (New York, 1932), p. 58.

[6] Brundage, *op. cit.*, p. 272.

[7] William Hickling Prescott, *The History of the Conquest of Peru* (Philadelphia, 1873), I, 356.

[8] Brundage, *op. cit.*, p. 301.

[9] John Hemming, *The Conquest of the Incas* (London, 1970), p. 45.

[10] Jay Monaghan, *The Great Rascal: The Life and Adventures of Ned Buntline* (Boston, 1952), pp. 326, 332.

[11] Clappe, Louise A. K. S., *The Shirley Letters* (Santa Barbara, 1970), p. 113; Thomas Robinson Warren, *Dust and Foam* (New York, 1859), p. 94.

[12] Means, *op. cit.*, p. 43.

[13] Brundage, *op. cit.*, p. 282.

[14] Hemming, *op. cit.*, p. 78.

[15] *Ibid.*, p. 82.

[16] Clements Robert Markham, *The Incas of Peru* (New York, 1910), p. 280.

[17] Brundage, *op. cit.*, p. 314.

[18] Tschudi, *op. cit.*, p. 211.

[19] Hemming, *op. cit.*, p. 152; Prescott, *op. cit.*, I, 487.

[20] Prescott, *op. cit.*, I, 465, 470.

[21] Brundage, *op. cit.*, p. 314; Prescott, *op. cit.*, I, 490.

[22] Hemming, *op. cit.*, p. 149; Donald M. Dozer, *Latin America* (New York, 1962), p. 65.

[23] John Edwin Pomfret, ed., *California Gold Rush Voyages* (San Marino, Calif., 1954), p. 144.

[24] George W. Peck, *Melbourne and the Chincha Islands* (New York, 1854), p. 142; Tschudi, *op. cit.*, p. 28; Wilkes, *op. cit.*, I, 251.

[25] Means, *op. cit.*, pp. 55–56; Tschudi, *op. cit.*, p. 43.

[26] Means, *op. cit.*, pp. 55–56.

[27] *Ibid.*, p. 71; Prescott, *op. cit.*, II, 183.

[28] Clements Robert Markham, *A History of Peru* (Chicago, 1892), p. 108; Prescott, *op. cit.*, II, 183–184; Tschudi, *op. cit.*, p. 54; Hemming, *op. cit.*, p. 262.

[29] Means, *op. cit.*, pp. 141, 291.

[30] *Ibid.*, p. 169.

[31] *Ibid.*

[32] Dozer, *op. cit.*, p. 73.

[33] Tschudi, *op. cit.*, p. 233.

[34] Jay Monaghan, *Australians and the Gold Rush* (Berkeley and Los Angeles, 1966), p. 55.

[35] Gwendolin B. Cobb, "Potosi, a South American Mining Frontier," in *Greater America: Essays in Honor of Herbert Eugene Bolton* (Berkeley and Los Angeles, 1945), pp. 40, 48; Tschudi, *op. cit.*, p. 236.

[36] Tschudi, *op. cit.*, p. 45.

[37] Jay Monaghan, ed., *The Private Journal of Louis McLane* (Los Angeles, 1971), pp. 38–39; Gilliss, *op. cit.*, p. 431; Prescott, *op. cit.*, II, 187; Warren, *op. cit.*, p. 95.

[38] Tschudi, *op. cit.*, p. 55.

[39] Means, *op. cit.*, p. 268.

[40] Andrew F. Rolle, *California: A History* (New York, 1964), pp. 31–32.

[41] Aurelio Miró Quesada Sosa, *Cervantes, Tirso y el Perú* (Lima, 1947), pp. 19, 21; Tschudi, *op. cit.*, p. 66.

42 Oscar R. Benavides, *Biblioteca de Cultura Peruana Patrocinada* (Paris, 1938), p. 57.

43 Gerald Brenan, *South from Granada* (New York, 1957), p. 90.

44 Benavides, *op. cit.*, pp. 203, 250.

45 Means, *op. cit.*, pp. 277, 279.

46 Interview with Dr. Emilio Romero, president of the Board of Directors of the Sociedad Geográfica de Lima; Tschudi, *op. cit.*, p. 201.

47 Basil Hall, *Extracts from a Journal* (London, 1840), Pt. I, p. 49; Kenneth F. Weaver, "The Five Worlds of Peru," *National Geographic* (Feb., 1964), p. 218.

48 John Gunther, *Inside South America* (New York, 1966), p. 367.

49 Means, *op. cit.*, p. 268.

50 Model in National Historical Museum, Lima.

51 Means, *op. cit.*, p. 241.

52 Peck, *op. cit.*, p. 266.

53 Tschudi, *op. cit.*, p. 117.

54 *Ibid.*, p. 28.

55 *Ibid.*, p. 117.

56 Pomfret, *op. cit.*, p. 144.

57 Peck, *op. cit.*, p. 266.

58 J. Fred Rippy, *Joel R. Poinsett* (Durham, N.C., 1935), p. 45.

59 Vernon Louis Parrington, ed., *The Connecticut Wits* (New York, 1926), p. xxxii.

60 Henry A. Beers, *The Connecticut Wits and Other Essays* (New Haven, 1920), p. 19.

61 Hall, *op. cit.*, Pt. I, p. 47; Frederick B. Pike, *The Modern History of Peru* (New York, 1967), p. 65.

62 Hall, *op. cit.*, Pt. I, p. 46.

63 Gilliss, *op. cit.*, p. 427; Peck, *op. cit.*, p. 147.

64 Hall, *op. cit.*, Pt. II, p. 15.

65 Tschudi, *op. cit.*, p. 34.

CHAPTER 8

1 Donald M. Dozer, *Latin America* (New York, 1962), p. 209.

2 Frederick B. Pike, *The Modern History of Peru* (New York, 1967), p. 52.

3 Basil Hall, *Extracts from a Journal* (London, 1840), Pt. II, p. 13.

4 Zoeth S. Eldredge, *The Beginnings of San Francisco* (San Francisco, 1912), I, 210–211.

5 J. Fred Rippy, *British Investments in Latin America, 1822–1949* (Hamden, Conn., 1959), pp. 21–22.

6 Pike, *op. cit.*, p. 92.

7 Jorge Basadre, *Historia de la República del Perú* (Lima, 1961–1968), II, 725, 798; Pike, *op. cit.*, p. 82; Charles Wilkes, *Narrative of . . . Exploring Expedition* (Philadelphia, 1845), I, 234.

8 William Ray Manning, *Diplomatic Correspondence of the United States: Inter-American Affairs, 1831–1860*, X (Washington, 1938), 528–530, 542–543; Manuel Ignacio Vegas García, *Historia de la Marina de Guerra del Perú* (Lima, 1929), p. 35.

9 Basadre, *op. cit.*, II, 727; John Edwin Fagg, *Latin America* (New York, 1966), p. 431.

10 Jay Monaghan, ed., *The Private Journal of Louis McLane* (Los Angeles, 1971), pp. 39–40.

[11] Basadre, *op. cit.*, II, 786, 825; Pike, *op. cit.*, pp. 103–112; Thomas Robinson Warren, *Dust and Foam* (New York, 1859), p. 363; Wilkes, *op. cit.*, I, 243.

[12] Robert N. Burr, *By Reason or Force* (Berkeley and Los Angeles, 1967), p. 75.

[13] Basadre, *op. cit.*, II, 795, 981–983; George W. Peck, *Melbourne and the Chincha Islands* (New York, 1854), p. 165.

[14] Basadre, *op. cit.*, II, 795, 981–983; James Melville Gilliss, *Chile: Its Geography, Climate* (Washington, 1855), p. 441; Peck, *op. cit.*, p. 158.

[15] Peck, *op. cit.*, p. 204.

[16] Oscar Lewis, *Sea Routes to the Gold Fields* (New York, 1949), p. 154.

[17] Basadre, *op. cit.*, II, 787; *El Peruano*, July 15, 1848, ff.

[18] *El Peruano*, May 17, 20, 1848.

[19] Arthur C. Wardle, *Steam Conquers the Pacific* (London, 1940), pp. 40, 55, 69.

[20] Victor M. Berthold, *The Pioneer Steamer* (Boston, 1932), p. 102.

[21] *El Comercio de Lima*, Nov. 6, 1848.

[22] *Ibid.*

[23] *Ibid.*, Nov. 4, 1848.

[24] *Ibid.*, Nov. 6, 1848.

[25] *Ibid.*, Nov. 9, 1848.

[26] *Ibid.*, Nov. 10, 1848.

[27] *Ibid.*, Nov. 9, 1848.

[28] *Ibid.*, Sept. 15, 1848.

[29] *Ibid.*,Nov. 15, 1848.

[30] *Ibid.*

[31] *Ibid.*

[32] *Ibid.*, Dec. 20, 1848.

[33] *Alta California*, Jan. 11, 1849.

[34] *El Comercio de Lima*, Nov. 28, 1848.

[35] *Ibid.*, Dec. 1, 1848.

[36] *Ibid.*, Dec. 13, 14, 1848.

[37] *Ibid.*, Dec. 14, 1848.

[38] Berthold, *op. cit.*, p. 35.

[39] Enrique Bunster, *Chilenos en California* (Santiago de Chile, 1965), p. 57.

[40] *El Comercio de Lima*, Dec. 18, 1848.

[41] Vegas G., *op. cit.*, p. 89.

[42] *El Comercio de Lima*, Dec. 28, 1848; John Edwin Pomfret, ed., *California Gold Rush Voyages* (San Marino, Calif., 1954), p. 218.

[43] *El Comercio de Lima*, Dec. 28, 1848; Pomfret, *op. cit.*, p. 218.

[44] Joseph Warren Revere, *Naval Duty in California* (Oakland, Calif., 1947), p. 5.

[45] Gilliss, *op. cit.*, p. 428; Wilkes, *op. cit.*, I, 233.

[46] Pomfret, *op. cit.*, p. 218.

[47] Gilliss, *op. cit.*, p. 428; Peck, *op. cit.*, pp. 142–143; Warren, *op. cit.*, pp. 108–109.

[48] Berthold, *op. cit.*, p. 34.

[49] Pomfret, *op. cit.*, p. 218.

[50] Revere, *op. cit.*, p. 8.

[51] Gilliss, *op. cit.*, pp. 428–429; Chester S. Lyman, *Around the Horn* (New Haven, 1924), p. 38; Pomfret, *op. cit.*, p. 219.

[52] Gilliss, *op. cit.*, p. 429.

[53] Pomfret, *op. cit.*, p. 219; Johann Jacob von Tschudi, *Travels in Peru*, (New York, 1847), p. 33.

[54] Lyman, *op. cit.*, p. 38.

[55] Peck, *op. cit.*, p. 145.

[56] *Ibid.*
[57] Wilkes, *op. cit.*, I, 231.
[58] Hall, *op. cit.*, Pt. I, p. 27.
[59] Pomfret, *op. cit.*, p. 135; Tschudi, *op. cit.*, p. 138.
[60] Warren, *op. cit.*, pp. 113, 359–360.
[61] Hall, *op. cit.*, Pt. I, p. 27; Lyman, *op. cit.*, p. 35.
[62] Hall, *op. cit.*, Pt. I, p. 27; Warren, *op. cit.*, p. 109.
[63] Tschudi, *op. cit.*, p. 41.
[64] Stephen Clissold, *Bernardo O'Higgins and the Independence of Chile* (New York, 1969), p. 35.
[65] Hall, *op. cit.*, Pt. I, p. 27.
[66] Peck, *op. cit.*, p. 232.
[67] Tschudi, *op. cit.*, p. 95.
[68] Gilliss, *op. cit.*, p. 430; Tschudi, *op. cit.*, p. 38.
[69] Pomfret, *op. cit.*, p. 142.
[70] Hall, *op. cit.*, App. I, p. 27.
[71] Pomfret, *op. cit.*, p. 218.
[72] *Ibid.*
[73] *El Comercio de Lima*, Sept. 18, 1848.
[74] Berthold, *op. cit.*, p. 35.
[75] Pomfret, *op. cit.*, p. 219.
[76] Berthold, *op. cit.*, p. 76.
[77] *El Comercio de Lima*, Jan. 10, 1848.
[78] Berthold, *op. cit.*, p. 50.
[79] *Ibid.*, pp. 49–50, 88.
[80] Vegas G., *op. cit.*, p. 89.
[81] *El Comercio de Lima*, Jan. 26, 1849.
[82] *Alta California*, March 29, 1849.
[83] *El Comercio de Lima*, Feb. 12, 1849.
[84] *Ibid.*, Feb. 21, 1849.

CHAPTER 9

[1] Basil Hall, *Extracts from a Journal* (London, 1840), Pt. I, p. 43.
[2] Kenneth F. Weaver, "The Five Worlds of Peru," *National Geographic* (Feb., 1964), p. 236.
[3] Robert B. Forbes, *Personal Reminiscences* (Boston, 1876), p. 105; Thomas Robinson Warren, *Dust and Foam* (New York, 1859), p. 121.
[4] Warren, *op. cit.*, p. 122.
[5] George W. Peck, *Melbourne and the Chincha Islands* (New York, 1854), p. 195.
[6] Hubert Howe Bancroft, *History of California* (San Francisco, 1884–1890), VI, 130; George W. Groh, *Gold Fever* (New York, 1966), p. 20.
[7] Victor M. Berthold, *The Pioneer Steamer* (Boston, 1932), p. 37; Edward C. Dunbar, *The Romance of the Age* (New York, 1867), p. 56; John Haskell Kemble, *The Panama Route, 1848–1868* (Berkeley, 1943), pp. 32, 33.
[8] Dunbar, *op. cit.*, p. 57.
[9] Berthold, *op. cit.*, p. 44.
[10] *Ibid.*, p. 36.
[11] *Ibid.*; Dunbar, *op. cit.*, p. 75.
[12] Dunbar, *op. cit.*, p. 80.
[13] Bancroft, *op. cit.*, VI, 125; Berthold, *op. cit.*, pp. 34, 35, 47; Dunbar, *op. cit.*, p. 77.

[14] Dunbar, *op. cit.*, p. 77.
[15] Berthold, *op. cit.*, p. 39; John Edwin Pomfret, ed., *California Gold Rush Voyages* (San Marino, Calif., 1954), p. 223.
[16] *California and New Mexico*, 33d Cong., 1st sess., H.R. Exec. Doc. 17 (Washington, 1850), pp. 174–175; Berthold, *op. cit.*, p. 39; Leonard Pitt, *The Decline of the Californios* (Berkeley and Los Angeles, 1966), pp. 55–56.
[17] Berthold, *op. cit.*, p. 39.
[18] *Ibid.*
[19] *Ibid.*; Pomfret, *op. cit.*, p. 177.
[20] Berthold, *op. cit.*, p. 42.
[21] *Ibid.*, p. 40.
[22] Dunbar, *op. cit.*, p. 78.
[23] *Alta California*, April 4, 1849.
[24] Berthold, *op. cit.*, p. 43.
[25] Pomfret, *op. cit.*, p. 223.
[26] Berthold, *op. cit.*, p. 52.
[27] Oscar Lewis, *Sea Routes to the Gold Fields* (New York, 1949), p. 225.
[28] Pomfret, *op. cit.*, p. 226.
[29] Berthold, *op. cit.*, p. 55.
[30] *Ibid.*, p. 51.
[31] *Ibid.*, p. 59.
[32] Pomfret, *op. cit.*, p. 226.
[33] Benjamín Vicuña Mackenna, *Pájinas de mi Diario* (Santiage de Chile, 1856), p. 11.
[34] Warren, *op. cit.*, p. 228.
[35] Vicuña Mackenna, *op. cit.*, pp. 10–11.
[36] Berthold, *op. cit.*, p. 54.
[37] Miguel de Toro y Gisbert, *Pequeño Larousse Illustrado* (Buenos Aires, 1968), p. 1205.
[38] Forbes, *op. cit.*, p. 100.
[39] Berthold, *op. cit.*, p. 57.
[40] *Ibid.*
[41] See *Alta California* lists in Jan., Feb., and March, 1849. See also Allen B. Sherman, ed., "Sherman Was There: The Recollections of Major Edwin A. Sherman," *California Historical Society Quarterly* XXIII (Sept., 1944), 259, 274.
[42] William Perkins, *Three Years in California* (Berkeley and Los Angeles, 1964), pp. 12, 80.
[43] Berthold, *op. cit.*, p. 49.
[44] *Ibid.*, p. 50.
[45] *Ibid.*, p. 61.
[46] *Alta California*, March 1, 1849.
[47] Berthold, *op. cit.*, p. 60.
[48] *Ibid.*
[49] *Alta California*, June 14, 1849.
[50] *Ibid.*, March 1, 1849; *El Comercio de Valparaiso*, Jan. 9, 1849; Reuben L. Underhill, *From Cow Hides to Golden Fleece* (Palo Alto, 1939), p. 179.
[51] *El Comercio de Valparaiso*, Jan. 9, 1849.
[52] Berthold, *op. cit.*, p. 63; Underhill, *op. cit.*, p. 179.
[53] Pomfret, *op. cit.*, p. 178.
[54] Berthold, *op. cit.*, p. 66.
[55] Pomfret, *op. cit.*, p. 178.
[56] Berthold, *op. cit.*, pp. 49, 89.
[57] *Ibid.*, p. 47.

CHAPTER 10

[1] Roberto Hernández Cornejo, *Los Chilenos en San Francisco* (Valparaiso, 1930), I, 92.

[2] *Ibid.*, p. 90.

[3] *Ibid.*, p. 91.

[4] *Ibid.*, p. 92.

[5] *Ibid.*, pp. 91–92.

[6] *Ibid.*, p. 91; Benjamín Vicuña Mackenna, *Pájinas de mi Diario* (Santiago de Chile, 1856), p. 7.

[7] Vicuña Mackenna, *op. cit.*, p. 8.

[8] Hernández C., *op. cit.*, I, 115.

[9] *Ibid.*, p. 92.

[10] Leonard Pitt, *The Decline of the Californios* (Berkeley and Los Angeles, 1966), p. 53.

[11] Hernández C., *op. cit.*, I, 91.

[12] *Ibid.*, p. 92.

[13] *Alta California*, Aug. 2, 1849.

[14] Sergio Sepúlveda G., *El Trigo Chileno en el Mercado Mundial* (Santiago de Chile, 1959), p. 43.

[15] Hernández C., *op. cit.*, I, 93.

[16] *Ibid.*

[17] Letters of Jan. 24 and June 8 in *ibid.*, pp. 90–95, 114–115.

[18] Hernández C., *op. cit.*, I, 94.

[19] *Butler's Lives of the Saints*, III (New York, 1956), 336.

[20] Felix Paul Wierzbicki, *California As It Is* (San Francisco, 1933), p. 30.

[21] *Ibid.*, p. 89.

[22] *Ibid.*, p. 30.

[23] Edna Buckbee, *The Saga of Old Tuolumne* (New York, 1935), p. 99.

[24] William Perkins, *Three Years in California* (Berkeley and Los Angeles, 1964), p. 103.

[25] John Haskell Kemble, ed., *To California and the South Seas* (San Marino, Calif., 1966), p. 76 ff.

[26] Perkins, *op. cit.*, p. 22.

[27] *Ibid.*, p. 24.

[28] Jay Monaghan, ed., *The Private Journal of Louis McLane* (Los Angeles, 1971), pp. 84–85; Wierzbicki, *op. cit.*, p. 18.

[29] Buckbee, *op. cit.*, p. 90; Perkins, *op. cit.*, p. 148.

[30] Buckbee, *op. cit.*, p. 1.

[31] Enos Christman, *One Man's Gold*, comp. and ed. Florence Morrow Christman (New York, 1930), p. 171.

[32] Perkins, *op. cit.*, pp. 26, 404.

[33] Thomas Robertson Stoddart, *Annals of Tuolumne County* (Sonora, Calif., 1963), p. 55.

[34] Perkins, *op. cit.*, pp. 103–104.

[35] Stoddart, *op. cit.*, p. 70.

[36] Buckbee, *op. cit.*, p. 343; Perkins, *op. cit.*, p. 101.

[37] Pitt, *op. cit.*, p. 54.

[38] Wierzbicki, *op. cit.*, p. 91.

[39] Vicuña Mackenna, *op. cit.*, p. 15.

[40] Gerald Brenan, *South from Granada* (New York, 1957), p. 109.

[41] Sigmund Spaeth, *History of Popular Music in America* (New York, 1948), p. 227.

[42] Perkins, *op. cit.*, p. 105.
[43] Stoddart, *op. cit.*, p. 75.
[44] Perkins, *op. cit.*, p. 117.
[45] Jay Monaghan, *Australians and the Gold Rush* (Berkeley and Los Angeles, 1966), p. 100; Perkins, *op. cit.*, p. 32.
[46] Perkins, *op. cit.*, pp. 29–30.
[47] *Hobart Daily Courier*, Oct. 20, 1849; Monaghan, *Australians and the Gold Rush*, pp. 119–120; Wierzbicki, *op. cit.*, p. 159.
[48] Perkins, *op. cit.*, p. 106.
[49] *Ibid.*, p. 107.
[50] Erna Fergusson, *Chile* (New York, 1943), p. 184.
[51] Pitt, *op. cit.*, p. 53.
[52] Buckbee, *op. cit.*, pp. 54–55; Rodman Wilson Paul, *California Gold* (Cambridge, 1947), p. 135.
[53] Otis E. Young, Jr., *How They Dug the Gold* (Tucson, 1967), p. 29.
[54] Paul, *op. cit.*, p. 112.
[55] Perkins, *op. cit.*, p. 26.
[56] Buckbee, *op. cit.*, p. 342.
[57] *Ibid.*, p. 341.
[58] Stoddart, *op. cit.*, p. 77.
[59] James J. Ayers, *Gold and Sunshine* (Boston, 1922), p. 81.
[60] Buckbee, *op. cit.*, p. 471.
[61] Perkins, *op. cit.*, p. 403.
[62] Christman, *op. cit.*, p. 169.
[63] Stoddart, *op. cit.*, p. 83; Perkins, *op. cit.*, p. 95.
[64] Buckbee, *op. cit.*, p. 441.

CHAPTER 11

[1] Sergio Sepúlveda G., *El Trigo Chileno en el Mercado Mundial* (Santiago de Chile, 1959), p. 42.
[2] *Alta California*, March 22, 1849.
[3] Vicente Pérez Rosales, *California Adventure*, trans. Edwin S. Morby and Arturo Torres-Rioseco (San Francisco, 1947), p. 37.
[4] *Ibid.*, p. 26.
[5] *Ibid.*, p. 27.
[6] *Ibid.*, p. 28.
[7] *Ibid.*, p. 29.
[8] *Ibid.*
[9] *Ibid.*
[10] *Ibid.*, p. 31.
[11] *Ibid.*, p. 32.
[12] *Ibid.*
[13] *Ibid.*, p. 29.
[14] *Ibid.*, p. 33.
[15] *Ibid.*
[16] *Ibid.*, p. 34.
[17] *Ibid.*, p. 35.
[18] *Ibid.*, p. 36.
[19] *Ibid.*, p. 37.
[20] *Ibid.*
[21] Richard Dillon, *Fool's Gold: A Biography of John Sutter* (New York, 1967), p. 283.

22 Pérez R., *op. cit.*, p. 38.
23 Dillon, *op. cit.*, p. 314.
24 Pérez R., *op. cit.*, p. 38.
25 *Ibid.*, p. 39.
26 *Ibid.*, p. 40.
27 *Ibid.*,p. 41.
28 Roberto Hernández Cornejo, *Los Chilenos en San Francisco* (Valparaiso, 1930), I, 101.
29 Pérez R., *op. cit.*, p. 42.
30 *Ibid.*, p. 43.
31 *Ibid.*
32 James Melville Gilliss, *Chile: Its Geography, Climate* (Washington, 1855), p. 68.
33 Pérez R., *op. cit.*, p. 44.

CHAPTER 12

1 Vicente Pérez Rosales, *California Adventure*, trans. Edwin S. Morby and Arturo Torres-Rioseco (San Francisco, 1947), p. 47.
2 *Alta California*, Feb. 22, 1849.
3 *Ibid.*, April 26, 1849.
4 Pérez R., *op. cit.*, p. 48.
5 *Ibid.*, p. 4.
6 *Ibid.*, p. 53.
7 *Ibid.*
8 *Ibid.*, p. 54.
9 *Ibid.*, p. 56.
10 *Ibid.*, p. 57.
11 *Ibid.*, p. 59.
12 *Ibid.*
13 Enrique Bunster, *Chilenos en California* (Santiago de Chile, 1965), p. 82; Roberto Hernández Cornejo, *Los Chilenos en San Francisco* (Valparaiso, 1930), I, 176; Ramón Pérez Yañez, *Forjadores de Chile* (Santiago de Chile, 1953), p. 257.
14 Pérez R., *op. cit.*, p. 59.
15 Felix Paul Wierzbicki, *California As It is* (San Francisco, 1933), p. 76.
16 Hernández C., *op. cit.*, I, 176.
17 Pérez R., *op. cit.*, p. 9.
18 *Ibid.*, p. 10.
19 *Ibid.*, p. 61.
20 *Ibid.*, p. 62.
21 *Ibid.*, p. 63.
22 Hernández C., *op. cit.*, I, 176; Pérez R., *op. cit.*, p. 65.
23 Bunster, *op. cit.*, p. 82.
24 *Alta California*, March 29, June 7, 1849.
25 Victor M. Berthold, *The Pioneer Steamer* (Boston, 1932), p. 22.
26 Hernández C., *op. cit.*, I, 114.
27 Bunster, *op. cit.*, p. 82.
28 Jorge Basadre, *Historia de la República del Perú* (Lima, 1961–1968), II, 788.
29 Pérez R., *op. cit.*, p. 66.
30 *Ibid.*

[31] James J. Ayers, *Gold and Sunshine* (Boston, 1922), p. 36; John Williamson Palmer, *The New and the Old* (New York, 1859), p. 78.
[32] Pérez R., *op. cit.*, p. 67.
[33] *Ibid.*, p. 68.
[34] Leonard Pitt, *The Decline of the Californios* (Berkeley and Los Angeles, 1966), p. 56.
[35] Letter from Atilio Zoppetti, Sept. 15, 1849, in Hernández C., *op. cit.*, I, 152–154.
[36] *El Comercio de Valparaiso*, Aug. 17, 1849.
[37] *Alta California*, July 12, 1849.
[38] Pérez R., *op. cit.*, pp. 70–72.

CHAPTER 13

[1] *Alta California*, Aug. 2, 1849.
[2] Susanna Bryant Dakin, *A Scotch Paisano: Hugo Reid's Life in California* (Berkeley, 1939), p. 175.
[3] Sergio Sepúlveda G., *El Trigo Chileno en el Mercado Mundial* (Santiago de Chile, 1959), p. 43.
[4] Roberto Hernández Cornejo, *Los Chilenos en San Francisco* (Valparaiso, 1930), I, 132.
[5] *Alta California*, June 28, 1849.
[6] *Ibid.*, Aug. 2, 1849.
[7] John Williamson Palmer, *The New and the Old* (New York, 1859), p. 79.
[8] Testimony of Domingo Cruz and Colonel Stevenson in *Alta California*, Aug. 2, 1849.
[9] Testimony of George Rigey in *ibid.*
[10] Palmer, *op. cit.*, p. 35.
[11] *Ibid.*, p. 206.
[12] *Ibid.*, pp. 211, 227, 229.
[13] Testimony of Alfred Miller in *Alta California*, Aug. 2, 1849.
[14] Letter from Atilio Zoppetti, Sept. 10, 1849, in Hernández C., *op. cit.*, I, 151–152; John Williamson Palmer, "Pioneer Days in San Francisco," *Century Magazine*, XLIII (Feb., 1892), 554.
[15] Frederick B. Pike, *The Modern History of Peru* (New York, 1967), p. 81.
[16] Jorge Basadre, *Historia de la República del Perú* (Lima, 1961–1968), II, 789; Hernández C., *op. cit.*, I, 142.
[17] Palmer, *The New and the Old*, p. 227.
[18] Testimony of Domingo Cruz in *Alta California*, Aug. 2, 1849.
[19] Letter from Atilio Zoppetti, Sept. 10, 1849, in Hernández C., *op. cit.*, I, 151–152.
[20] Hernández C., *op. cit.*, I, 132.
[21] *Alta California*, Aug. 2, 1849; Palmer, "Pioneer Days in San Francisco," p. 547.
[22] Frank Soulé, John H. Gihon, and James Nisbet, *The Annals of San Francisco* (New York, 1855), p. 558.
[23] *Alta California*, Aug. 2, 1849.
[24] *Ibid.*
[25] Soulé et al., *op. cit.*, p. 559.
[26] *Alta California*, Aug. 2, 1849.
[27] *El Mercurio*, Sept. 1, 1849.

CHAPTER 14

[1] Roberto Hernández Cornejo, *Los Chilenos en San Francisco* (Valparaiso, 1930), I, 73; Enrique Bunster, *Chilenos en California* (Santiago de Chile, 1965), p. 79.

[2] *El Comercio de Valparaiso*, Jan. 1, 10, 15, 20, 31, 1849.

[3] Hernández C., *op. cit.*, I, 69.

[4] *Ibid.*, p. 70.

[5] *Ibid.*, pp. 79–80, 85; Allen B. Sherman, ed., "Sherman Was There: The Recollections of Major Edwin A. Sherman," *California Historical Society Quarterly*, XXIII (Sept., 1944), 277.

[6] Oscar Lewis, *Sea Routes to the Gold Fields* (New York, 1949), p. 149.

[7] Sergio Sepúlveda G., *El Trigo Chileno en el Mercado Mundial* (Santiago de Chile, 1959), p. 45.

[8] George P. Hammond, ed., *The Larkin Papers* (Berkeley and Los Angeles, 1951–1964), VII, 353.

[9] Sepúlveda G., *op. cit.*, p. 43; Charles Wilkes, *Narrative of . . . Exploring Expedition* (Philadelphia, 1845), I, 201.

[10] Sepúlveda G., *op. cit.*, p. 46.

[11] *Ibid.*, p. 45.

[12] *Ibid.*

[13] José Pelaez y Tapia, *Historia de "El Mercurio"* (Santiago de Chile, 1927), p. 83.

[14] Hernández C., *op. cit.*, I, 79.

[15] Frederick Gerstaecker, *Narrative of a Journey round the World* (New York, 1853), p. 127; James Melville Gilliss, *Chile: Its Geography, Climate* (Washington, 1855), p. 227.

[16] Basil Hall, *Extracts from a Journal* (London, 1840), Pt. I, p. 28.

[17] Hernández C., *op. cit.*, I, 75.

[18] Jay Monaghan, *The Great Rascal: The Life and Adventures of Ned Buntline* (Boston, 1952), pp. 175 ff.

[19] Hernández C., *op. cit.*, I, 75.

[20] *Ibid.*, p. 76.

[21] *Ibid.*, p. 77.

[22] *El Comercio de Valparaiso*, Feb. 5, 1849.

[23] *Ibid.*, Feb. 6, 1849.

[24] Hernández C., *op. cit.*, I, 162.

[25] Ramón Pérez Yañez, *Forjadores de Chile* (Santiago de Chile, 1953), p. 252.

[26] Hernández C., *op. cit.*, I, 82.

[27] *El Mercurio*, Oct. 10, 1849.

[28] *Ibid.*, Feb. 13, 1849.

[29] Hernández C., *op. cit.*, I, 83.

[30] *Ibid.*, p. 85.

[31] Diego Barros Arana, *Un Decenio de la Historia de Chile* (Santiago de Chile, 1913), p. 310; Ralph J. Roske, "The World Impact of the California Gold Rush, 1849–1857," *Arizona and the West*, V (Autumn, 1963), 201.

[32] "Influencia de California," in *El Comercio de Valparaiso*, May 17, 1849.

[33] Victor M. Berthold, *The Pioneer Steamer* (Boston, 1932), p. 106.

[34] Gerstaecker, *op. cit.*, p. 34; Roske, *op. cit.*, p. 201.

[35] Gilliss, *op. cit.*, p. 359; Johann Jacob von Tschudi, *Travels in Peru* (New York, 1847), pp. 24–25.

[36] Dick Smith and Robert Easton, *California Condor, Vanishing American* (Santa Barbara, Calif., 1964), p. 38.

[37] Gerstaecker, *op. cit.*, p. 121.
[38] *Ibid.*, pp. 119–120.
[39] Jay Monaghan, *Australians and the Gold Rush* (Berkeley and Los Angeles, 1966), p. 54.
[40] *El Mercurio*, July 6, 1849.
[41] Hernández C., *op. cit.*, I, 116.
[42] *El Mercurio*, July 3, 1849.
[43] *Ibid.*, Aug. 4, 1849.
[44] John Williamson Palmer, *The New and the Old* (New York, 1859), pp. 100–106.

CHAPTER 15

[1] Diego Barros Arana, *Un Decenio de la Historia de Chile* (Santiago de Chile, 1913), pp. 310, 347.
[2] *El Mercurio*, Aug. 6, 1849.
[3] *Ibid.*, Aug. 2, 1849; Jordi Fuentes and Lia Cortes, *Diccionario Político de Chile, 1810–1966* (Santiago de Chile, 1967), p. 63; Ralph J. Roske, "The World Impact of the California Gold Rush, 1849–1857," *Arizona and the West*, V (Autumn, 1963), 200; Doris Marion Wright, "The Making of Cosmopolitan California: An Analysis of Immigration, 1848–1870," *California Historical Society Quarterly*, XIX (Dec., 1940), 326.
[4] *El Mercurio*, Aug. 3, 1849.
[5] Roske, *op. cit.*, p. 201.
[6] James Melville Gilliss, *Chile: Its Geography, Climate* (Washington, 1855), p. 465.
[7] Roberto Hernández Cornejo, *Los Chilenos en San Francisco* (Valparaiso, 1930), I, 172.
[8] Enrigue Bunster, *Chilenos en California* (Santiago de Chile, 1965), p. 81; Hernández C., *op. cit.*, I, 172.
[9] Wright, *op. cit.*, p. 326.
[10] *El Mercurio*, Nov. 15, 1849; Barros Arano, *op. cit.*, pp. 250–252.
[11] Maurice Tourneux, "Jacques-Etienne-Victor Arago," *La Grande Encyclopédie* (Paris, n.d.), III, 522.
[12] Ivor Guest, *The Romantic Ballet in Paris* (Middletown, Conn., 1966), pp. 203, 226.
[13] *El Mercurio*, Aug. 8, 14, 1849.
[14] Guest, *op. cit.*, p. 260.
[15] Hernández C., *op. cit.*, I, 127.
[16] Frederick Gerstaecker, *Narrative of a Journey round the World* (New York, 1853), p. 127.
[17] *El Mercurio*, Aug. 14, 1849.
[18] *Ibid.*, Aug. 15, 1849.
[19] Barros Arana, *op. cit.*, p. 338.
[20] Hernández C., *op. cit.*, I, 127–128.
[21] *El Mercurio* and *El Comercio de Valparaiso*, Aug. 20, 21, 22, 1849.
[22] *El Comercio de Valparaiso*, Aug. 29, 1849.
[23] *Ibid.*, Sept. 7, 1849.
[24] Gerstaecker, *op. cit.*, p. 132.
[25] *Ibid.*, p. 133.
[26] Letters in *El Mercurio*, July 6, 1849, ff.
[27] *El Comercio de Valparaiso*, Aug. 23, 1849.
[28] Hernández C., *op. cit.*, I, 124.

29 *El Comercio de Valparaiso*, Aug. 28, 1849.
30 Hernández C., *op. cit.*, I, 124–125.
31 *El Mercurio*, Oct. 1, 1849.
32 *Ibid.*, Oct. 2, 1849.
33 *El Comercio de Valparaiso* and *El Mercurio*, Oct. 2, 1849.
34 *El Comercio de Valparaiso* and *El Mercurio*, Oct. 3, 1849.
35 *El Comercio de Valpariaso*, Sept. 24, 1849.
36 *El Mercurio*, Sept. 26, 1849.
37 Hernández C., *op. cit.*, I, 130.

CHAPTER 16

1 *El Comercio de Valparaiso*, Nov. 29, 1849.
2 Diego Barros Arana, *Un Decenio de la Historia de Chile* (Santiago de Chile, 1913), pp. 349.
3 Roberto Hernández Cornejo, *Los Chilenos en San Francisco* (Valparaiso, 1930), I, 121.
4 *Ibid.*
5 Barros Arana, *op. cit.*, p. 349.
6 *Ibid.*, pp. 349–351.
7 Hernández C., *op. cit.*, I, 140–146.
8 Jorge Basadre, *Historia de la República del Perú* (Lima, 1961–1968), II, 789.
9 Hernández C., *op. cit.*, I, 142, 147–148.
10 *Ibid.*, p. 148.
11 Enos Christman, *One Man's Gold*, comp. and ed. Florence Morrow Christman (New York, 1930), p. 51.
12 *El Comercio de Valparaiso*, Aug. 20, 1849; Barros Arana, *op. cit.*, pp. 349–350. Hernández C. (*op. cit.*, I, 144) says this measure received a favorable vote but was not converted into law.
13 Hobart *Colonial Times and Tasmanian*, Jan. 18, 1850.
14 Hernández C., *op. cit.*, I, 140.
15 *El Comercio de Valparaiso*, Oct. 4–10, 1849.
16 James Melville Gilliss, *Chile: Its Geography, Climate* (Washington, 1855), p. 229.
17 *El Comercio de Valparaiso*, Oct. 3, 1849.
18 Hernández C., *op. cit.*, I, 171.
19 *El Mercurio*, Oct. 10, 1849.
20 *Ibid.*
21 *Ibid.*, Dec. 13, 14, 1849.
22 *Ibid.*, Nov. 4, 1849.
23 *Ibid.*, Nov. 12, 1849.
24 *Ibid.*, July 3, Oct. 22, Nov. 3, Dec. 28, 1849.
25 *El Comercio de Valparaiso*, Aug. 25, 1849.
26 *El Mercurio*, Nov. 3, 1849.
27 *Ibid.*, Nov. 15, 1849.
28 Hernández C., *op. cit.*, I, 173.
29 Ramón Pérez Yañez, *Forjadores de Chile* (Santiago de Chile, 1953), p. 455.
30 Gilliss, *op. cit.*, p. 135.
31 Enrique Bunster, *Chilenos en California* (Santiago de Chile, 1965), p. 81; Hernández C., *op. cit.*, I, 67.
32 Sergio Sepúlveda G., *El Trigo Chileno en el Mercado Mundial* (Santiago de Chile, 1959), p. 37.
33 Gilliss, *op. cit.*, p. 173.

[34] *Ibid.*, pp. 104–105.
[35] *Ibid.*, p. 174.
[36] *Ibid.*, p. 175.
[37] *Ibid.*, p. 177.
[38] *Ibid.*, p. 197.
[39] Charles Wilkes, *Narrative of . . . Exploring Expedition* (Philadelphia, 1845), I, 201.
[40] Gilliss, *op. cit.*, p. 117.
[41] *Ibid.*, p. 477.
[42] Christman, *op. cit.*, p. 49.
[43] Hernández C., *op. cit.*, I, 172.
[44] Christman, *op. cit.*, p. 53.
[45] *Ibid.*, p. 49.
[46] *Ibid.*
[47] *Ibid.*, p. 52.
[48] *Ibid.*, p. 49.
[49] *Ibid.*, p. 51.
[50] Oscar Lewis, *Sea Routes to the Gold Fields* (New York, 1949), pp. 138–142.
[51] Christman, *op. cit.*, p. 67.
[52] Lewis, *op. cit.*, pp. 138–142.
[53] Christman, *op. cit.*, p. 61.
[54] *Ibid.*, p. 62.
[55] *Ibid.*, p. 61.
[56] *El Mercurio*, Oct. 4, 1949.
[57] Felix Paul Wierzbicki, *California As It Is* (San Francisco, 1933), p. 13.
[58] *El Comercio de Valparaiso*, Oct. 4, 1849.
[59] *Ibid.*, Oct. 5, 1849.
[60] Erna Fergusson, *Chile* (New York, 1943), p. 52.
[61] *El Mercurio*, Nov. 30, 1849; Frederick Gerstaecker, *Narrative of a Journey round the World* (New York, 1853), p. 115.
[62] *El Mercurio*, Dec. 12, 1849.
[63] Christman, *op. cit.*, p. 54; Thomas Robinson Warren, *Dust and Foam* (New York, 1859), p. 116.
[64] *El Mercurio*, Nov. 5, 1849; Benjamín Vicuña Mackenna, *"Terra Ignota," o sea Viaje del país de la crisis al mundo de las maravillas* (Valparaiso, 1930), p. 18.
[65] Wierzbicki, *op. cit.*, p. 77.
[66] *El Mercurio*, Dec. 31, 1849.
[67] *Ibid.*, Nov. 5, 1849; Hernández C., *op. cit.*, I, 176–177.
[68] Bunster, *op. cit.*, p. 82.
[69] *El Mercurio*, Dec. 31, 1849.
[70] Hernández C., *op. cit.*, I, 178.

CHAPTER 17

[1] Enos Christman, *One Man's Gold*, comp. and ed. Florence Morrow Christman (New York, 1930), p. 62; Robert B. Forbes, *Personal Reminiscences* (Boston, 1876), p. 250; Frederick Gerstaecker, *Narrative of a Journey round the World* (New York, 1853), pp. 59, 80, 86–88; James Melville Gilliss, *Chile: Its Geography, Climate* (Washington, 1855), p. 6.

[2] Basil Hall, *Extracts from a Journal* (London, 1840), Pt. I, p. 8; Gerstaecker, *op. cit.*, pp. 38, 57–58; Jay Monaghan, *The Overland Trail* (Indianapolis, 1947), p. 366.

[3] Edward Hungerford, *Wells Fargo* (New York, 1949), p. 84.

[4] Gerstaecker, *op. cit.*, pp. 66–67, 93.

[5] Gilliss, *op. cit.*, p. 393.

[6] Gerstaecker, *op. cit.*, pp. 33, 108; Tito Saubidet Gauche, *Vocabulario y Refranero criollo* (Buenos Aires, 1943), p. 156; Charles Wilkes, *Narrative of . . . Exploring Expedition* (Philadelphia, 1845), I, 96.

[7] Gilliss, *op. cit.*, p. 359.

[8] George McCutcheon McBride, *Chile: Land and Society* (New York, 1936), p. 58; Wilkes, *op. cit.*, I, 190.

[9] Saubidet Gauche, *op. cit.*, p. 204.

[10] Johann Jacob von Tschudi, *Travels in Peru* (New York, 1847), p. 213.

[11] Gilliss *op. cit.* p. 361; Hall, *op. cit.*, Pt. I, p. 35.

[12] Gerstaecker, *op. cit.*, p. 108.

[13] Gilliss, *op. cit.*, p. 356.

[14] *Ibid.*, p. 355.

[15] Wilkes, *op. cit.*, I, 191–193.

[16] Nora Barlow, ed., *Charles Darwin and the Voyage of the Beagle* (New York, 1946), pp. 106–107.

[17] Erna Fergusson, *Chile* (New York, 1943), p. 244; Hall, *op. cit.*, Pt. II, p. 7.

[18] Gilliss, *op. cit.*, p. 451; Wilkes, *op. cit.*, I, 179.

[19] McBride, *op. cit.*, p. 212.

[20] Gerstaecker, *op. cit.*, p. 33.

[21] Gilliss, *op. cit.*, p. 344; McBride, *op. cit.*, p. 154.

[22] Fergusson, *op. cit.*, p. 196.

[23] Gilliss, *op. cit.*, p. 346.

[24] *Ibid.*, p. 344.

[25] Hubert Herring, *Good Neighbors* (New Haven, 1941), p. 214.

[26] George W. Peck, *Melbourne and the Chincha Islands* (New York, 1854), p. 266.

[27] McBride, *op. cit.*, p. 50.

[28] Hall, *op. cit.*, Pt. 1, pp. 30, 32.

[29] *Ibid.*, p. 30.

[30] Joseph Henry Jackson, *Bad Company* (New York, 1939), p. 9.

[31] *Ibid.*, p. 19.

[32] Roberto Hernández Cornejo, *Los Chilenos en San Francisco* (Valparaiso, 1930), I, 183.

[33] John Rollin Ridge, *The Life and Adventures of Joaquin Murieta* (Norman, Okla., 1955), p. xxxv.

[34] Georgie Anne Geyer, "Leftist Chilean Poet Controversial Figure," *Los Angeles Times*, May 8, 1969.

[35] Pablo Neruda, *Fulgor y Muerte de Joaquín Murieta* (Santiago de Chile, 1967), p. 78.

[36] *Ibid.*

[37] *Ibid.*, pp. 78–80.

[38] David F. Belnap, "Chile Author Casts U.S. as Villain of Piece," *Los Angeles Times*, March 16, 1969.

[39] Ramón Pérez Yañez, *Forjadores de Chile* (Santiago de Chile, 1953), pp. 457–458.

[40] Hubert Howe Bancroft, *History of California* (San Francisco, 1884–1890), VII, 203; Theodore H. Hittell, *History of California*, IV (San Francisco, 1897), 712–726.

CHAPTER 18

[1] Johann Jacob von Tschudi, *Travels in Peru* (New York, 1847), p. 26.

[2] James Melville Gilliss, *Chile: Its Geography, Climate* (Washington, 1855), p. 41.

[3] Tschudi, *op. cit.*, p. 26.

[4] Ralph Lee Woodward, Jr., *Robinson Crusoe's Island* (Chapel Hill, 1969), pp. 6–15.

[5] *Ibid.*, p. 37; J. Ross Browne, *Crusoe's Island* (New York, 1867), p. 154.

[6] Browne, *op. cit.*, p. 33.

[7] Pedro Pablo Figueroa, *Diccionario Biográfico de Chile* (Santiago de Chile, 1897–1901), II, 458.

[8] Stephen Clissold, *Bernardo O'Higgins and the Independence of Chile* (New York, 1969), p. 138.

[9] Richard Henry Dana, *Two Years before the Mast* (Boston, 1886), p. 46.

[10] Oscar Lewis, *Sea Routes to the Gold Fields* (New York, 1949), p. 150.

[11] Browne, *op. cit.*, p. 12.

[12] *Ibid.*, p. 21.

[13] *Ibid.*, p. 31.

[14] *Ibid.*, p. 34.

[15] Tschudi, *op. cit.*, p. 26.

[16] Roberto Hernández Cornejo, *Los Chilenos en San Francisco* (Valparaiso, 1930), I, 110.

[17] *Ibid.*

[18] Browne, *op. cit.*, pp. 141–142.

[19] Lewis, *op. cit.*, p. 158.

[20] *La Aurora* (Cajamarca, Peru), Feb. 21, 1849.

[21] William Ray Manning, *Diplomatic Correspondence of the United States: Inter-American Affairs, 1831–1860*, X (Washington, 1938), 265.

[22] Hernández C., *op. cit.*, I, 144.

[23] *Ibid.*, p. 142.

[24] *El Comercio de Lima*, April 10, 1849.

[25] Hernández C., *op. cit.*, I, 144.

[26] *El Comercio de Lima*, March 31, 1849.

[27] *Ibid.*

[28] Dated April 30, 1849.

[29] Jorge Basadre, *Historia de la República del Perú* (Lima, 1961–1968), II, 788; Hernández C., *op. cit.*, I, 143.

[30] Manuel Ignacio Vegas García, *Historia de la Marina de Guerra del Perú* (Lima, 1929), p. 89.

[31] Gilliss, *op. cit.*, p. 427.

[32] Thomas Robinson Warren, *Dust and Foam* (New York, 1859), p. 361.

[33] *Report on Consulate at Valparaiso*, 31st Cong., 1st sess., Senate Exec. Doc. 16 (Washington, 1850), VI, 1–7.

[34] John Edwin Pomfret, ed., *California Gold Rush Voyages* (San Marino, Calif., 1954), p. 148.

[35] George W. Peck, *Melbourne and the Chincha Islands* (New York, 1854), p. 147.

[36] Tschudi, *op. cit.*, p. 70.

[37] Pomfret, *op. cit.*, p. 148.

[38] Peck, *op. cit.*, p. 193.

[39] Frederick Gerstaecker, *Narrative of a Journey round the World* (New York, 1853), p. 126.

[40] Pomfret, *op. cit.*, p. 141.
[41] Charles Wilkes, *Narrative of . . . Exploring Expedition* (Philadelphia, 1845), I, 237.
[42] Gilliss, *op. cit.*, p. 439.
[43] *Ibid.*, p. 436; Peck, *op. cit.*, p. 252.
[44] Basil Hall, *Extracts from a Journal* (London, 1840), Pt. I, p. 23; Pomfret, *op. cit.*, p. 144; Peck, *op. cit.*, p. 246.
[45] Nora Barlow, ed., *Charles Darwin and the Voyage of the Beagle* (New York, 1946), p. 243.
[46] Pedro Pablo Figueroa, *Diccionario Biográfica de Estranjeros en Chile* (Santiago de Chile, 1900), pp. 173–174; Kenneth F. Weaver, "The Five Worlds of Peru," *National Geographic* (Feb., 1964), p. 222.
[47] Tschudi, *op. cit.*, p. 70.
[48] Gilliss, *op. cit.*, p. 434.
[49] Wilkes, *op. cit.*, I, 239.
[50] Pomfret, *op. cit.*, p. 144.
[51] Tschudi, *op. cit.*, p. 93.
[52] *Ibid.*, p. 97.
[53] *Ibid.*, p. 196.
[54] Burr Cartwright Brundage, *Empire of the Inca* (Norman, Okla., 1963), p. 309.
[55] Tschudi, *op. cit.*, p. 242.
[56] *Ibid.*, p. 243.
[57] *Ibid.*, p. 205; Weaver, *op. cit.*, p. 228; Wilkes, *op. cit.*, I, 261, 269.
[58] John Hemming, *The Conquest of the Incas* (London, 1970), p. 33.
[59] Tschudi, *op. cit.*, p. 267.
[60] *La Aurora* (Cajamarca, Peru), Nov. 18, 1848; Jan. 6, 27, Feb. 7, 1849.
[61] *Ibid.*, Feb. 28, 1849.
[62] *Ibid.*, Jan. 3, 1849.
[63] *Ibid.*, Jan. 27, 1849.
[64] *Ibid.*, Feb. 7, 1849.
[65] Tschudi, *op. cit.*, p. 260.
[66] *La Alforja* (Ayacucho, Peru), March 1, 1850.

CHAPTER 19

[1] *El Mercurio*, Oct. 10, Dec. 13, 14, 1849.
[2] *El Correo del Sur* (Concepción), Nov. 24, 1849; *El Comercio de Valparaiso*, Dec. 4, 1849; Roberto Hernández Cornejo, *Los Chilenos en San Francisco* (Valparaiso, 1930), I, 182.
[3] *El Comercio de Valparaiso*, Dec. 4, 1949.
[4] Enrique Bunster, *Chilenos en California* (Santiago de Chile, 1965), p. 82.
[5] Benjamín Vicuña Mackenna, *Pájinas de mi Diario* (Santiago de Chile, 1856), p. 6; Felipe Wiegand's translation of speech in *Consular Reports between United States and Chile, 1910–1929*, encl. no. 4, dispatch no. 413.
[6] Hernández C., *op. cit.*, I, 160.
[7] Vicuña Mackenna, *op. cit.*, p. 4.
[8] *Ibid.*, p. 9.
[9] Letter from a physician, in Hernández C., *op. cit.*, I, 93; John Williamson Palmer, *The New and the Old* (New York, 1859), p. 241.
[10] Vicuña Mackenna, *op. cit.*, p. 6.
[11] *Ibid.*

[12] Jay Monaghan, *Australians and the Gold Rush* (Berkeley and Los Angeles, 1966), p. 125; Frank Soulé, John H. Gihon, and James Nisbet, *The Annals of San Francisco* (New York, 1855), p. 241.

[13] Vicente Pérez Rosales, *California Adventure*, trans. Edwin S. Morby and Arturo Torres-Rioseco (San Francisco, 1947), p. 95.

[14] Hernández C., *op. cit.*, I, 179.

[15] *Ibid.*

[16] *Ibid.*

[17] *Ibid.*, p. 176; Benjamín Vicuña Mackenna, *"Terra Ignota," o sea Viaje del país de la crisis al mundo de las maravillas* (Valparaiso, 1930), p. 18; Ramón Pérez Yañez, *Forjadores de Chile* (Santiago de Chile, 1953), p. 257.

[18] Pérez R., *op. cit.*, p. 80.

[19] Bunster, *op. cit.*, p. 82; Hernández C., *op. cit.*, I, 176; Pérez Y., *op. cit.*, p. 257.

[20] John Haskell Kemble, ed., *To California and the South Seas: The Diary of Albert G. Osbun, 1849–1851* (San Marino, Calif., 1966), p. 34; Leonard Pitt, *The Decline of the Californios* (Berkeley and Los Angeles, 1966), p. 58.

[21] Jay Monaghan, *Civil War on the Western Border, 1854–1865* (Boston, 1955), pp. 29 ff.

[22] Kemble, *op. cit.*, p. 33.

[23] *Ibid.*, pp. 37, 42.

[24] Allen B. Sherman, ed., "Sherman Was There: The Recollections of Major Edwin O. Sherman," *California Historical Society Quarterly*, XXIII (Dec., 1944), 350–351; Pitt, *op. cit.*, p. 58.

[25] Leonard Pitt, "The Beginnings of Nativism in California," *Pacific Historical Review*, XXX (Feb., 1961), 26.

[26] Andrew F. Rolle, *California: A History* (New York, 1964), p. 214.

[27] Pitt, *Decline of the Californios*, p. 52.

[28] Owen Cochran Coy, ed., *Pictorial History of California* (Berkeley, 1925), p. 31.

[29] Stockton *Placer Times*, July 9, 1849; *Alta California*, July 26, 1849.

[30] Bunster, *op. cit.*, p. 84.

[31] James J. Ayers, *Gold and Sunshine* (Boston, 1922), pp. 46–58.

[32] *Alta California*, June 2, 1849.

[33] Bunster, *op. cit.*, p. 84.

[34] Ayers, *op. cit.*, p. 50.

[35] *Alta California*, Dec. 13, 1849.

[36] *Ibid.*, Jan. 2, 1850.

[37] *Ibid.*

[38] Ayers, *op. cit.*, p. 53.

[39] *Ibid.*, p. 56.

[40] *Ibid.*, p. 57.

[41] *Alta California*, Jan. 2, 1850.

[42] *Ibid.*

[43] *Ibid.*, Jan. 7, 1850.

CHAPTER 20

[1] Helen Miller Bailey and Abraham P. Nasatir, *Latin America: The Development of Its Civilization* (Englewood, N.J., 1968), p. 413.

[2] Jay Monaghan, *Australians and the Gold Rush* (Berkeley and Los Angeles, 1966), p. 271.

[3] Rodman Wilson Paul, *California Gold* (Cambridge, Mass., 1947), p. 345.

[4] Leonard Pitt, *The Decline of the Californios* (Berkeley and Los Angeles, 1966), p. 52; Ramón Pérez Yañez, *Forjadores de Chile* (Santiago de Chile, 1953), p. 259.

[5] Jorge Basadre, *Historia de la República del Perú* (Lima, 1961–1968), II, 848.

[6] Pitt, *op. cit.*, p. 56.

[7] Miguel Luis Amunátegui Aldunate, *Ensayos Biográficos* (Santiago de Chile, 1893–1896), II, 212–221.

[8] James Melville Gilliss, *Chile: Its Geography, Climate* (Washington, 1855), p. 492.

[9] *Ibid.*

[10] J. Fred Rippy, *Joel R. Poinsett, Versatile American* (Durham, N.C., 1935), pp. 43–45.

[11] Gilliss, *op. cit.*, p. 492.

[12] Luis Galdames, *A History of Chile*, trans. and ed. Isaac Joslin Cox (Chapel Hill, 1941), p. 524.

[13] Gilliss, *op. cit.*, p. 505.

[14] Galdames, *op. cit.*, p. 288.

[15] Gilliss, *op. cit.*, p. 298.

[16] *Ibid.*, p. 499.

[17] *Ibid.*, p. 501; Galdames, *op. cit.*, p. 288.

[18] Ricardo Donoso, *Las Ideas Políticas en Chile* (Santiago de Chile, 1967), p. 294.

[19] Pérez Y., *op. cit.*, pp. 175–176.

[20] Domingo Faustino Sarmiento, *Sarmiento's Travels in the United States in 1847*, trans. Michael Aaron Rockland (Princeton, 1970), p. 10.

[21] Gilliss, *op. cit.*, p. 68.

[22] Roberto Hernández Cornejo, *Los Chilenos en San Francisco* (Valparaiso, 1930), I, 58.

[23] Pedro Pablo Figueroa, *Diccionario Biográfico de Chile* (Santiago de Chile, 1897–1901), II, 459; Pérez Y., *op. cit.*, pp. 211–214.

[24] Basadre, *op. cit.*, pp. 825, 830; Frederick B. Pike, *The Modern History of Peru* (New York, 1967), p. 114.

[25] Donoso, *op. cit.*, p. 126; Erna Fergusson, *Chile* (New York, 1943), p. 112; George McCutcheon McBride, *Chile: Land and Society* (New York, 1936), p. 113.

[26] *El Mercurio*, Nov. 29, 1849.

[27] Enos Christman, *One Man's Gold*, comp. and ed. Florence Morrow Christman (New York, 1930), p. 52; Gilliss, *op. cit.*, p. 226.

[28] Pérez Y. *op. cit.*, p. 468.

[29] Sergio Sepúlveda G., *El Trigo Chileno en el Mercado Mundial* (Santiago de Chile, 1959), p. 44.

[30] Pérez Y., *op. cit.*, pp. 460–461.

Sources

(The following is a list of works used in citations, not a complete bibliography.)

BOOKS AND ARTICLES

Acevedo Hernández, A. *Joaquin Murieta.* Suplemento Excelsior no. 1. Santiago de Chile, 1936.

Amunátegui Aldunate, Miguel Luis. *Ensayos Biográficos.* 4 vols. Santiago de Chile, 1893–1896.

Anderson Imbert, Enrique. *Genio y Figuro de Sarmiento.* Buenos Aires, 1967.

Atherton, Gertrude. *My San Francisco: A Wayward Biography.* Indianapolis, 1946.

Ayers, James J. *Gold and Sunshine: Reminiscences of Early California.* Boston, 1922.

Bailey, Helen Miller, and Abraham P. Nasatir. *Latin America: The Development of Its Civilization.* Englewood, N.J., 1968.

Banco Popular del Peru. *El Peru: Breve Divulgación Artística, Geográfica, Histórica, Ofrecida al Turista.* Lima, 1944.

Bancroft, Hubert Howe. *California Pioneer Register and Index, 1542–1848.* Baltimore, 1964.

——. *History of California.* 7 vols. San Francisco, 1884–1890.

Barlow, Nora, ed. *Charles Darwin and the Voyage of the Beagle.* New York, 1946.

Barros Arana, Diego. *Compendio de Historia Moderna.* Santiago de Chile, 1881.

——. *Historia Jeneral de Chile.* Santiago de Chile, 1884.

——. *Un Decenio de la Historia de Chile (1841–1851).* Santiago de Chile, 1913.

Basadre, Jorge. *Historia de la República del Perú.* 11 vols. Lima, 1961–1968.

Beers, Henry A. *The Connecticut Wits and Other Essays.* New Haven, 1920.

Belnap, David F. "Chile Author Casts U.S. as Villain of Piece," *Los Angeles Times,* March 16, 1969.

Bemis, Samuel Flagg. *The Latin American Policy of the United States.* New York, 1943.

Benavides, Oscar R. *Biblioteca de Cultura Peruana Patrocinada.* Paris, 1938.

Berthold, Victor M. *The Pioneer Steamer, "California," 1848–1849.* Boston, 1932.

Bieber, Ralph P. "California Gold Mania," *Mississippi Valley Historical Review,* XXXV (June, 1948), 3–28.

Billingsley, Edward Baxter. *In Defense of Neutral Rights: The United States Navy and the Wars of Independence in Chile and Peru.* Chapel Hill, 1967.

Boletín de Fourento (Lima), 1912. This publication contains articles by the secretary of agriculture on Peruvian saddles.

Boletín de la Sociedad Geográfica de Lima. Vol. LXXXII (Jan.–July, 1964).

Borges, Jorge Luis. *The Aleph and Other Stories, 1933–1969.* New York, 1970.

———. *A Personal Anthology.* Edited with a foreword by Anthony Kerrigan. New York, 1967.

Bowers, Claude G. *Chile through Embassy Windows, 1939–1953.* New York, 1958.

Brenan, Gerald. *South from Granada.* New York, 1957.

Browne, J. Ross. *Crusoe's Island: A Ramble in the Footsteps of Alexander Selkirk.* New York, 1867.

Brundage, Burr Cartwright. *Empire of the Inca.* Norman, Okla., 1963.

Bryant, Edwin. *What I Saw in California.* Minneapolis, 1967.

Buckbee, Edna. *The Saga of Old Tuolumne.* New York, 1935.

Bunster, Enrique. *Chilenos en California.* Santiago de Chile, 1965.

Burr, Robert N. *By Reason or Force: Chile and the Balancing of Power in South America, 1830–1905.* Berkeley and Los Angeles, 1967.

Butler's Lives of the Saints. Vol. III. New York, 1956.

California and New Mexico. 33d Cong., 1st sess., H.R. Exec. Doc. 17. Washington, 1850.

Chambers, Charles H. *A General View of the State of California, Past and Present; with a Glimpse of the Probable Future.* Sydney, 1850.

Christman, Enos. *One Man's Gold: The Letters and Journals of a Forty-niner.* Comp. and ed. Florence Morrow Christman. New York, 1930.

Clappe, Louise A. K. S. *The Shirley Letters: Being Letters Written in 1851–1852 from the California Mines.* Introd. by Richard Oglesby. Santa Barbara, 1970.

Clark, Arthur H. *The Clipper Ship Era: An Epitome of Famous American and British Clipper Ships, Their Owners, Builders, Commanders, and Crews, 1843–1869.* New York, 1912.

Clissold, Stephen. *Bernardo O'Higgins and the Independence of Chile.* New York, 1969.

Cobb, Gwendolin B. "Potosi, a South American Mining Frontier." In *Greater America: Essays in Honor of Herbert Eugene Bolton.* Berkeley and Los Angeles, 1945.

Combet, Pedro Isidoro. *Recuerdos de California.* Santiago de Chile, 1859.

Coy, Owen Cochran, ed. *Pictorial History of California.* Berkeley, 1925.

Dakin, Susanna Bryant. *A Scotch Paisano: Hugo Reid's Life in California, 1832–1852.* . . . Berkeley, 1939.

Dana, Richard Henry. *Two Years before the Mast.* Boston, 1886.

Dillon, Richard. *Fool's Gold: A Biography of John Sutter.* New York, 1967.

Donoso, Ricardo. *Las Ideas Políticas en Chile.* Santiago de Chile, 1967.

Dozer, Donald M. *Latin America.* New York, 1962.

Dunbar, Edward E. *The Romance of the Age; or the Discovery of Gold in California.* New York, 1867.

Egan, Ferol. *The El Dorado Trail: The Story of the Gold Rush Routes across Mexico.* New York, 1970.

Eldredge, Zoeth S. *The Beginnings of San Francisco.* 2 vols. San Francisco, 1912.

Fagg, John Edwin. *Latin America: A General History.* New York, 1966.

Feliú Cruz, Guillermo. *Andrés Bello y la redacción de los documentos oficiales de gobierno de Chile.* Caracas, 1951.

———. *Vicente Pérez Rosales: Diccionario de "El Entrometido"; Sueños que parecen verdades y verdades que parecen sueños.* Santiago de Chile, 1946.

———. *Vicente Pérez Rosales: Ensayo crítico.* Santiago de Chile, 1946.

———. "Vicente Pérez Rosales, escritor," *Boletín de la Biblioteca Nacional,* 2d ser., IV (Dec., 1933).

Fergusson, Erna. *Chile.* New York, 1943.

Figueroa, Pedro Pablo. *Diccionario Biográfico Chileno, 1550–1887.* Santiago de Chile, 1887.

———. *Diccionario Biográfico de Chile.* 3 vols. Santiago de Chile, 1897–1901.

———. *Diccionario Biográfico de Estranjeros en Chile.* Santiago de Chile, 1900.

Findlay, Alexander George. *A Directory for the Navigation of the South Pacific Ocean.* London, 1863.

Forbes, Robert B. *Personal Reminiscences.* Boston, 1876.

Ford, Thomas R. *Man and Land in Peru.* Gainesville, Fla., 1955.

Fuentes, Jordi, and Lia Cortes. *Diccionario Político de Chile, 1810–1966.* Santiago de Chile, 1967.

Galdames, Luis. *A History of Chile.* Trans. and ed. Isaac Joslin Cox. Chapel Hill, 1941.

Gay, Theressa. *James W. Marshall, the Discoverer of California Gold: A Biography.* Georgetown, Calif., 1967.

Gerstaecker, Frederick. *Narrative of a Journey round the World.* New York, 1853.

Geyer, Georgie Anne. "Leftist Chilean Poet Controversial Figure," *Los Angeles Times,* May 8, 1969.

Gilliss, James Melville. *Chile: Its Geography, Climate, Earthquakes, Government Social Condition, Mineral and Agricultural Resources, Commerce, &c.* Washington, 1855.

Groh, George W. *Gold Fever: Being a True Account Both Horrifying and Hilarious, of the Art of Healing (so-called) during the California Gold Rush!* New York, 1966.

Guest, Ivor. *The Romantic Ballet in Paris.* Middletown, Conn., 1966.

Gunther, John. *Inside South America.* New York, 1966.

Hall, Basil. *Extracts from a Journal Written on the Coasts of Chile, Peru, and Mexico in the Years 1820, 1821, 1822.* London, 1840.

Hammond, George P., ed. *The Larkin Papers.* 10 vols. Berkeley and Los Angeles, 1951–1964.
Hanson, Earl Parker, ed. *South from the Spanish Main.* New York, 1967.
Hawgood, John Arkas. *First and Last Consul: Thomas Oliver Larkin and the Americanization of California.* San Marino, Calif., 1962.
Hemming, John. *The Conquest of the Incas.* London, 1970.
Hernández, José. *El Gaucho Martín Fierro y la Vuelta de Martín Fierro.* Buenos Aires, 1937.
Hernández Cornejo, Roberto. *Los Chilenos en San Francisco de California.* 2 vols. Valparaiso, 1930.
Herring, Hubert. *Good Neighbors: Argentine, Brazil, Chile.* New Haven, 1941.
Hittell, Theodore H. *History of California.* Vol. IV. San Francisco, 1897.
Hungerford, Edward. *Wells Fargo: Advancing the American Frontier.* New York, 1949.
Hunter, Daniel J. *A Sketch of Chile, Expressly Prepared for the Use of Emigrants from the United States and Europe to That Country.* New York, 1866.
Jackson, Joseph Henry. *Bad Company.* New York, 1939.
Jenkins, Olaf P., ed. *The Mother Lode Country.* San Francisco, 1948.
Jerez, Francisco de. "Verdadera Relación de la Conquista del Perú y Provincio del Cuzco." Ed. Enrique de Vedia. In *Biblioteca de Autores Españoles.* Madrid, 1862.
Jones, Howard Mumford. *America and French Culture, 1750–1848.* Chapel Hill, 1927.
Judd, Laura Fish. *Honolulu: Sketches of Life in the Hawaiian Islands from 1828 to 1861.* Ed. Dale L. Morgan. Chicago, 1966.
Kelsey, Vera. *Seven Keys to Brazil.* New York, 1946.
Kemble, John Haskell. *The Panama Route, 1848–1869.* Berkeley, 1943.
Kemble, John Haskell, ed. "Journal of Lieutenant Tunis Augustus Craven," *California Historical Society Quarterly,* XX (Sept., 1941), 193–234.
———. *To California and the South Seas: The Diary of Albert G. Osbun, 1849–1851.* San Marino, Calif., 1966.
Kinsbruner, Jay. *Bernardo O'Higgins.* New York, 1968.
Lewis, Oscar. *Sea Routes to the Gold Fields.* New York, 1949.
Lyman, Chester S. *Around the Horn to the Sandwich Islands and California, 1845–1850.* New Haven, 1924.
McBride, George McCutcheon. *Chile: Land and Society.* New York, 1936.
Manning, William Ray. *Diplomatic Correspondence of the United States: Inter-American Affairs, 1831–1860.* Vols. V, X. Washington, 1935, 1938.
Markham, Clements Robert. *A History of Peru.* Chicago, 1892.
———. *The Incas of Peru.* New York, 1910.
———. *Narratives of the Rites and Laws of the Incas.* London, 1873.
Markham, Clements Robert, ed. *Reports on the Discovery of Peru.* New York, n.d.
Marryat, Florence. "Memoir of Captain Marryat." In *Works of Captain Marryat.* I, 7–14. New York, n.d.
Marryat, Frederick. *Frank Mildmay or, The Naval Officer.* London, 1863.

Means, Philip A. *Fall of the Inca Empire and the Spanish Rule in Peru, 1530–1780*. New York, 1932.

[Merwin, Mrs. C. B.] *Three Years in Chile*. New York, 1963.

Miró Quesada Sosa, Aurelio. *Cervantes, Tirso y el Perú*. Lima, 1947.

Monaghan, Jay. *Australians and the Gold Rush: California and Down Under, 1849–1854*. Berkeley and Los Angeles, 1966.

———. *Civil War on the Western Border, 1854–1865*. Boston, 1955.

———. "Did Expansion of the Traditional American West Stop at the Pacific?" In *The Westward Movement and Historical Involvement of the Americas in the Pacific Basin*. San Jose, Calif., 1966.

———. *The Great Rascal: The Life and Adventures of Ned Buntline*. Boston, 1952.

———. *The Overland Trail*. Indianapolis, 1947.

Monaghan, Jay, ed. *The Book of the American West*. New York, 1963.

———. *The Private Journal of Louis McLane, U.S.N., 1844–1848*. Los Angeles, 1971.

Nasatir, Abraham Phineas, ed. "A French Pessimist in California: The Correspondence of J. Lombard, Vice-Consul of France, 1850–1852," *California Historical Society Quarterly*, XXXI (June, Sept., Dec., 1952), 139–148, 253–260, 307–324.

Navarro Jil, Ramón. "Los Chilenos en California en 1849 y 1850." Series of articles in *El Correo del Sur* (Concepción, Chile), 1853–1854.

Neruda, Pablo. *Fulgor y Muerte de Joaquín Murieta, bandido chileno injustíciado en California el 23 de julio de 1853*. Santiago de Chile, 1967.

Nunis, Doyce B., Jr., ed. *The California Diary of Faxon Dean Atherton, 1836–1838*. San Francisco, 1964.

Palmer, John Williamson. *The New and the Old; or, California and India in Romantic Aspects*. New York, 1859.

———. "Pioneer Days in San Francisco," *Century Magazine*, XLIII (Feb., 1892), 541–560.

Parrington, Vernon Louis, ed. *The Connecticut Wits*. New York, 1926.

Parsons, George F. *The Life and Adventures of James W. Marshall, the Discoverer of Gold in California*. Sacramento, 1870.

Paul, Rodman Wilson. *California Gold: The Beginning of Mining in the Far West*. Cambridge, Mass., 1947.

———. *The California Gold Discovery Sources*. Georgetown, Calif., 1966.

———. "Mining Frontiers in the Americas and the British Commonwealths." In *The Westward Movement and Historical Involvement of the Americas in the Pacific Basin*. San Jose, Calif., 1966.

Peck, George W. *Melbourne and the Chincha Islands; with Sketches of Lima and a Voyage round the World*. New York, 1854.

Pelaez y Tapia, José. *Historia de "El Mercurio": Un Siglo de periodismo chileno*. Santiago de Chile, 1927.

Pereira Salas, Eugenio. *Bibliografía Chilena sobre el "Gold Rush" en California*. N.p., n.d.

———. *Colección de artículos, noticias y capítulos de cartas con respecto a California. . . .* Santiago de Chile, 1949.

Pérez Rosales, Vicente. "Algo sobre California." In *Revista de Santiago*. VI, 1–10, 127–136, 185–193. Santiago de Chile, 1850.

————. *California Adventure*. Translation of *Recuerdo del Pasada* by Edwin S. Morby and Arturo Torres-Rioseco. San Francisco, 1947.

————. *Diario del Viaje a California, 1848–1849*. Santiago de Chile, 1951.

————. *Diccionario de "El Entrometido."* Santiago de Chile, 1946.

————. *Recuerdos del Pasada, 1814–1860*. Santiago de Chile, 1943.

Pérez Yañez, Ramón. *Forjadores de Chile*. Santiago de Chile, 1953.

Perkins, Dexter. *The United States and Latin America*. Baton Rouge, 1961.

Perkins, William. *Three Years in California: . . . Journal of Life at Sonora, 1849–1852*. Berkeley and Los Angeles, 1964.

Pike, Frederick B. *The Modern History of Peru*. New York, 1967.

Pitt, Leonard. "The Beginnings of Nativism in California," *Pacific Historical Review*, XXX (Feb., 1961), 23–38.

————. *The Decline of the Californios: A Social History of the Spanish-Speaking Californians, 1846–1890*. Berkeley and Los Angeles, 1966.

Pomfret, John Edwin, ed. *California Gold Rush Voyages, 1848–1849: Three Original Narratives*. San Marino, Calif., 1954.

Prescott, William Hickling. *The History of the Conquest of Peru*. 2 vols. New York, 1847. Philadelphia, 1873.

Public Statutes at Large. Vol. VIII. Boston, 1846.

Quaife, Milo Milton, ed. *Pictures of Gold Rush California*. Chicago, 1949.

Report on Consulate at Valparaiso. 31st Cong., 1st sess., Senate Exec. Doc. 16. Washington, 1850.

Revere, Joseph Warren. *Keel and Saddle: A Retrospect of Forty Years of Military and Naval Service*. Boston, 1872.

————. *Naval Duty in California*. Oakland, Calif., 1947.

Rickard, Thomas Archer. *Journeys of Observation*. San Francisco, 1907.

Ridge, John Rollin. *The Life and Adventures of Joaquín Murieta. . . . With* introduction by Joseph Henry Jackson. Norman, Okla., 1955.

Rippy, J. Fred. *British Investments in Latin America, 1822–1949*. Hamden, Conn., 1959.

————. *Joel R. Poinsett, Versatile American*. Durham, N.C., 1935.

————. *Latin America: A Modern History*. Ann Arbor, 1958.

Riva Agüero, José de la. *Por la Verdad, la Tradición, y la Patria*. Lima, 1938.

Rolle, Andrew F. *California: A History*. New York, 1964.

Romero, Emilio. *Historia Económica del Perú*. Buenos Aires, 1949.

Roske, Ralph J. "The World Impact of the California Gold Rush, 1849–1857," *Arizona and the West*, V (Autumn, 1963), 187–232.

Sarmiento, Domingo Faustino. *Life in the Argentine Republic in the days of the Tyrants; or, Civilization and Barbarism, with a biographical sketch of the author, by Mrs. Horace Mann*. New York, 1868.

————. *Sarmiento's Travels in the United States in 1847*. Trans. Michael Aaron Rockland. Princeton, 1970.

Saubidet Gauche, Tito. *Vocabulario y Refranero criollo, con textos y dibujos originales de Tito Saubidet*. Buenos Aires, 1943.

Schneider, Robert. *Gold von Peru und andere Schatzgräbergeschichten hereausgegeber von Robert Schneider*. N.p., n.d.

Sepúlveda G., Sergio. *El Trigo Chileno en el Mercado Mundial: Ensayo de Geografía Histórica*. Santiago de Chile, 1959.

Sherman, Allen B., ed. "Sherman Was There: The Recollections of Major

Edwin A. Sherman," *California Historical Society Quarterly*, XXIII
(Sept., Dec., 1944), 259–281, 349–377; XXIV (March, June, Sept.,
1945), 47–52, 165–180, 271–279.
Sherman, William Tecumseh. *Memoirs of General William T. Sherman by
Himself.* 2 vols. Bloomington, Ind., 1957.
————. *The Sherman Letters: Correspondence between General and
Senator Sherman from 1837 to 1891.* Ed. Rachel Sherman Thorndike.
New York, 1894.
Silva Castro, Raúl. *Panorama Literario de Chile.* Santiago de Chile, 1961.
————. *Prensa y Periodismo en Chile, 1812–1956.* Santiago de Chile,
1958.
Smith, Dick, and Robert Easton. *Californian Condor, Vanishing Ameri-
can.* Santa Barbara, Calif., 1964.
Soulé, Frank, John H. Gihon, and James Nisbet. *The Annals of San Fran-
cisco.* New York, 1855.
Spaeth, Sigmund. *History of Popular Music in America.* New York, 1948.
Stackpole, Edouard. *The "Charles W. Morgan": The Last Wooden Whale-
ship.* New York, 1967.
Stoddart, Thomas Robertson. *Annals of Tuolumne County.* Sonora. Calif.,
1963.
Tompkins, Walker A., and Horace A. Sexton. *Fourteen at the Table: An
Informal History of the Life and Good Times of the Sexton Family of
Old Goleta.* Santa Barbara, Calif., 1964.
Toro y Gisbert, Miguel de. *Pequeño Larousse Ilustrado.* Buenos Aires,
1968.
Tourneux, Maurice. "Jacques-Etienne-Victor Arago." In *La Grande En-
cyclopédie.* III, 522. Paris, n.d.
Trevor-Roper, H. R. *The Crisis of the Seventeenth Century.* New York,
1968.
Tschudi, Johann Jacob von. *Travels in Peru, during the years 1838–1842.*
New York, 1847.
Underhill, Reuben L. *From Cow Hides to Golden Fleece: A Narrative of
California, 1832–1858.* . . . Palo Alto, 1939.
Varigny, Charles Victor Crosnier de. *L'Océan Pacifique. Les derniers can-
nibales; îles et terres océaniennes;* . . . *San Francisco.* Paris, 1888.
————. *Los Orijenes de San Francisco de California.* Valparaiso, 1887.
Vedia, Enrique de. *Biblioteca Autores Españoles, desde la formación del
lenguaje hasta nuestra dias.* Madrid, 1862.
Vegas García, Manuel Ignacio. *Historia de la Marina de Guerra del Perú,
1821–1924.* Lima, 1929.
Velasco, José Francisco. *Noticias estadísticas del estado de Sohora, acom-
pañadas de ligeras reflecsiónes.* Mexico City, 1850.
————. *Sonora: Its extent, population, natural production, Indian tribes,
mines, mineral lands, etc.* Trans. from Spanish of Francisco Velasco by
Wm. F. Nye. San Francisco, 1861.
[Venegas, Miguel.] *Noticia de la California.* 3 vols. Madrid, 1757.
Vicuña Mackenna, Benjamín. *Contribución para el Centenario de Vicuña-
Mackenna "Terra Ignota," o sea viaje del país de la crisis al mundo de
las maravillas.* Valparaiso, 1930.

————. *Cronicas de Valparaiso.* Valparaiso, 1931.

————. *De Valparaiso a Santiago. Datos, impresiónes, noticias, episodios de viaje.* Santiago de Chile, 1877.

————. "Don Carlos Wooster," *La Justicia* (Talcahuano), XXVI, no. 2.558.

————. *Miscellanea: Colección de articulos, discursos, biografías, impresiones de viaje.* . . . Santiago de Chile, 1874.

————. *Obras completas.* Santiago de Chile, 1938.

————. *Pájinas de mi Diario durante Tres Años de Viajes, 1853–1854–1855.* Santiago de Chile, 1856.

————. *"Terra Ignota," o sea Viaje del país de la crisis al mundo de las maravillas.* Valparaiso, 1930.

Wardle, Arthur C. *Steam Conquers the Pacific: A Record of Maritime Achievement, 1840–1940.* London, 1940.

Warren, Thomas Robinson. *Dust and Foam; or, Three Oceans and Two Continents.* New York, 1859.

Weaver, Kenneth F. "The Five Worlds of Peru," *National Geographic* (Feb., 1964), pp. 212–267.

Wiegand, Felipe, director, Naval School of Engineering at Talcahuano. Translation of speech eulogizing Carlos Wooster at time of visit to Cincinnati. "Consular Reports between United States and Chile, 1910–1929." Dispatch 413, enclosure no. 4, National Archives, microfilm roll 489.

Wierzbicki, Felix Paul. *California As It Is & As It May Be; or, A Guide to the Gold Regions.* San Francisco, 1933.

————. *What I Saw in California.* Launceston, Tasmania, 1850.

Wilder, Thornton. *The Bridge of San Luis Rey.* New York, 1928.

Wilkes, Charles. *Narrative of the Unites States Exploring Expedition during the years 1838, 1839, 1840, 1841, 1842.* 5 vols. Philadelphia, 1845.

Willison, George Findlay. *Here They Dug the Gold.* New York, 1931.

Woodward, Ralph Lee, Jr. *Robinson Crusoe's Island: A History of the Juan Fernández Islands.* Chapel Hill, 1969.

Wright, Doris Marion. "The Making of Cosmopolitan California: An Analysis of Immigration, 1848–1870," *California Historical Society Quarterly,* XIX (Dec., 1940), 323–343; XX (March, 1941), 65–79.

Young, Otis E., Jr. *How They Dug the Gold.* Tucson, 1967.

NEWSPAPERS

La Alforja (Ayacucho, Peru)
Alta California
La Aurora (Cajamarca, Peru)
Californian
California Star
California Star and Californian
El Comercio de Lima
El Comercio de Valparaiso
El Correo del Sur (Concepción)
Hobart *Colonial Times and Tasmanian*
Hobart Daily Courier

Hobart Town Advertiser
Marysville [California] *Herald*
El Mercurio de Valparaiso
Nantucket *Inquirer*
El Peruano: Periódico Oficial (Lima, Peru)
Sacramento Transcript
Sonora [California] *Herald*
Stockton *Placer Times*
Stockton Times

MANUSCRIPTS

Converse, Henry. Journal of cruise to California during gold rush. Special Collections, University of California, Santa Barbara.

"Gold Rush Days: Vital Statistics Copied from Early Newspapers of Stockton, California, 1850–1855." Mimeographed by San Joaquin Genealogical Society of Stockton, 1958.

McLane, Louis. A naval officer's journal in California, 1844–1848. Santa Barbara Historical Society.

Neville, Richard A. "Santiago de las Montaña y San Francisco de Borja: Ensayo histórico sobre las cuidades antiquas del Ponga de Manseriche." Thesis, Universidad Nacional Mayor de San Marco, Lima, 1950.

Acknowledgments

This study was supported in part by a grant from the Penrose Fund of the American Philosophical Society, and I am indebted to Professors Ray Allen Billington, John Caughey, and the late Allan Nevins for encouragement in the project. Research in a foreign country always presents problems, and personal contacts are important. Donald M. Dozer, professor of history at the University of California, Santa Barbara, and a world authority on South America, gave me a list of his friends in Peru and Chile who might help. On arriving in the capitals of these countries, I called first on the cultural affairs officer at the United States embassy in each city for further suggestions. In Lima this officer, Francis Cooke, made an appointment for me to meet Señor Guerva Lohmann Villena, director of the Biblioteca Nacional, who assigned me a seat in the Rare Newspaper Room of his splendid building. I went to this room by climbing the grand stairway to the second floor and walking along the patio gallery to the sanctuary where Señora Graciela Sánchez Cerro's capable assistant helped me locate files of the early papers. Señora Sánchez C. also graciously obtained for me the photostats of newspapers which I have used for illustrations in this book.

A foreign city's leading newspaper is often a valuable source of historical information. In Lima, Señora Miriam Beltrán, co-owner of *La Prensa*, made helpful suggestions, although her newspaper was not in existence during the period in which I am working. Ella Dunbar Tempé, professor of history at San Marcos University, cordially invited me to her attractive, neocolonial residence where she and her secretary gave me valuable advice on pertinent sources for my research. Ella Barta, Jefe de Venta, of Librerías A.B.C., checked the list of publications I sought, and Dr. Emilio Romero, president of the Sociedad Geográfica de Lima, was generous and untiring in answering questions concerning the folklore and history of Peru.

For a while I was frustrated by the apparent lack of a file of Lima newspapers published during the gold rush. Revolutions and invasions of enemy neighbors seemed to have destroyed all of them. Then an eminent historian, Jorge Basadre, whose books are essential to any study of Peruvian history, came to my rescue, telling me that a complete file of *El Comercio* had been preserved in the library of the Catholic University. At the main entrance to that institution I stepped through a small doorway in the huge formal portal and found myself in a vacant patio with no one in sight. I climbed the steps to the second-floor gallery surrounding the patio. Here, at the open door into a small room, I saw a studious padre sitting at a table. He directed me to an inner patio downstairs where Sr. Alysendrio Lastaneau assigned me a work table, and a helpful clerk brought out the papers I was so eager to find.

Donald Dane Johnson, a North American living in Peru, prepared for me an excellent microfilm of the file of *El Comercio*, which is now owned by the library of the University of California, Santa Barbara. Two other North American residents of Lima, John Reilly and his wife, Ursula, who have lived in Latin America for years, told me many interesting facts about Peru not to be found in books.

In Santiago, Chile, the cultural affairs officer at the United States embassy, S. C. McCulloch, had just arrived from Washington, D.C. He apologized for his lack of acquaintances at a new post but his assistant, Enrique Salas, a skillful historian, showed genuine interest in my problems and lent me some of his own books, which I took to the hotel and read in the evenings. Paul Miles, library coordinator for the universities of Chile and California, was scheduled to leave for his vacation on the day after my arrival. Before departing he introduced me to the intelligent, resourceful, and attractive Señorita Ana Lya Yaikin, who accompanied me up O'Higgins Boulevard to the Biblioteca Nacional. There she introduced me to the eminent Chilean historians, Dr. Guillermo Feliú Cruz and Sr. Roque Estaban Scarpa. I was then assigned to Ernesto Gallano, whose efficient staff members during the days that followed were patient and persevering in finding the material I sought.

I am also indebted to a bookseller I met by chance in Santiago while visiting bookstalls along Alonzo Ovalle. Sr. David Nutels, an authority on Dante, was an expert scout for rare books, many of which were later purchased by the library of the University of California, Santa Barbara; these additions helped to build up the library's rich collection of books in the Hispanic-American field. I also want to express my thanks to Christián Guerrero Yoacham of Centro de Investigaciónes de Historia Americana, University of Chile, for his detailed suggestions concerning works I should consult. Last, but by no means least, I am indebted to Dr. Engel Sluiter, professor of history, University of California, Berkeley, who was in Santiago on sabbatical leave. A student of the rise and fall of Dutch imperialism, he explained its relation to Chilean history and suggested the names of helpful archivists in Santiago.

In the United States I am indebted to Tony Nicolosi, assistant curator of Special Collections at Rutgers University, for research concerning the New Jersey bark, *Undine*, which was built on the nearby Raritan River. Joseph Alsop, of Washington, D.C., generously answered my questions concerning his ancestors' participation in the early South American trade. Howard Bird, in San José, Málaga, Spain, called my attention to the possible Spanish source of the song, "Clementine." Mary Isabel Fry, in charge of reader services at the Huntington Library, San Marino, California, rechecked citations I had made from French sources there. Dr. John H. Kemble, national authority on ocean vessels, lent me a volume from his personal library and gave me important bits from his vast knowledge about the sea.

In Santa Barbara, Margaret Mallory, a member of the famous New Bedford clipper-ship family, suggested sources for my research. Paul Sweetser, retired attorney and former president of the Santa Barbara Historical Society, who has served and befriended Latin Americans for years, gave me the names of Chileans who had settled in Santa Barbara. Walker Tompkins, author of many books about Santa Barbara city and county, related stories he has heard about early-day Chileans in this area. Eric Wendelin, former foreign service officer in the United States Department of State, and his wife, Dorothy, generously lent me a rare volume of gaucho expressions which I would otherwise have overlooked. Mr. and Mrs. Clifford Neville, who lived in Lima for some time, generously allowed me to borrow a unique publication of the Banco Popular del Peru, as well as a copy of their son's doctoral thesis which was written as a partial requirement for his degree from San Marcos University in Lima. Dr. Neville and his charming Peruvian wife have generously responded to a curious man's questions about their country. Jorge Nef, a Chilean graduate student at the University of California, Santa Barbara, suggested books and articles with a modern point of view which have been of great assistance in this study. Robert E. Wilson, veteran foreign service officer and now lecturer in Spanish at UCSB, lent me an unusual Hispanic publication unavailable in any of the University of California's libraries. Professor Roberto de Souza explained unusual Spanish-American slang.

Margaret Orchowski of Santa Barbara, a resident of Latin America for three years, translated for me with careful accuracy a long letter written by a doctor who traveled from Chile to San Francisco in 1849. I am also everlastingly indebted *a el simpático amigo*, the late Dr. Samuel A. Wofsy, former chairman of the Spanish Department at UCSB, and his enthusiastically helpful wife, Frances. Another Spanish Department member, the late Andrés Rodríguez Ramón, who lived for many years in Spanish colonial areas, always had time to explain some odd provincial idiom when we met on campus. Professor Philip W. Powell, specialist in the history of both Spain and Spanish America at UCSB, has invariably known all the answers to my perplexing questions and stimulated my interpretation of Chile and Peru. His ever gracious Colombian wife, Maria, has been equally helpful.

University Librarian Donald C. Davidson's efficient development of the library on the Santa Barbara campus has provided materials invaluable to this study. Under his administration the library has become outstanding in Spanish and Spanish-American sources. Martha Peterson, associate university librarian, arranged for the purchase from Chile of a long list of books unavailable in other libraries of the university. Donald Fitch, head of the Reference Department, has shown ingenuity in finding sources relating to my inquiries. His assistant, Ann Pritchard, now Mrs. Kreyche, with marvelous persistence found for me the birth date of a sixteenth-century Peruvian writer unavailable in English and Spanish biographical dictionaries. Carolbeth Gibbens and Patricia Gebhard have both been untiring in seeking solutions to my problems. Herbert Linville, head of serials and government publications, has helped many times with an appropriate document. Richard Duprey, order librarian, located and ordered microfilms of California newspaper files important to the period of history covered by this study. In the map room, Larry Carver and Barbara Christy have been quick to find the maps I needed in the library's comprehensive and well-catalogued collection. Robert Crittenden and Linda Sanchez invariably produced with a smile the books I requested through interlibrary loan. In the library's department of Special Collections, Christian Brun, Dolores Ritchie, and Sherry Fondren have always been helpful and cheery fellow workers. As in two earlier volumes, I want to thank Luella Howard for giving up many of her scanty leisure hours to type this manuscript with her usual speed, accuracy, and intelligence.

The preparation of this book has entailed years of grinding work and incredible isolation, but it has also included high adventure shared by my wife, Mildred. Together we roamed the crowded streets of Spanish-American cities and explored the Chilean Andes where Pérez R. had smuggled cattle. Together we watched horsemen in the narrow streets of tile-roofed villages and hoped we were envisioning life in a vanished age. Mildred read the first draft of this book with the same patient understanding she showed when I wandered away seeking folk knowledge under the thatched roofs and among the suspended hammocks of an Indian village, or in the cloth booths of a city market. Perhaps the best praise of her unfailing interest in this project was the surprising question voiced by a stewardess on our plane as we dived from a 35,000-foot altitude down through a cloud ceiling and skimmed out over the breathtaking peaks of the Andes. "Excuse me for asking," the young lady said, "but are you two bride and groom?"

J. M.

Index